# TennyBoots!
## A Memoir by Judy Edwards

**A Baby Boomer Daughter's Decade Of Caring for Her Aging, Independent Mother**

# TENNYBOOTS!

# Copyright Page
Copyright © 2019 by Judy Edwards

All rights reserved.
Published in the United States by knecting dots publishers

knectingdotspublishers.com (goes live in January 2020)
facebook.com\writethebookyouwanttoread
646.410.2622

Library of Congress Cataloging-in-Publication Data is available upon request

ISBN: 978-1-7342738-1-6

**PRINTED IN THE UNITED STATES OF AMERICA**

*Book design by Publishing by Pinkie*
*Jacket Design by Publishing by Pinkie*
*Jacket illustration by Elijah Davis*
*Epigraph illustration by Chloe Davis*

13 11 19

**First Edition**
First Edition:November 2019
*(Paperback Edition first published 2019)*

*This is a work of creative non-fiction some parts have been fictionalized in various degrees or various purposes. Notwithstanding those purposes the events and conversations in this book have been set down to the best of the author's ability, although some names and details have been changed to protect the privacy of individuals.*

# TENNYBOOTS!

## Dedication and Acknowledgments

***TENNYBOOTS!*** is dedicated to the Ancestors on whose shoulders we stand and to Mama—Florence Edwards, Flo, Big Mama, Pie—who lives through her stories, her great big personality and the love her family and community has for her. I must acknowledge the following people who not only helped to make this book a reality, but also helped to make my life, that of a perpetual caregiver—easier: My wonderful only child, my daughter, Cricket, acting as editor, whose brutal honesty gave me permission to leave thousands of words in the netherworld of the delete toggle; to my babies who double as grandchildren, Chloe and Elijah whose drawings illustrate the cover and pages, and whose very existence makes me want to write our way to a just and fair world; to my first grandson, Miles; to my first niece, Pinky, an author of three books who fell back when my sister, Edie, convinced her that this story was mine to write; to Ashley and Russell, my right and left hands in helping to care for Mama; to my cousin, Myrna, whose active love for Aunt Pie, and her willingness to shoulder my complaints were a blessing to me; to Deborah Burrows, a lifelong friend who found me again at just the right time in our mutual caregiving roles; to Lucille Finney Jacobs, and my little *sister*, Sheila Brown, whose lifelong friendships appear perennially at the times I need it most; to Dr. Betty Salley Stevens, PhD, and Valerie Brown Sistrunk, my day ones who I can call on any time of day or night; to the Loti Sisterhood: Leslie Gallagher, Holly Argent-Tariq, Sandy Fernandez Shechy, and O.J. Nelson, whose honest counsel and strong shoulders kept me from sinking into the mud and staying there; to Audrey Peterman, my dear sister friend and fellow author for the virtual handholding, hugs and support that propped me up during the publishing process; to all Mama's friends in the Foster Projects, and LaGree Baptist Church, who made my job easier and are too many to name, but especially Wanda Hendrix, Belinda White, Audrey Frasier, Deacon Dorothy Williams, Pastor Wayland Williams, and Sister Ethel Hunter; to mothers, daughters, fathers, sons, and caregivers everywhere who have finished the task, especially: William Simmons, Tony Major (R.I.P.) Suzanne Meyers (R.I.P.); and those boomers and caregivers who are still toiling in the vineyard, wondering if it will ever end and feeling guilty about those thoughts.

****

## Sunday Morning Mama

an alarm pierces the early
morning
followed by the jingle of my
cell phone
pithy interrogatives rent the
air:
you coming for me
you got my slip?
more an accusation than a
question
answers in the affirmative
bring
more interrogatives: what
time, what color?
all devoid of pleasantries
no extras. compact
like the years that remain?
minutes later i am in the car
the car knows the routine
a right, 4 avenues, double
rights.
there she waits
with an audience as usual
at the gate
in the tradition of the
ancestors
holding court
she gets to her feet
hardscrabble like
climbs into the car
the ease and grace of youth
escaped long ago
courage and iron will
marshaled against
the dying of the light
propel her forward.
landing with a plop
in a heap
on the seat
1st Sunday white in a pile
our eyes meet
hers-embarrassed and
apologetic
for being old
and having witnesses
to its indignities.
mine-reassuring
as to a child, encouraging
grudgingly proud of the fight
especially when it's directed
elsewhere.
now comes the memories
tweaked over the years
told in a stream of
consciousness
I know them all by heart.
memorialize this moment in
writing
now comes the chorus
blessed, lucky, blessed, lucky
blessed, lucky, blessed.

**Judy Edwards**

# TENNYBOOTS!

## Table of Contents

| | |
|---|---|
| Acknowledgments | |
| Foreword | |
| Chapter One | Hot |
| Chapter Two | Red Summer Baby |
| Chapter Three | TennyBoots |
| Chapter Four | Bonaparte King and His Children |
| Chapter Five | Black Gal |
| Chapter Six | Heartbroken and Migrating |
| Chapter Seven | From the Field to Factories |
| Chapter Eight | Susetta. Fire |
| Chapter Nine | Judy Ain't My Mother |
| Chapter Ten | Mama and Me: Stickin' Plaster |
| Chapter Eleven | Red Blood Cells |
| Chapter Twelve | Ain't Carrying No Load |
| Chapter Thirteen | Sunday Morning Mama Brings in a New Year |
| Chapter Fourteen | All the Sentimental Reasons |
| Chapter Fifteen | New Pantsuit |
| Chapter Sixteen | Ballerina and Mind Pictures |
| Chapter Seventeen | Bored Impatient and Talking Loud |
| Chapter Eighteen | Mt. Sinai Takes Her Back |
| Chapter Nineteen | Shawnee Yellow Bracelet as North Star |
| Chapter Twenty | Jim Crow and Dr. Buzzard |
| Chapter Twenty-One | VIP Hits Turbulence |
| Chapter Twenty-Two | Saturday Night Revelry |
| The Final Chapter | |
| Epilogue | |
| Glossary | |
| Who's Who in the Family | |
| About the Author | |

# TENNYBOOTS!

## Foreword

### by Holly Argent-Tariq LNHA, MS, MFT

Some believe we choose our parents while still in the spirit world. I am one of those people. We venture into the moment of conception and get here. I wondered whether my own mother was happy when she found out I was there. Was she worried? Was she afraid? I heard her voice before all others. It was muffled like ears with cotton earplugs and absorbed by walls and water, and I knew her before I saw her. Then I saw her. She was 40 years old when I saw her as a woman. She was Mami and she was formidable. Nothing stopped her. She was a force of nature. But on this day, she was suffering a miscarriage and bled through her clothing. I was a teenager and was horrified and disgusted by her sexuality and vulnerability. I was *so* angry, and she was *so* human. I was a girl/woman, and everything was about me. One day, I would understand this deep loss as a mother/ woman myself, as I lived through lost pregnancies.

Years later, we mourned the loss of my Nana. Nana -my other mother; her mother. Mami and I shuffled places in the hierarchy of women in the family. She was now The matriarch, and I, the sous chef. We enjoyed this relationship until her illness required me to lose all remnants of youth and secondary womanhood in the family.

Although she continued to reign supreme with the men and boys in the family, she relinquished her authority to me. She trusted me. She loved me. One evening, as I tried to make her bed, with her still in it, she admonished me to "calm down, take it easy." By morning, she was gone. I had ascended.

I miss her and have voice recordings I listen to and remember that hers was the first voice I ever heard, muffled like cotton earplugs and absorbed by walls and water. My daughter chose me and has all the fire of my mother. Next time Mami may choose me as the vehicle to return from spirit, and I will be her Mami.

# TENNYBOOTS!

The stories in this book speak so eloquently to the complexity of that profound mother-daughter relationship. This is literally a book for the ages: every reality grounded person—male, female, young or old—who has struggled at times with the emotion of a human relationship will find themselves on the pages of this Memoir.

****

# TENNYBOOTS!

# Chapter One

## Hot

The August heat held us all hostage. Unending days of temperature readings and humidity indexes approaching 100s had held sway since the month began with no respite in sight. Summer weather, welcomed after a chilly July, by the 3rd week in August we were already over it and dreaming of a crisp fall. Heat Alerts, targeting the elderly, kept flashing on breaking news, posting addresses of cooling centers for people without air conditioning. Public pools were staying open late, and they were reminding the elderly to hydrate. Adults and children were flocking to open hydrants—water parks for the urban poor—providing refuge from the heat under the cool spray of the water.

It wasn't quite 9 A.M. and the rising mercury on the vintage kitchen thermometer, at 98 degrees, was threatening to explode its glass tubing. The heatwave came early one morning and lingered all night like an adolescent boy on a first date. The scorching day's heat cleaved to the nights and renewed its intensity each dawn. Leaving my apartment to walk four blocks to Mama's was not on my agenda this morning. Three ceiling fans and five window unit air conditioners going night and day had displaced and cooled enough hot air to render my apartment comfortable—Con Edison electric

# TENNYBOOTS!

bill be damned. But voicemail, and not Mama, picked up on my morning call to her. Either she had died in her sleep, or against my advice to stay in, she left the apartment early in the morning and was still sitting outside on the bench on one of the hottest days of the year. As soon as I opened my apartment door, a blanket of hot, stale air trapped with nowhere to go in the hallway, mugged me. I gasped for air and retreated backward into my cool apartment. It was a good thing because in my haste to check on Mama; I had forgotten my keys on the sideboard by the door. Common sense coaxed, no, pleaded with me to stay home. But I could not.

Neither heatwaves, nor rain, nor admonitions to the contrary would stop Mama, at 95 years old, from doing what she wanted to do when she wanted to do it. Last night when I'd spoken to her, I suggested that she stay upstairs in her air-conditioned room because they were predicting another scorcher. She had thrown, "I'll see," into the space between us that separated unsolicited advice from common sense; I may as well have been talking to a wall because I knew then that Mama would damn well do what she pleased. But I had to go because there was no way to be sure.

With the hot, humid air turning my clothing into dishrags of sweat, I walked the 4 blocks to the projects where Mama had lived since I was born—over 60 years. Even though it was early, on every block between my place and Mama's, people were filling the sidewalks and sitting on stoops, escaping apartments rendered uncomfortable by the stifling heat. Resigned that my warnings for Mama to stay upstairs were most likely unheeded, and to squelch the anxiety that was taking root in my head and causing my heart to race, I assumed the best under the circumstance—
that Mama was alive and well—just hardheaded. On Mama's corner, I stopped at the store and bought a large bottle of water to keep her hydrated. I also bought what she had requested yesterday—a box of vanilla wafers cookies and a ham sandwich. From halfway down the block, it relieved me to see the bush of white hair on Mama's head sticking out from the crowd at the bench. It also pissed me off.

# TENNYBOOTS!

When I got near the bench, I heard someone say, "here comes Judy," and she had turned towards me but changed her mind, which put her in an awkward position. Steeling herself for a reprimand; yet trying to act disinterested, she began fidgeting with something in her lap. After saying hello to the people on the bench, I turned my attention to Mama. She was sitting on the seat of her walker in her usual spot, opposite the bench, by a wrought-iron fence that separated the parking lot from the walkway. An assortment of black, bodega plastic bags hung near her on the fence—personal-sized bottles of soda and water, snacks and other goodies that the neighbors plied her with. Mindful of my tone, and parsing my words so as not to trumpet my angst or displeasure, I greeted her.

"Hey, Mama."

"Hi Ju."

On the asphalt pathway in front of the building where the benches sit, it was boiling. It was still two hours shy of noon and yet, the sun was bright in the sky. The Sycamore shade trees that framed the benches had lost the battle with the sun today, there was no shade to give and their leaves drooped in defeat. An errant mylar balloon, long escaped from its celebration, hung tangled in the Sycamore's branches for perpetuity. Its ribbon dangled, unable to sway as there was not a scintilla of wind to be had. Mama's white hair was limp in places and sticking to her forehead. Droplets of perspiration greased the side of her face like sideburns slicked down with Royal Crown hair grease. The straw hat I had bought to shield her head from the sun hung on the handle of her walker, like a dejected lover cast aside, but still not wanting to go. To suggest that she put it on was out of the question. I knew better. She caught me looking at it, and opened her mouth in protest, but before she could form the words, I turned away as though I did not even see the old straw hat. I pulled the bottle of water out of the bodega bag, and unscrewed the top to offer her a sip, when she began:

"I ain't drinking that old water!"

"Mama, you need to hydrate yourself in this heat."

# TENNYBOOTS!

"I told you, you can't play in this heat, Ms. Florence," her friend, Linda interjected.

"I asked her if she's hot, she said she's not hot," her friend Ms. Frasier added.

"I told y'all I'm full and I-don't-want-no-water," Mama was shaking her head from side-to-side and drawing out the syllables of the last four words, accentuating each with her hand poised as to stop me from giving her the water.

"Where my cookies?" "Give em here."

She flicked her protest wrist with the nimbleness of a beggar. I prayed for strength. Bad enough it was hot, but being hot and aggravated by Mama would be too much.

"Bout time you brought my stuff. I'm dying from starvation over here."

I froze with the bottle of water suspended in mid-air, the bottle cap in my left hand, and had a mind to douse her with it. But I refrained.

"Ms. Florence, all that you ate already this morning, you cannot be starving," reminded Ms. Frasier.

I knew better than to add that she just contradicted herself because she said that she was full. Instead, I stood as still as the breeze that refused to blow that morning, taking deep breaths with my mouth open to calm myself, and hoping that her friends would shame her into taking a sip of water.

The momentary calm I created for myself was interrupted when Mama shouted, "The hell I am. She told me she was bringing this stuff yesterday." "Hmmmph!"

Her voice rose to a crescendo signaling that she believed she won and the round was over. Smug with satisfaction that I was beaten, she sat upright in her seat, back propped against the

# TENNYBOOTS!

fence, as a boxer retreats to his corner to prepare for the next round.

Linda shakes her head and says, "Ms. Florence, you are too much."

I give Mama her cookies and hook my bodega bag with the ham sandwich and water onto a spike on the fence. It hangs alongside the other bodega bags, vivid contradictions of Mama's claims of *starving*. As I turn to leave, Mama as instigator lobs parting shots at my back.

"You ain't gonna say bye?"

Willing myself not to respond, I half walked, half ran towards Lenox Avenue, where I caught the downtown subway to my office. Since I was already out, I could save myself from leaving the apartment tomorrow. My refusal to answer her taunt angered her, and she continued to call after me.

"Ju," then louder, "Judy!"

Resigned that I would not turn around, Mama's last taunt was lethal.

"Go on with your fat ass. Don't come back."

The laughter from her friends, like exclamation marks, broadcast my humiliation. Tears—that I had blinked back, and willed not to fall more often in the past five years than I care to keep track of—again prick my eyes. I struggle to prevent them from spilling onto my cheeks and into my mouth, a cascade of salty anger, frustration, and fatigue. To wipe my eyes with Mama and her friends watching would signal defeat. Mama had zero respect for those she could bully. It would only make my job more difficult. With all my might marshaled against the spilling of tears that needed to fall, I made it to Lenox Avenue with dry eyes.

Dammit, Nothing is ever easy. Every single time Mama had an audience, she would do this shit: I was 13 all over again, standing in the kitchen of apartment 9A, and in my teenaged way, I was challenging Mama about some decision she made. My two friends, Fay and Marilyn, were waiting for me to go outside. I told Mama that after all that I'd done for her, whatever it was we were arguing about was as though she were spitting in my face. Mama crowed, "spitting in your face huh, you want to see what that feels like?" Then, she hawked up phlegm, and with all the contempt she could muster, spat. By God's Grace, and bad aim, the hawked-up spit fell short of its target-my face. But I didn't realize it. Stunned, in disbelief, and reacting without processing the depths of what Mama had just done, I ran past my friends—who stood with their hands covering their mouths, more in disgust than awe, and then to hide laughter. I wound up in the bathroom, grabbing the pretty washcloths Mama kept hanging on the fancy towel rack for show, searching for the spit to wash off of me.

Mama, laughing through her disdain, had found me in the bathroom and said, "next time I won't miss." Her claim that she hadn't aimed to hit me, but to teach me a lesson, fell on deaf ears. The ridicule was real. Whether she missed spitting in my face by error or intent, the impact remained the same. It was a public humiliation of me at 13 when I could least afford it. My friends told all the Playgirls (a teenaged girls club we formed in 1965) and the Romantics (a rival club of girls who lived in building 1370) that Mama had hawked up phlegm and spat in my face. That she missed me was absent from the story, like a zealous game of telephone. The humiliation and embarrassment were real even if the story had holes.

Mama said I was overreacting and was never sorry and never apologized. I buried the hurt and moved on. That was my first tangible recognition of being the subject of Mama's scorn, papered over by the sense that she was my Mama, and I loved her. Over the years, she had perfected her ability to bring me right back to that moment with layers of additional hurts piled on. When she pushed those buttons, it triggered all of my insecurities. Fifty years later, that wound had never healed and God damn it, here it was again in all its putrid festering threatening to bring me down again. I would not, *could* not allow it.

# TENNYBOOTS!

As fast as I could in the heat, now eclipsed by the hurt, I walked to the corner of Lenox Avenue and 116th Street and took each step one at a time, minding my clumsiness and bad knee, so as not to fall downstairs into the not air-conditioned Subway station, hot as Hades in this August heat. As I swiped my metro card in the turnstile, a train was coming into the station. It was a Number Three Train that began its route four stops ago in Harlem, so more than likely I would get a seat. As the train slowed to a stop, I saw a seat from the window and jockeyed to it when the door opened.

Seated and in the air-conditioned subway car, I felt safe and was getting my bearings. There was a man, about my age, standing next to my seat by the door. He was speaking with a younger man, half his age. Although I assumed my subway persona, (as only those who've grown accustomed to sharing urban public space with strangers can do), I kept hearing snippets of their conversation. The younger man had asked after the older man's mother. I couldn't hear everything but "bitch," and "horrible," and "detest," pierced the din of the subway car, and rode the peals and pitches of the train as it navigated around the curve at the 110th Street station. Intrigued, I allowed the way the train was moving to bring me closer to the man and started listening to his conversation. The older guy twisted his face into an ugly scowl and spat out, "… she died in February at 96, and by the time the bitch died I didn't want to have anything to do with her, but I am the only one who could deal with her, so I did. I was at the nursing home four times a week…"

I gave the older guy a knowing glance and inquired, "your mother?" Annoyed, not so much by my intrusion, but by the thought of his dead mother—the bitch whom he detested—he nodded his head. My own battles with Mama, fresh in my mind from the debacle at the bench, compelled me to validate his sentiments. I told him I understood because I had one of my own who was hard to deal with. I was about to parrot his description using the word that rhymes with witch. But I refrained. The younger man managed an uneasy laugh as though it embarrassed him how the son had spoken of his dead mother in earshot of others. My valiant effort to validate the son's rage fell on deaf ears. He could not receive it. Six months after his mother's death he was still too angry at her to put distance between the hurt that his caring for her had brought and the fact that it was now over.

Recognizing the wicked script, I had no need for the particular details. Five years caring for Mama, it was clear: Baby Boomers harmed and neglected themselves while caring well for aging parents. Mama and I were moving down that same road. I couldn't validate that man's experience on the subway that day, but he sure as hell validated mine. Relieved to know my plight was typical, yet it disheartened me because I could see myself in that man. It was only a matter of time. That evening when I got home I Googled "irascible aging parents" and found hundreds of posts about adult children, Baby Boomers like myself, who had now become their parents' caregivers lamenting about how hard it was, how unappreciated they felt, and how it endangered their health. I sat at my laptop, late into the night and read each painful post while crying big, snot-filled sobs of relief. My situation was not unique. I was not alone. It was not just me! There were many of us out there, battle-weary and wounded children who were caregivers, still doing what we had to do, regardless of the toll it was taking on us. The statistics of caregivers who died within one year of the person they were caring for was alarming. Some articles had it as low as 35% or as high as 70%.

The revelation that what we were going through was typical comforted me. Relieved, yes! But the alarming statistics had me dreading the future. I did not want to emulate that man on the subway. Cursing Mama's last days, six months after her death was not my goal—no matter how hard it got. And making it out alive was paramount. Right on cue, the telephone rings at 3 A.M. and it's Mama. (Mama's expression, "thinking bout the devil and the devil appears" comes to my mind.) Drained and not wanting to invite any more drama, I don't answer the phone until the fourth ring, certain my voice doesn't register any emotion.

"Hey Ma,"

"Hey Ju, you sleep? "

Mama's voice is pleasant and devoid of her earlier nastiness.

# TENNYBOOTS!

"Nope, not sleep."

"Oh, I saw on the News that some trains had problems and I was worried about you. I fell asleep and forgot to call you. I'm glad to hear that you wasn't on the trains. They are still stuck down there."

I think to myself; you mean the train with the man who had a mother who acted like you and he was calling her a bitch and I wanted to call you the same thing. I don't say that. I reply to her genuine concern:

"I got back early. Ma. How are you?"

"I'm okay. I came up early too. It was too hot out there. Girl, I have my air conditioner on full blast, and I have my fan blowing right on me. They can have that heat out there."

"Good to hear, Ma, good to hear." Wanting to end on a good note, I asked no questions and signed off with Goodnight Ma.

It was this Mama who worried about my welfare and safety that kept me caring for her. This Mama, who many years ago rode with me—when taking my daughter to and from Camp in Vermont—to "protect" me from the road terrors that befell women and children riding alone in parts of the country where we were unwelcomed—is the woman I want to care for. This is the Mama that I wanted to help live out the rest of her life aiding her independence, and with as much dignity as she could.

*TennyBoots!* began as the *Sunday Morning Mama Stories*: essays I wrote to vent the many ways I was vexed, angered, and frustrated, by the role reversal playing itself out in my care for Mama. Every Sunday after dropping Mama off at church, I would go home and write about the week before and post it on my social media page. Posting the stories on social media kept me honest, and after a following developed, it kept me consistent. Ours is a story of how Mama sees me when my role changes from daughter to *dictator* in her mind. Her way of seeing me makes my caregiving role difficult.

It's also a story of two imperfect women thrown into a codependent relationship after years of forging our own paths and doing things our own way.

Mama tells her own account of her stories——a double memoir, so to speak. Her stories are candid and unfiltered, in her own words and told how and when she desired. They are her past that holds the secrets of her present, couched in the memories she holds dear, that are never very far from her these days.

Before the onset of cataracts interrupted her perfect vision and halted her reading and writing without eyeglasses, she had written out pages and pages of her memories. Her telling of her stories has become more honest. Advancing age and being the last one left of her birth family has chipped away at family secrets; the need for pretensions buried with the family members she no longer needs to protect. I've taped some of her stories to be true to her voice. Thus, I've recounted her stories here almost verbatim, where I could. I played them again and again in transcribing her stories for this book. I laughed where she laughed in the telling. I cried at the parts where she stopped to cry about family members long departed. And, I got sad, choked up, and angry in the places where her frail and shaky voice trumpeted the hurt of some long-ago slight——still painful almost a century after its first sting.

****

## Chapter Two

### The Red Summer Baby
### Born 23 October 1919

Woodrow Wilson was President in 1919, the year Mama was born. An avowed racist, one of his first tasks, after he came to office, was to re-segregate the Federal Government. Wilson demoted, marginalized or outright fired, Black people, who had held high federal positions after Reconstruction.[1] An assault on voting rights disenfranchised many, Jim Crow laws became more entrenched, and threats of extralegal, violent reprisals and lynchings were common and tolerated threats against Black people. Wilson did nothing to stop it and everything to encourage it.

The year before, 1918, across the country and to a great extent, the Black South was reeling from the horrific lynching of 19-year-old Mary Turner. Vigilantes had had rounded up, accused and lynched her husband, Hayes, for being Black. Mary Turner, pregnant and distraught, spoke out against her husband's heinous and unlawful treatment. A swarm of whites set out to teach her a lesson; they caught, stripped her naked and hung Mary, 8 months pregnant, by her ankles to a tree. They poured gasoline on her body

---

[1] Remembering President Wilson's Purge of Black Federal Workers bunkhistory.org

and the mob watched while a fire was lit and they roasted Mary alive. The 8-month-old soon-to-be-born child that she was carrying was still alive when a white man from the mob reached up and gutted her abdomen with a hunting knife. Mary's unborn child fell to the ground with a thump, cried out in protest before the mob stomped the baby to death.[2] This happened as a bloodthirsty crowd of white men, women, and children, hollering for more, bore witness to the horror. Mary Turner's story has been rumored to be the story behind Josephine Baker's song *Strange Fruit*. Hayes and Mary Turner's lynchings were just two incidents that fueled the uprisings that erupted during the Red Summer of 1919, the year Mama was born.

    They called it the Red Summer because of the enormous amount of bloodshed by both Blacks and whites. By the time it was over white mobs and militias had killed hundreds of Black people, in the North and South United States, and a fair number of white lives were taken too. It was the end of World War I and Black soldiers coming back from Europe had fought to keep the country free. Returning home, they had zero tolerance for the discrimination that greeted them with open arms when they returned to the Jim Crow South. The Black men and women who worked in the war effort at home were ready to take their rightful place as citizens of this country. Black people embraced the second amendment, armed themselves and took a stand against lynching, Jim Crow and rampant inequality on the rise after the failure of Reconstruction.

    In the year of Mama's birth, uprisings spread like wildfire across the North and South. Claude McKay, writing that year about the violence and upheaval he saw around him, penned the lines of the poem, *If We Must Die*, which ends with the famous words, "pressed to the wall dying, but fighting back."[3]

---

[2] #SayHerName:100 Years Ago, Mary Turner Was Lynched
verysmartbrothas.theroot.com
[3] If We Must Die by Claude McKay published July 1919 issue of the Liberator

# TENNYBOOTS!

As the uprisings of the hot summer limped into the much-needed respite of the fall, in this 1919 Red Summer of upheaval, on October 23, 1919, Mama was born. A tiny thing, the story goes. She was so small that she fit into the palm of her Momma's hand. Her head reached the tip of her Momma's tallest finger, her feet barely brushed her wrist. She was so small that her bed was a dresser drawer. Mama tells the story that her skin was as smooth as cream skimmed off freshly gathered cow's milk and black as pure coal——but her hair, attached in tight curls to her small, rounded head, was a brilliant red.

Small and fighting to live, Mama entered this world as the third daughter of George Wilson and Malinda King, daughter of Boneparte "Bonney" King and Mary Woods. Mama was the only one of her mother's five children born at the country hospital, and not at home. Only if you press her, will she tell you that the hospital in St. Landry's Parish was little more than a lean-to for *Coloreds*, propped up on the side of the road. But it's a particular point of pride that she, of all of her sisters, came into this world in the quasi-sterile confines of a hospital, rather than her mother's bed with Madame Toute Toute, the Creole midwife, using her only tools——a pot of boiled water sterilizing rags——and hollering, "pu-sh, pu-sh," when the baby's head crowned the cervix. From her grand hospital birth, Mama returned to the land and the house that her grandfather, Bonney King, owned. Her father George, who had lost an arm in a sawmill accident, died before Mama was born, she never even met him.

Her Momma's marriage to Steve Allen and the birth of two more children secured Mama's place as the middle child of five daughters. Before she turned a year old, her Momma and Stepfather and her two older sisters, Mildred and Fannie, moved from Bonney King's home. Similar to legions of Black folks, imperiled by the failure of Reconstruction, they became sharecropping farmers on a red clay plantation near Interstate 10 in St. Landry's Parish, Opelousas, Louisiana. This move away from her grandfather's land secured her fate.

Mama is equal parts strong-willed, independent, and relentless like the Red Summer that birthed her. She is unmovable in that what she desires, she must have. These traits have remained constant in my lifetime, a jagged framing of Mama's other qualities——wonderful mother, grandmother, great grandmother, friend, cheerleader, and abundant provider of things. Faithful, religious, praying mother that she is, she has covered her family in her constant prayers. She sometimes has a heart of gold. I cannot understate her love for her family. But sometimes Mama's noble heart bumps right up against her pride; when that happens, pride———borne from the ridicule of being Black and poor—wins every single time, extinguishing any hope of rational thought or action. At those times, no amount of pleading, cajoling, or reasoning has ever shaken Mama loose from her beginnings or got her to change her mind or course of action. Events that occurred in Mama's life before she became a woman are the irreversible foundation of who she is. Neither old age, nor time passing has diminished this quality.

Marked by the fighting spirit of the year she was born, fighting back is what Mama has done her whole life. She fights now against time, waning independence, and old age. Pressed to the wall, with more of her living behind her than ahead of her, but she is not giving up——she's fighting back—and giving us a lesson of how to age without becoming old. Blossoming in her ninth decade, she is a charismatic guru in her community. From a distance, I am impressed, inspired by, and grateful for the fight left in this *Red Summer* baby. But up close, as the person who gets in her way, I am also bloodied.

****

# Chapter Three

## TennyBoots!

The towers fell on September 11, 2001, and Mama quit working her day job. Mama's quitting was apocalyptic in the sense that she had vowed never to stop working. But the tragic day shook her to her core. "Enough," she had decried. She was 82 years old and still doing *day's work* cleaning apartments, scrubbing bathtubs and floors on her hands and knees. The last of the little boys she cared for had grown up, and she was too old to get more babysitting work; jobs cleaning apartments were plentiful. Frightened and confused by the events of 9/11 which imperiled hordes of New Yorkers, Mama left work and walked miles to get home, with no certainty that the home she had known was intact. My ex-husband, daughter and I went looking for her and found her a mile and a half from home, walking north on 100th Street and First Avenue. Scared, but pressing forward, when she saw us, she fell into the car and only then cried a baby's cry, forceful and loud with no shame. As soon as landlines were transmitting calls again, she called the woman she worked for and told her she quit. But, soon bored and living longer than she could have imagined, she began to rue the day she retired.

# TENNYBOOTS!

Until that time, I had no memories of Mama ever not having a job. Each day she left the projects in Harlem, traveling by bus and train sometimes to Washington Heights, or Bayside, Whitestone or Forest Hills, Queens, or the Upper East Side, or Lawrence, or Syosset, Long Island, and even to New Jersey. Cleaning woman, babysitter, or caterer for different members of two Jewish families by day and weekends; during the evenings, she cleaned the 4th, 5th and 7th floors of an office building at 233 West 49th Street in midtown Manhattan. Her sister, Fannie, who had gotten her the job, cleaned the 3rd, 8th, and 9th floors. A third woman, Ms. Elizabeth, cleaned the 2nd and 6th floors. Yves, a dear Haitian man, cleaned the lobby and pulled the garbage onto the street.

From 5:00 in the evening until 10:00 at night, Mama pushed an old metal cart with smelly, burlap garbage bags attached to small hooks that jutted out from the rim of the metal wagon. The wagon sometimes lead and sometimes followed Mama as she cleaned and mopped bathrooms, emptied trash cans and ashtrays, dusted desks and vacuumed floors. At 8:00 each evening, during her 15-minute break she sat at someone's desk and called to check on us, at home alone. On weekends and holidays, she cared for other people's children, or catered Bar Mitzvahs and Passovers, Pinya Habins and Bris, Thanksgivings and even Easters and Christmas for the same Jewish families. Into her late 70s she cared for four boys from two families, one Irish and one Protestant. She loved those boys as she loved us, and the families treated her well.

I spent many an evening alongside Mama at the office building—emptying trash cans and wiping ashtrays clean using the dirty, wet rag that hung at the side of the metal cart—with a strong reprimand from Mama not to touch anyone's belongings. Making Mama shame was taboo. Avoiding embarrassing her was paramount.

Mama learned how to work hard and long early in life from lack and shame. Mama tells the story again and again, although it's too painful to remember, she never allows herself to forget.

# TENNYBOOTS!

After church this Sunday she is in a good mood. There's no way of telling what pushes a specific memory to the forefront on a particular day. Today it's a foundational memory. Her need to speak it aloud, as though the telling relieves its pain, demands my participatory silence as I actively listen to a story over 90 years old:

"*I remember it as though it was yesterday…*" Mama says as she tells me the story again at age 98, while I am driving her home from church:

*I was so excited when Momma told me that a friend who lived in town invited me to a birthday party for her little girl, Kitty, five years old and in my grade at school. Momma was the cook at the boss man's house and the missus had given Momma her white curtains that she had took from the windows and left for trash. They was wide curtains, plenty yardage. Momma made me a dress that made me feel like we was rich. The lace of the curtain was at the tail of the dress. Momma bought a shiny satin ribbon and tied it round the waist. It was the prettiest dress I'd ever seen. Momma scraped around and could buy me a new pair of black and white tennys to wear with the dress. I couldn't sleep the night before Kitty's birthday party.*

*We didn't have a buggy then so Momma and Papa Steve took me to the party in the wagon. Now the wagon was for hauling and farming. A slide but with sides. When we got near Kitty's white house with the white picket fence, I jumped out the wagon cause I didn't want them to see me riding up to the party in a old farm wagon. The girls was playing in the yard, and they was singing 'ring around the rosies pockets full of posey…' I was so glad to get to the party. The kids wore fancy dresses. But my dress was prettier than theirs.*

*I ran right to the ring around the rosies group and shimmied my way into the circle. So happy to be there. Then one girl pointed at my feet and said, 'Oh look at Florence, she's wearing tenny boots.' And then they all started to point and sing 'tennyboots, tennyboots Florence is wearing tennyboots.' I tried not to let the tears fall from my face. But the tears came faster than I could hold them back and I started to cry. Kitty's mother made the girls stop singing tennyboots at me.*

*All the girls, most of them who lived in town, was wearing nice little patent leather shoes or white kidskin sandals. Not one of them wore tenny boots. I felt so out of place and wanted to curl my feet up and hide them. I knew*

# TENNYBOOTS!

*I didn't belong there. We was so poor. I wanted to leave that party so bad, but I had to wait until Momma and Papa Steve came back with the wagon to get me.*

*I'll never forget that day. Oh boy, we had it so hard. They laughed at me 'cause they had on black patent leather shoes or white sandals. You can imagine how I felt. But I couldn't stop. I tried to jump around and play ring around the rosies and the other games they was playing. They called me tennyboots the whole party when Kitty's mother had left the room. 'Tennyboots come here, tennyboots do this, do that.' I answered, cause I knew that's what they was calling me.*

*When Momma and Papa Steve came back for me, I ran and jumped in the old wagon and buried my head in the hay. Every time that story come to mind, I can smell the wagon and the hay. When Momma asked if I had a nice time, I began to cry again. She said, 'what's the matter didn't you have fun?' I told her yeah, I had fun, but she knew something was wrong. She asked again, 'what happened Florence?' I told her they laughed at me cause I had wore tennys. Momma told me don't let that hurt you cause you look as pretty as they did. So I, So I...*

Mama stammers. After 98 years, the pain of remembering is too much for Mama to continue, but forgetting is a choice she will not allow herself. She sobs—noisy, shoulder-shaking sobs. When she collects herself, she shakes her head and says she doesn't want to finish the story today. Pulling over to stop the car, I take a tissue, reach into the back seat and wipe her eyes. I caress the softness of her white hair and tell her it's okay; she is a long way from that party. I tell her that what didn't kill her made her stronger, and that she had to either root hog or die poor pig and she had root hog. The Gullah expression that I learned from my mother-in-law, Irene, made her laugh. It was a favorite of hers. But Mama rebuffs my desire to console her today. She needs to dwell in her melancholy. Taking the cue to be quiet, I touch her hair once again, and turn around and drive home. Each to our own thoughts, Mama and I ride in silence the rest of the way home. TennyBoots has impacted Mama's entire life and has made her who she is, who she was, and who she wasn't. Two years short of a century of living, it still grieves her and informs most of our struggles.

****

# TENNYBOOTS!

# Chapter Four

## Bonaparte King and His Children

Shame is Mama's agency—it compels her to act or not. But lack made her a striver. Hunger and going without were familiar childhood companions. Twin societal evils of being Black and poor in post-Reconstruction Opelousas mired the family in poverty to be sure, but the move from her grandfather's land to a sharecropping plantation had circumscribed their fate. Mama labored to cast off the shame and burden of being poor. Those hard years, of being Black and shamed and poor and hungry cling to her subconscious emotions like the parasites they are, feeding on her inability to rise above her raising. The reason she revisits these memories so often over ninety years after they happened is unclear to me. But each time she retells a familiar story, In silence, I listen for the cadence of her voice and her loyalty to the retelling to dislodge undiscovered revelations. Today her early years are forefront in her mind:

*My grandfather, Bonaparte "Bonney" King, was born in the 1860s, right after his father was man'mitted so he was never in slavery. His father, Robert King, had been born during slavery times in South Carolina. That's all we know about him. Bonney's mother was named Melinda too. Just like Momma but with an 'e.' She was Creole, named Melinda Mouton before she married my grandfather.*

*We called him PaPá-you know, Creole potwash. But my Uncle Jack's kids called him KaPa. Momma kinda favored Papá. He would give you the shirt off his back and never spoke to us children in a cross tone. He was easygoing. Something like Momma. My grandmother, Mary Woods, his wife, died in childbirth with their sixth child, Irene. Irene later died too. So PaPá raised five children alone. He never got married again. His kids was my Uncle Jack, Aunt Nettie, Momma who was Malinda, named after PaPa's mother, Aunt Bessie and Aunt Annie. Four girls and one boy, and he raised them all by hisself.*

*PaPá's mother, Melinda Mouton King had three children that we know. PaPá had a sister named Mitty, and a brother, Lewis. Lewis died before I was born so I didn't know him. We called her Aunt Mitty, she was a widow. Aunt Mitty died sitting up. They found her one day sitting by the old wood stove, dead. Nobody knew how long she had been dead. Looked like she had just nodded off, they said. Just as peaceful-like. A day, two days, nobody knew. The last person who saw her alive couldn't quite remember the day.*

*PaPá had a big house and a lot of land. Some people say he got his 40 acres and a mule, but he was born near when slavery ended so I think he bought it hisself. Some say his Mother Melinda Mouton's boss man had give her land when she got free. I don't know the truth behind that story. But he had a big house with a front porch, a back porch, and a side porch. I was born when we was living in Papa's house. They put me in the dresser drawer for a crib; I was so tiny, Momma said.*

*My grandfather was good with horses, and his only son, Uncle Jack, was good with horses too. PaPá and Uncle Jack kept beautiful horses and saddles. He would put a saddle on his horse and pace that horse all the way to town. He wouldn't run him, or lope him, he would let him take a few steps at a time, just pacing. Momma said everybody would come to see him about horses.*

*Momma was the middle girl of five children. Just like me. That's why we got along so good. Born in 1896—she was the second girl. Malinda was Momma's name, after my grandfather's mother, but they called her Lindy. She was easygoing and kind. She never had cross words with anybody.*

*Momma married George Wilson when she was 17. Or she said she did. We think they may have just jumped a broom. Momma told us that the marriage license was behind the picture over the table that set in the front room. But one time my oldest sister, Mildred, looked and we couldn't find no license. Then one time Momma slipped and said they had to choose between eating and buying the license, and they choose to eat. We never said nothing bout it cause we* didn't want her to feel shame. Lots of those old people got married by jumping the broom in those days. Momma and George Wilson had three girls, my oldest sister, Mildred, Fannie, and then me. Me and Fan was close in age. Fan was the knee baby, and I was the arm baby. And we always was that close. I loved my sister, Fan. Our father, George Wilson, had been working at a sawmill when he got his arm cut off. Momma was pregnant with me but she couldn't stand to be with a one arm man. Momma told us that all he had to do was shake that lil nub where the arm used to be, and she would be gone. She kept running home to PaPá. One time she left before I was born and she said she couldn't go back. That nubby arm scared the shit out of her, and my father was very mean to her after he got his arm cut off. I always told Momma I couldn't blame her for leaving him. I would've left too. And later, hot dammit, when I got married I be damned if my husband didn't get a nub too. I was sure glad me and Eddie wasn't still living together when he got his leg cut off. One time he shook that nub at me and scared me half ta death. So I can't say I blame Momma for leaving a man with a nub.

They say that my father grieved the loss of his arm and Momma, and he died before I was born a lonely, sad man. Momma said that the wound got infected, they never took care of it properly at the hospital, and it poisoned his whole body. So that's how I got to be born at the hospital, cause Momma was living with her father.

But by the time Momma ran off from Wilson and moved back with my grandfather, my Uncle Jack was living there with his wife, Hattie, and they six kids. So me, Momma, and my two older sisters and PaPá all lived in one room.

Momma met Papa Steve in 1919 when she was pregnant with me, after my father died. After I was born, Momma and Papa Steve got married— this time they had a marriage license. They had two more babies. Susie Mae was born three years after me, and Nettie was born two years after Susie.

Since Momma and Papa Steve didn't have no farm equipment after they got married, we all moved from PaPá's house onto the white man's plantation and started sharecropping. Papa Steve was no farmer, but he was a good hunter. He would hunt at night with a light round his head that would blind the birds. They would be sleep in the tree and he would take his stick—he call em ricans—and thrash them down to the ground. He would have a sack that he would put them in. They would be good eating them robin redbreasts.

# TENNYBOOTS!

*We would gut 'em down the back—not the front cause we would mess up the good meat. We'd clean 'em out, pick the feathers off over a kettle of hot water and fry them up. Oh boy that was good eating when Papa Steve would go hunting. Them birds was so good they'd make you slap yo mama.*

*But a lot of times we ain't have much to eat. When it was time to take the cotton to the gin, we would make a bale of cotton, we thought. We would pack that bale of cotton all night so Papa Steve could be one of the first ones at the cotton gin. Because there'd be lotsa people going to gin the cotton, we would try to get our cotton ready early. Your bale had to weigh at least 400 and some pounds. Poor Papa Steve would get up early in the morning, hitch up his wagon and there he'd go. All the cotton, tall, white and pretty, going to the gin. When he got there, the bale would only weigh about 300 pounds, then he had to pay a fine cause it didn't weigh enough. The only thing he had free was the cotton seeds—then he could sell them back. Most people kept they seeds, but Papa Steve sold his cotton seeds back every time he went. We would have to get new seeds from the boss man, and bout time we'd pay him back, all the money be gone, and we worked another season for nothing. Later we found out that our field was on the worst piece of land on the plantation.*

*But that didn't stop us from hoping. Every time, we would wait for Papa Steve to come back with a package of French bread and cans of sardines for each one of us. When he returned, we would drop everything and meet him halfway down the road. But we could tell by the way he was coming if he had something. He'd come back looking sad. No bread, no sardines, no package. Oh boy, you talking about some sad lil kids. I was always greedy, I'd been tasting the sardines and bread. I cried. No bread! No sardines! Nothing! When Momma found out she would say, 'that's all right, I will make y'all a cornbread.'*

*Even the trees in our yard was bad luck. Everybody else had fig trees, pecan trees and other fruit-bearing trees. We had a thorn tree. Nothing on it but thorns! When the new boss man came, Mr. Charlie Bohanne, he moved our house to a better piece of land. Then he added on what used to be a real dollhouse for the white kids to play in, to our house. Mr. Robert Nash would move houses; he hitched it onto our two rooms and we finally got us a kitchen, instead of the kitchen being in the bedroom in our two-room house. So that gave us three rooms and a pantry. We put a safe in the kitchen, a safe where you put your dishes and glasses. And things got a little better.*

# TENNYBOOTS!

*We had it hard but I don't remember Momma ever being raped though. For some women, it wasn't so easy. Any white man would come to the field and call out, 'hey nigger, tell your wife to come here.' The poor nigger man would say, 'Yesssuh!' One man it happened to would tell his wife, 'Barbara go, he calling you.' Barbara would say, 'I don't wanna go.' But the old white man would take her in her house where she lived with her family and have his way with her and then give her a few dollars. Barbara had a half-white baby. And she raised her right there long with her other children and her husband. The only difference was she was light. They used to call me 'shine' I was so black. I used to ask Momma why she didn't let them take her. I wouldn't have been so black.*

*My sister Fannie got married at 14, she was just a kid. But she was beautiful and a lot of men picked at her. A lot of the girls got married early so the older men wouldn't mess with them. Our mothers thought it was better for us to be married to a man, rather than 'low a man to fool round with us unmarried. Momma didn't want Fannie to leave home, so they added another two rooms onto the house; one room for Fan and her husband, and a bedroom for us, so it made a bigger house. Her husband, Frank, was mean and jealous. He got killed in a saloon not too long after they got married and Fan got pregnant, so Fannie and her son, Frank Jr, we called him Sonny, stayed with us until she met and married her second husband, a Creole man named Joseph Mac Chavis.*

*It was a big deal when Fan's husband, Frank Sam, got killed. He got into a fight, got stabbed and was bleeding bad. It was late at night and his friends had put him in the wagon to take him to the hospital. They swung by our house and got Momma and Fannie and continued on to the old country hospital. By the time they got there, he had bled out. Then there was a big stink cause the men who did it wasn't arrested. You see, they worked on another plantation. And they owner was boasting about his niggers going free. Everybody was waiting to see what Bohanne was gon do. Bohanne was the owner of our plantation at that time. So Bohanne went to the sheriff and they say he pitched a bitch. The sheriff arrested the men who killed Frank Sam—they went to jail for a while. Bohanne was bragging and everybody was saying don't mess with Bohanne's niggers. He was a lawyer, so he knew his way round the law.*

*All our mules was half dead. Whenever the white folks had a old mule they knew was gon die, they would say, 'Hey Steve, wanna buy a mule for 25 cents?' Papa Steve would fall for it every time. He would buy the old mule* thinking he was getting a bargain, and damn if the mule didn't die that day or soon after. Then Papa Steve would have to haul the dead mule all the way out to the country. Them old white folks was dirty like that. Always getting somebody to do they dirty work. And Papa Steve was always trusting them, he was such a good soul. One time he bought a old half-dead mule that fell dead right there on the plow, didn't even finish one row. Pa Steve was hitting the old mule with the rawhide whip, saying 'git up git up.' I said, 'Papa Steve that mule done died. The old mule was dead as a doorknob but Papa Steve couldn't believe it. We had to unhitch him from the plow and drag his ass into the woods where the buzzards would eat him. Last time I seen the old mule two black buzzards had his guts flying away. Papa Steve cried like a baby. No work was gone get done that day. A day lost in the field was a day you could never get back.

In all the time we was cropping we had one good mule, his name was 'Jimmy.' He was the last mule we had, and he was a pretty lil mule, fat and everything. He was the nicest mule we ever had too. Mules can be stubborn. They don't like to work unless you make em.

Oh, we had horses too. We had a horse named Belle. Poor Belle—we had rode her so much without a saddle that her back got sore. One day me and Fannie put a coat over her sore spot and rode off on poor Belle. We had been drinking something Papa Steve had, some old moonshine; or maybe we was chewing his tobaccy or something and we got a lil dizzy. We fell off old Belle into a pile of red ants that was biting our ass. Good thing poor Belle had more sense than we had. When old Belle went back with a coat on her back and no riders, Momma wondered where we was. Momma went to look for us in the direction Old Belle had come. She found us in the pile of ants. We was drunk or high or something. Me and Fan swore we would never drink or chew tobaccy again. And we didn't. Till this day, I only drink communion wine or Manischewitz wine. And Fan never drank either. Momma wanted to cut our behinds, but those red ants had us itching and swelling. Momma made some poultices and put on us and gave us some tonic to ward off a fever.

We had other animals too. I once had a pet pig named Suki. Suki had been the runt of the litter, so she wasn't slaughtered and ate. Momma said I could have her for a pet. Suki was a cute lil pig, but she couldn't get to the tit. I would get some milk for her and then feed her with a baby bottle. We'd feed her the scraps, and whatever I had, I gave Suki some. Suki used to follow me everywhere. Like that nursery rhyme, the only time Suki couldn't follow me was when I had to go to school. After a while Suki fattened up. But she was a pet then, so Momma promised we wouldn't kill and eat her. One day I came home from school and no Suki. She used to be waiting for me by the gate. I asked Momma and everybody if they seen Suki. Nobody seen her... I went all round the field, and then I went all round the house calling Suki Suki. Then it dawned on me that my Aunt's in-laws had probably stole her. They used to steal everything. I went over to their house looking for Suki, and I asked them if they saw Suki. They said they hadn't been over our way. But I saw blood running from the old lady's skirts. They had butchered Suki up and was fixin to cook her. The old woman had sat on top of the pig when I came in and tried to cover it with her skirts. After I saw the blood running out from under her skirts, I ran from there hollering for Momma. Momma was sad too, but she said don't worry. Momma was not the type to go over and confront them. She was content to let God handle them. 'Jesus will whip em,' she said. After they ate Suki, they came to our house wanting to fight. They told Momma to come out of the gate. Momma said, 'Now you done ate the pig up and got your bellies full and want to fight. We ain't gon fight you.' They had a big knife that was used for cutting cane and they was swinging it and cutting at the air. I started crying, 'Momma don't go out the yard, they gon kill you.' Momma was not scared of them even though they was some bad people.

Along with working the fields, Momma was the cook and Aunt Bessie was the wash woman for the boss man. Some days Momma would let me go to work with her at the boss man's house. She would sit on the couch and read the Times Picayune. She had learned how to read before I was born, I guess, cause I never knew her not to read. I would clean the house up and down and she would cook. Sometimes she would tell me what she was reading in the Times Picayune. It wasn't all bad days when I think about it now. Momma would've made a perfect Missus of the house, she was kinda proper like that.

That boss man was Herbert—he was a gambler. He lost his money in gambling debts. Everybody said the wife killed herself when they begin to get poor. Her first husband was a rich man, and he died. And then she married Herbert. He would gamble his last penny away. The wife saw them getting poorer and poorer. One day she tried to kill herself and they took her in a long car—ambulance, to the hospital. She told them, 'If you save me today, you will bring me back tomorrow.' And sure nough the next day she was dead. Their kids was all big by then. And Mr. Herbert kept on gambling until he lost the property. That's when Bohanne came.

# TENNYBOOTS!

  *People never escaped from sharecropping. Some did better than others but nobody ever really broke free. Except the ones who got killed in the war, they family would get a lil pension and enough to buy a house in town. And except my brother-in-law, Jerome. After my oldest sister, Mildred got married, she and her husband stayed in Opelousas for a while. Her father-in-law, old man Jerome was a white man. Her mother-in-law was half Indian, half Black. Old man Jerome loved Madame Jerome, and the boss man in Opelousas had married them.*

  *When my sister Mildred and her husband first got married Jerome was cropping, and he didn't make the amount he was supposed to make. The boss man repossessed his mule. Without a mule, Jerome didn't have no team to plow, so he was working with his mother and father, just barely making ends meet. Momma got so mad at the boss man, Herbert, and was cussing Herbert out—the only time you could get Momma to cuss was if you did something to her children—telling him how dirty he was, that he didn't have to take the only mule they had away from the kids. She told him that he know they didn't have nothing, he know they just started out. Old boss man Herbert turned red-faced and picked up a walking cane and he got behind Momma. Momma started running and hollering. Just then PaPá, Momma's father, happened to be coming cross the field. He said, 'Come on Lindy, run to your Daddy, come on I'll fight him.' Herbert turnt round on his heels, went through his kitchen—they had a big house and he parked the car in front of the house—out the front door. When I looked I couldn't see nothing but dust, Herbert had jumped in his car and hauled ass. I don't know if PaPá could fight, he was walking with a cane then, but he sure scared old Herbert off. The next day the boss man was sweet as pie.*

  *But Jerome was mad as hell and never got over it. One day Jerome stopped the whole operation in the middle of the row. He stopped the plow. He said, 'Whoa!' Stopped the mule, and said, 'Fuck you!' He left everything right there in the field and walked to Galveston, Texas—barefoot. He hitchhiked on the freight train, and buggies and wagons. He went to Galveston where his sister T-bed lived with her husband, a pure African. Jerome was a hero to all the sharecroppers. They told that story for years how Jerome stuck the plow in the field and said 'Fuck you!' and never looked back.*

  *There was no cropping in Galveston. Jerome's brother-in-law was working on the sea. But Jerome could build a house with his own bare hands. He built his own house in Galveston and when he went to New York City*

# TENNYBOOTS!

years later, he sold it for a good price. He worked in Galveston until he got enough money to send for his parents, old man Jerome and Madam Jerome, and my sister and their children.

When old man Jerome and his wife, Madame Jerome, got to Galveston, they wasn't allowed to be married. She was half Indian, half Black. Old man Jerome was ostracized for marrying a nigger. They took the old white man, and they separated the old man from his half Indian, half Black wife. It worried old man Jerome so much he got sick and went blind. He suffered so much. He used to walk to town every day, him and that cane, falling down, getting up, cause he was half blind, to get a dime worth of coffee and nickel worth of sugar. The townspeople all felt bad for him and finally they let him go back with his Black Indian wife. He was really old and sick by that time. He didn't live too much longer after they let him go back with his wife. He loved her so much.

****

## Chapter Five

### Black Gal

Mama has a habit of calling people black and ugly. Self-hatred she learned as a child also has her calling herself the same names. A man had just walked past us on the bench and she had smiled and spoke nicely to the fellow, but once he was out of earshot, she began her name-calling.

"Boy, he is blaaack and ugly. But he's nice though."

"You black yourself Ma. You ain't ugly but you sure are black."

"Oh yeah, I am ugly. This old ugly face of mine scare all the babies. They see this black face against this white hair and the first thing they do is turn up their face to cry. I'm used to it. Hell, you black too Judy,"

"Black and proud, Ma. And you ain't ugly. But you don't hear me denigrating people by calling them black and ugly."

"Shit. I was den-a-gated too. I'm just used to it."

"Den-i-gr-ated Ma."

# TENNYBOOTS!

"Oh hell, denagated, denigrated, whatever the word is. I was called black all my life. Ain't bother me none."

"Well just cause you got used to it doesn't mean other people want to be called black in a bad way. I really wish that you would stop it."

"Oh, Judy, please! They called me 'Black Gal' or 'Shine' cause I was so black. The white folks used to beckon their fingers and call "Shine, come here Shine." And I'd go cause I knew my name. And the colored folks called me, 'Black Gal.'"

"That's my point, Ma. So why do you call other people black if it made you shame?"

*I wasn't shame. That sun had me so black and it had my already red hair—bright red. My oldest sister Mildred would plait big old braids in my hair. One braid be going to the sun and the other to the moon. I was a sight for sore eyes. The name, 'TennyBoots' stuck with me for a long time. Other kids called me and my sisters 'rag-a-muffins.' We had been used to walking everywhere bare feet, but after we got older, Momma bought us some tennys for our feet. When we was going to the country school the white people had a bus that pass by our house and go down in the woods and pick up one lil white boy and bring him to school. The bus pass right in front of our house and the driver would step on the gas to make the bus go fast and the dust fly up on us. It would cover our whole body including our face and hair and the old driver would laugh his ass off. He had dusted up the niggers again. We would beat the dust off of us as much as we could, and bout the time we get to the school, the kids would laugh and say here come the dust bugs. It was a lot we had to take...Y'all don't know how easy y'all have it. We went to school about three miles from where we lived in the country. The Couteau School was a one-room schoolhouse with one side for girls and one side for boys, with eight rows of seats on each side. The school went from primer to 6th grade. I can see it like it was yesterday. We had to bring our lunch to school cause there was no such thing as a school lunch then. Momma bought us lunch pails. We would have rice with butter; when we didn't have butter we would have rice with lard. When we had made some money sometimes we would have rice and sardines. The kids who wasn't as poor as we was would have bread and jelly or bread and figs. Their parents would put preserves away, or have a lot of fig trees and make them nice fat sandwiches fill with preserves.*

# TENNYBOOTS!

*At school, kids would swap they lunches. I always ask to swap with the other kids. They would always say, 'I'll give you a piece of mine, but I don't want any of yours.' Nobody wanted the rice and lard or rice and sardines. My older sister would never bring lunch if she had to bring that old rice and lard or butter or sardines. Sometimes at school she would be so hungry, she was bout ta faint. On those days, she would sneak around us and ask for a spoonful of the rice and sardines, but she wouldn't let the other kids see her eating it. One day I was bargaining for a piece of another kid's sandwich and I looked up and our teacher, Ms. Hattie Locks, was looking down on me from the window. She smiled, but I felt so shame. I was dealing with that girl for some of her sandwich. I said sheepishly, 'Ms. Hattie, what you doing looking out the window?'*

*Momma only had these old irons you would heat them by the fireplace, and she would put starch in our clothes until they could stand up by themself. Then she would iron the clothes and the smut from the iron would get on the clothes. I had a navy-blue jacket, that I wore to school one morning and the kids laughed at me. Momma could only wash it on the weekend so it would get dry. I sat next to Kitty Brooks, the pretty little girl who birthday party I went to. One day the teacher said, 'Wilson, why would you wear that coat and sit next to Kitty?' She scorned me for wearing it. I felt so small. But Kitty was nice. When we got out of school she said, 'It's okay Wilson, just wash your jacket before you come to school.' I said 'Okay'. I couldn't tell her that it didn't matter, after walking miles to school, even a clean jacket would be dusty, so that's all I said to her. I went home and told Momma that evening after school. All Momma said was, 'I can't do any better baby.'*

*After we finished at that school, we went to the big St. Landry's Colored School on Academy Street in town. Professor Solete and her husband ran that school. That's when all hell broke loose. Cause we didn't have no city clothes. Momma and Aunt Bessie would buy material for 5 cents a yard and they would sew all night. Momma didn't have no sewing machine, but Aunt Bessie did. They used to make me a dress called the bellbottom dress. When we started school in the city, the city kids had nice clothes and nice shoes like the city kids at the party. We barely had tenny boots. But* we made it. *Momma couldn't do any better cause she was always sickly. Come to think of it, Momma may have been a lil lazy too, now that I think about it.*

*I went to the 6th grade in the country, but when I got in 7$^{th}$ grade at the city school I didn't know my maths. I didn't know how to invert the terms. I* didn't even know what it meant to invert the terms. I was at the blackboard one day and the teacher told me to invert the terms. Shit, I wrote the terms upside down. Hell, I had never heard bout inverting terms. I heard some kids laughing behind my back, but it ain't help to invert the terms. The teacher told me I had to go back to the 6th grade. I went to the professor who ran the school, I said, 'Professor Solete, Ms. Matilda is putting me back in the 6th grade.' She said, 'I agree you don't know the $6^{th}$ and 7th.' I cried and went home and told Momma and she said, 'Well that's what you have to do baby.' Momma was not bout to put up no fight with the school. So that's what I started to do. It was just me who had to go back to the country school with my younger sisters, Susie and Nettie.

Well, I went on back for a few days a week. Then Momma had a friend who job was to clean the porches of some white folk's houses every day. She asked me if I wanted to earn money. She paid me a dollar a week to clean some porches for her every day. I would stop on my way to school and clean the porch. I used the money I earned to buy Momma's medicine. That's why I finally quit school cause I didn't have no school clothes and shoes and Momma needed medicine. It was just easier to go to work.

When I got to be 11 and 12 years old during the time they was rationing food and stuff, we didn't have much money. We was working on 'halfs' on sharecropping. We had to give the boss man half of what we make. Some people was on thirds but we had to use the boss man's equipment so we was on halfs. The boss man was giving Momma and Papa Steve five dollars a month and they had to pay it back after the harvest. During harvest time we had to pull the corn off the stalk, and dig white potatoes and yams. We would pick gallons of blackberries and we would walk four miles to town and knock on the white folks' back doors and we would get ten cents or fifteen cents a gallon and they would make jam out of the blackberries. Then it had pecan trees on the land, men used to get up in the trees and thrash them with a rican and beat all the pecans down. There was pecan trees going down in rows, they call it a pecan arbory and we would go down the row and pick up gallon buckets full and we would sell it fifteen cents or twenty cents a gallon. Momma also used to make pies and praline candies and we would sell them at the golf club for a quarter. We would go home and give the money to Momma. Since Momma was sickly a lot of the work was on us.

It had a swamp in the back of our house where crawfish and catfish would be plenty in the swamp. We used to go back there and take a cane and *'bear' for fish and crawfish. We'd get maybe two to three gallons of crawfish and Momma would boil 'em, take the tails off and either make gumbo or stew the crawfish tails. And we would eat that, and that was a good meal.*

*One night, Momma went to town and told us to stay in the house till she come back. But our cousin came by and said, 'We going to catch some crawfish y'all wanna go?' We went into the swamp, the water would catch you to your knees, but if you muddied the water up, then the crawfish would come to the top. We did, and we each got a gallon of crawfish. We just knew Momma would be proud of us. But she had come home and had been calling us, she didn't know where we was. Near our house, there was a big old bayou of water, the Callahan, but we never went crawfishing in the bayou cause they ain't had no crawfish in there. They had snakes in there, and dangerous lampeels. Momma didn't know whether we had gone there and got drowned or what. She went all in the bayou and then the swamp with a stick feeling round for us. She was calling, 'Mildred', 'Sister' (that's what we called Fan) 'Florence' for me and my two older sisters. And finally, we heard her. It was too dark to see her. We each had a gallon of crawfish we had struck gold that day. We thought Momma would be glad. But she give us all a whipping. She said, 'Glad, nothing. I been all in the dam looking for y'all.' Then afterwards, she was sorry, and she cooked the crawfish, made the gumbo and put some up for another day. Momma apologized for beating us that day and we was all friends again.*

*Sometimes we sold eggs for money. Chickens would make a nest on the side of the road in the briar patch. And they would hatch. They would wait till they got about 12 eggs and they would set on the eggs till the chicks would hatch. We would find those eggs and take them to the store; we could get a nickel for two eggs. Them chickens would be going round, 'cluck cluck cluck, cluck cluck cluck,' looking for them eggs. We didn't know how long them eggs had been there. Didn't know if a chicken was bout to hatch or what, we sold them eggs. Mr. Moses at the old general store would ask, 'Is they good?' We'd say, 'Yessir they's good!' I hope whoever got them got what they wanted. What a life...*

*When we all moved away from home, Papa Steve and Momma did better. Finally, they left the country and moved into a house on Mill Street in town. They lived out they lives in that old house on Mill Street.*

****

## Chapter Six

### Heartbroken
### Migrating

Migrating away from the hot, red, dusty fields of Opelousas, Louisiana where work was hard and living was even harder, was not a question of if, but when, for Malinda King Allen's five daughters. They left behind the days of endless sun and back breaking toil for the same reason six million Black people left the fields and brutal racism of the Jim Crow rural south from 1916 to 1970 traveling to cities in the North, the Midwest and the West.[4] All five of my grandmother's daughters followed many who had gone before, migrating away from their ancestral home. Four of them came north to New York City and died there. Aunt Annie, Mama's aunt was the catalyst for the family's migration from Louisiana to Texas and then to Harlem, New York. The fifth sister, Aunt Susie settled in Galveston, Texas. She was the only one of the four who returned to Opelousas to live out her life until she died.

Sitting on the bench with Mama, it's just her and me. None of her friends are out yet. Mama complains of boredom and is cranky when she begins a familiar longing for her Momma.

"I sure miss Momma. If only I could see her one more time."

"I can imagine. What do you miss about your mother, Ma?"

---

[4] The Great Migration (African American) en.m.wikipedia.org

"I miss everything. I even miss sitting on the porch with her on that old plantation. You know when Mama and Papa Steve moved to the city I was already living in New York. So most of my memories are in the field or on the plantation."

"But Ma, you always say that you hate Opelousas and that you would never return. After Grandma Lindy died that was it for you."

"Yeah, I know. I was glad to leave that old hot dusty place. Look like the sun never went down, and when it did the night was too dark and too long. I threw some of that old red dust over my shoulder and said I wouldn't be back. You know they used to say if you don't wanna come back to someplace when you leaving throw salt or the dirt over your left shoulder and the place won't pull you back. But when I think about it now, although the leaving part was easy maybe staying gone was too hard. It makes me sad. I wish I had pictures of our old house. First two rooms, then with the dollhouse attached, then after Fanny built two more rooms on it. Now with everybody gone, those memories of them in Opelousas at our old house, in the fields and on the plantation, is all that I have of my family."

"Hey, what are we? Chopped liver?"

That gets a chuckle from Mama and interrupts her longing for a moment.

"No, Well, you know, my family who knew me before I knew myself. My family who knew me in the fields, on that old plantation; in Lake Charles and Galveston. Y'all my family too but y'all came after. Maybe if I had gone back. You know we had mineral rights when we sold Mama's old house. I think we each got five hundred dollars. We should've hung on to that house. But nobody lived there. Susie was in Galveston. Well, we had cousins there. But they was tired watching over the house. That's what made Mildred sell it. We had minerals you know. You ever find out anything bout those mineral rights?"

"Nope. You didn't mention it until 50 years later."

# TENNYBOOTS!

"I know. I know."

"But anyway, Momma and Fan and them always come around. I talk to them. They keep me company. I tell them I'll join em when God is ready for me to come. I don't know what he waiting on. I'm ready to go."

"Ma, you're ready to leave us?"

"Y'all will be all right. I can leave now."

Biding her time until God is ready for her to join her Momma and sisters, Mama keeps the longing at bay by keeping company with her memories: where her deceased loved ones still live. When she reminisces, her eyes are closed and she's having such a good time, I push my back towards the back of the bench, making myself less prominent in her stories.

*It was funny how all of us but Susie wound up here. Aunt Annie was the reason. When Aunt Annie Mae left Texas, she was the first to travel to New York City. Little by little she sent for different family members to come to Harlem, where she was living. The first time she sent for me to come, it was to babysit her first child, my cousin, Betty. I was only 14 and traveled to New York on the train. It was 1933 or 1934. I sat wide-eyed all the way to New York City. Aunt Annie was living in Harlem, and I moved in with her to care for Betty. It went okay for a while, but Aunt Annie's husband, John, was a fresh old man, and he would pick at me. His sister, who was living with them too, told Aunt Annie to make him leave me alone. Aunt Annie decided it would be better if I went back home to Momma. She sent me back to Louisiana telling me she did not need me anymore.*

*I came back home around 16 years old and I worked at home for a while for this family who had a little girl named, Myrna Baines. I was babysitting her before I went to New York and she missed me and cried all the time. They was happy to have me come back and soon as I got back to Opelousas, I started working for them again. I named my sister, Fannie's second daughter, Myrna, after Myrna Baines.*

*Then, Lil'yan, my cousin, one of Uncle Jack's children had married a guy from Lake Charles, Louisiana—the ugliest nigger I ever seen in my life,*

# TENNYBOOTS!

and she went to Lake Charles with him. He was real good to her though. Later, Lil'yan's sister, cousin Willimae, (one twin, Willie and Willimae), we called her 'Titter' decided she would go to Lake Charles and live with Lil'yan. When Titter got there, she met a guy named Wilson. She already had a baby, Geraldine, and she took her baby with her. She met a man named Wilson and they fell in love and got married. Titter and Wilson built a two-room house behind his mother's house. I went to live with them. Wilson was working at the lakefront and he had a friend who used to work on the lakefront with him. Every morning around 5 A.M. the friend would stop by the house to pick Wilson up for work. Titter would fix them coffee and breakfast before they left. Me and Geraldine, who was the baby then, was sleeping in the kitchen since there was only two rooms. I would hear the guy every morning and I thought the guy sounded nice. One morning I got up early, I was barefoot and only had on my gown. Titter introduced me to him, 'This is my cousin Florence,' she said. We said hello and every morning after that I made it my business to greet him in my street clothes when he came.

One morning he asked me for a date, to go to the movies. His name was Moses Booth. Soon we was going out and we went together as girlfriend and boyfriend for a long time, maybe two years. One day he came home with me to Opelousas to visit Momma. Fannie and her husband, Mac was living there and Fannie had just had a baby and Momma's house was a mess. Momma wasn't a good housekeeper cause she was always sick and clothes was all over everywhere. When we walked in the door, I saw how he looked around at everything. Mac was home, and there was a county fair in town, I was so shame so I asked Mac to take Moses with him to the fair. Mac and Moses went to the fair, and I stayed at the house with Momma and Fannie and helped to get the house together. This woman Sadie, a friend of Mac's would run after men. While they was at the fair, Moses met Sadie. I didn't know it but I noticed when Mac and Moses came back he was acting strange. Me and Moses came on back to Lake Charles, but he wasn't acting the same.

I had moved from Titter's house after she had the new baby, cause they needed the room. My sister, Susie, had come to Lake Charles for a while. Two years younger than me, but she was a go-getter. Had already got married to a man from home, his last name was Lyons. She got pregnant, and his folks didn't want her to marry him, Momma didn't either, cause his folks was high class and we was poor. But Susie and the guy got married, anyway. And she had the baby, a lil boy. But when he was a few weeks old and Susie was working in the fields, Momma gave him some straight cow milk and it was too

# TENNYBOOTS!

strong for him. The poor lil boy died soon after that. Then Susie and her husband broke up. So, Susie followed me to Lake Charles, and we rented a room in a house full of boarders. This was about 1940. I was working as a servant, doing housework, and Susie got a job doing the same thing. We was each making $10 a week. I was sending most of my money home to Momma and saving the rest. Soon, Susie left Lake Charles and went to live in Galveston. Our oldest sister, Mildred and her husband had moved there after Jerome stuck his plow in the field, said, 'fuck you' and walked in his bare feet all the way to Galveston. They was doing okay there.

When Susie left for Galveston, I rented a room on Lake Charles Boulevard, in a house with a woman who had six boys. My room was on the back porch. She had put up screens and windows and that's what she rented me. Moses used to come over every Sunday. This Sunday he didn't come round. One of the woman's sons had kept trying to get in the window to get to me. I was waiting to tell Moses about it. But he didn't come that Sunday. And he didn't come the next Sunday either. It was not like Moses.

Titter had just had Gertrude and had brought the new baby to see me. Across from the house where I was living on the boulevard was a hotel. We was sitting on the porch, me, Titter and the woman who owned the house. And hotdammit Moses and Sadie got out of a cab and went into the hotel. We was all shocked. I called to him, and said, 'Moses, what you doing?' He put Sadie upstairs in the hotel. Then he come back over to me. I asked him what was he doing with Sadie. He told me he went south to pick her up and brought her here to live. I asked him, 'Is she your girlfriend now?' He said, 'Yeah.' Just like that. No explanation. Just like it was normal. I felt awful, but I kept talking—cause if I stopped, I would bust out crying—and told him about one boy trying to get in the window to bother me. He got the boy and told him if he bothered me he would kill him, right in front of the boy's mother. After that she pulled my bed into the kitchen and that's where I slept.

I had a male friend named Amos. He was just a friend, not a boyfriend. One day I wanted to go to the movies, I was feeling so blue. Amos said that he would walk me there. After we started out walking we didn't know that Moses and Sadie came out of the hotel and got in a cab. Titter told me that later. They went to the same movie that I was going to. Amos had turned around and left when we got there. I bought my ticket and without knowing sat on the same seat where Moses and Sadie was sitting. When I realized I was sitting down beside them I was mad as hell. But I wouldn't leave. I sat there and nagged the hell out of them. I made them move over and over till they got up and left. Then, I followed them out. Moses got a cab, and I sat in the cab. It was three of us in the back seat, and the cab drove off. I had them all screwed up there together. When we reached the hotel, I got out. They ran on upstairs to they room, and I crossed the boulevard and sat on the porch. Titter had just come over with the two babies to see me, and she and the owner was sitting on the porch. They saw the three of us get out the cab. I felt so shame. They told me not to worry that Sadie didn't mean Moses no good.

I asked my brother-in-law Mac, why he didn't tell me Moses had met Sadie. He said he didn't have nothing to do with it. But Moses was a good-looking light-skinned guy. See, that's what stopped me from marrying him earlier. He had asked me to marry him twice.

I was shame that his people would call me black and wouldn't want him to marry me, but we had a lot of fun together. Sadie was light-skinned too. She was nice looking and had pretty teeth. Her mother and them had a nice looking house in the city. I was a little shamed of myself and felt that I wasn't as much as other people. I was working doing housework. If you didn't have a education you couldn't get a big job, I only went to the 7th grade.

Last I heard, Moses and Sadie had moved away, and got married. I was still feeling heartbroken bout Moses and I didn't want another boyfriend. Years later, in 1968 when we went south to bury Momma, we went to Lake Charles to see our cousins. Wilson told me, you wouldn't even know Moses Booth now. He sits on the street he's been to jail. Moses didn't like his women round no other men, and Sadie was chatting with a man one day and Moses killed the man. I'm sure it was more than that. He made six years in jail and was never the same. He and Sadie had five pretty girls. Moses was good looking and Sadie was good looking so I would expect them to have pretty, light-skinned children. I told Wilson good for him, bet Sadie was the cause, running round with another man. I would have made a good wife with Moses, but he ran off with Sadie and broke my heart.

I left Lake Charles when I was about 21, 22 and followed Susie and Mildred and Jerome to Galveston, Texas. I didn't know how to quit my job, so I told the people I was working for that I had to go home cause my mother was sick. I told them as soon as I bought a suitcase I would pack my things and leave. They said all right, and the man loaned me his suitcase. I didn't want to take it, but anyway I packed up his suitcase full of my clothes. They expected me to come back in a week. He wanted to take me to the station to catch the train. But I told him I would get to the station by myself. I didn't want him to see I was traveling to Texas, not Opelousas.

Now, Susie, my younger sister was fearless. She had gone to Galveston and met a guy, an older man as usual. She hooked up with him and they got a apartment. I went to Galveston and stayed with Susie and old man Bradley. Three of us sisters was now in Galveston. My sister, Mildred, had two little girls, and I loved to play with them. Susie didn't live very far from Mildred. I stayed there with her and her old man for a while. Then Susie rented me a room at 37 Avenue H, and I stayed there until I left for Harlem. I remember that old rooming house like it was yesterday. A Black man owned the house we lived in. He had boarders. Had a woman there they called her, 'Baby.' She had a old man for a husband too. He worked at the waterfront and he made good money. He would bring her his check and put it in her lap. I wanted that kind of man like Baby had. My room was on the third floor. Baby and her old man rented the kitchen and a downstairs bedroom. The owner had some other boarders there too. One of them died when I was there. Likedta scared me to death. Then people said that his ghost was still there. We did hear a lot of bottles rattling at times. And the man who died always had bottles rattling too. Boy, If those walls could talk... A lot of stuff went on there but that's a whole nother story. I had to tell Momma that I was living with Susie and Old man Bradley. Momma would not have approved of me living in a place like that by myself. But really, it was fine. We all lived like one big family.

I had bought myself a yellow bicycle to ride to get around. My nieces, Erdie Mae and Georgie used to come over every Saturday to ride the bicycle. When my sister, Fannie, wrote and told me to come back to New York, I give them the bicycle. They was so happy they rode the wheels off the old bicycle.

Aunt Annie had told my sister, Fannie's husband, Mac, to come to New York so he could get a better job. Mac was working at the department store on Academy Street in Opelousas. He packed up when Aunt Annie called and moved to Harlem. Soon after he got there, he got a job working on the railroad. When he got all settled in Harlem, he sent for my sister Fannie to come.

But Fannie was lonely in New York and wanted me to come and live there. Mac had gone to work with Pullman as a sleeping car porter on the railroad. He was away from home a lot. Them porters had to work something

# TENNYBOOTS!

like 400 hours or 11,000 miles each month. The pay was better than the department store, but not by so much. Mac was earning close to $1,000 per year. But the job had a lot of prestige for Black men, so he didn't want to leave it. My sister, Fan, was there alone most of the time. Fan was my closest and favorite sister. When she wrote me to come back to New York, there was no way that I was not gonna go. I got on the bus with a ticket as long as my arm. They would tear off a piece every time you change towns. My sisters, Mildred and Susie, had fried me some chicken and made a box for me to eat. Just couldn't tell the people I was working for that I was leaving, so I had Susie to tell them after I left. It took a whole week to get from Galveston, Texas, to New York City. There was no paved roads, just rocks, and dirt roads. Only when you got into New York City, that guy, what's his name—Robert Moses—was just starting to put cement down. The bus ride was long and dusty. I had never traveled on the bus that far before, but I couldn't afford a train ticket. Black folks had to sit all the way on the back seat, only three seats, the long seat and two side seats. I got a squeezed-up seat where four people sat in the space for two, and sat down. Sometimes I got up and sat on my suitcase. We would stop at different towns and would go round to the back to the colored bathroom, and a lil restaurant door. They would throw you a sandwich for about thirty-five cents to a dollar. My food ranned out about the third day and I had to buy the old sandwiches.

# TENNYBOOTS!

## Chapter Seven

### From the Fields to the Factory
### Cleaning House is Honest Work

    *A taxi cab driver ripped me off my first time taking one in New York City. That's why I don't take them now. They will rip you off. When I got to the bus station in New York City, I took a taxicab to west $126^{th}$ Street. The taxi driver brought me all the way upstairs with my bag, but he charged me five dollars. The meter only had two dollars on it. When we got upstairs, I told Fannie I did not want to pay him no five dollars for a two-dollar ride. He said, 'Yeah, but I brought you upstairs.' Hell, I was dumb. I didn't know better, I thought Taxi Cab drivers took you upstairs too. But I wasn't dumb enough to think if the meter said two dollars that I owed him five dollars. Fannie was always easygoing and said 'Give it to him Florence, pay him the five dollars.' I only had one bag. He charged me five dollars to bring one bag up five flights of stairs. I ain't trust taxi drivers since then.*

    *Fannie was renting a room from a old Creole lady named Mrs. Poole. She was short but proud. She lived in that fancy building on St. Nicholas Avenue where the Schrafft's Restaurant was on the street level. Ms. Poole rented a room to another man, Mr. Vanilla. He was a longshoreman. Mac was working on the railroad, and then when the war broke out he had gone to the Army, so Fannie was alone often. When I got there, I was sleeping on the couch in the living room. Ms. Poole didn't like that and objected after two weeks. Fannie's children—Sonny, Jeanie, and Boo, whose real name was Joe after his father—was living with Momma in Opelousas until Fannie got on her feet. So, me and Fannie found a apartment from Mr. Douglas, a Negro man, who owned the building at 365 West $126^{th}$ Street. We got a apartment on the fifth*

# TENNYBOOTS!

floor. It was a old railroad flat, with a front room and two bedrooms—five rooms with the kitchen and bathroom. Once we got the apartment, Fannie got her kids from Louisiana and brought them back to New York. We was so happy to have the kids with us. While we was living there, Myrna was born. I named her after the little girl I babysit for in Opelousas.

Fannie was a beautiful woman, she was tall and light-skin. Everybody said we look alike, but she was yellow and I was Black. Where Fan was tall, I was short. I didn't see it cause Fan was beautiful, and I knew I was ugly. But she was good and kind and always was easygoing. We both had red hair. Fan's was browner than mine. Momma said I was supposed to be light-skinned like Fan, but this woman thought Momma was fooling round with her old husband and when Momma got pregnant with me, she hoodooed the baby to be black and ugly. And that's why I came out blacker than Fan.

"Hold up, Mama, do you really believe that?"

I try not to interrupt Mama when she is reminiscing, but this is the biggest piece of self-hatred bullshit yet.

"Yeah, you don't know everything Judy. Everybody was hoodooing everybody else."

"Ma, let's get this straight. You believe that but for the hoodoo spell that hexed you, you would be the same complexion as Aunt Fannie?"

"Sure do. I would be bright yellow."

I can't decide if she truly believes this or if she's pulling my leg. I suck my teeth, so that Mama can hear me, and roll my eyes in her direction. Such damn nonsense...I thought it was over, but she's hell-bent on getting to the end of this story, so I fade back into the bench giving her all the space she needs to push her memories into the wind. It's a slow morning, not prime bench sitting weather, and only a few people had passed the bench and said hello to Mama. So engrossed in her stories, she hadn't heard them, and the people had waved and kept on walking. I never got to spend so much uninterrupted time with Mama on her bench. Everyone was Mama's friend, and she had to stop each person who walked by to ask of their Mother, Father, sister, brother, children,

# TENNYBOOTS!

cousins or whoever. She knew each one's name and remembered intimate details about all of their lives. They obliged her inquiries, and each was willing to catch her up on the latest details. Mama was in every peas pickin. At least today, I didn't have to compete with her community for her attention.

*Where was I... oh, I know...When I got to New York City this time, it was during the war. Things were rough and food and other things like nylon stockings, gas and tires was being rationed. Everything had to be saved for the war. Fannie was working at a factory sewing the collars on jackets for the soldiers. Some factory workers had to stuff the collar with an airbag so it wouldn't sink when the soldiers hit the water. Fannie took me on that job and the foreman hired me right away. Dumb and had never done factory work before, I didn't know you had to make so many each day. I was making 50 a day, cutting the threads off the jackets. Boy, I thought I was doing good. But the foreman told Fannie I wasn't producing enough work and that he had to let me go. Fannie told me I was supposed to put out 100 to 200 pieces a day, minimum. She asked them to give me a little more time. The guy came to me and said, 'Florence let me show you. Don't hold your scissors like that. Hold your scissors in your two fingers down by the points, not through the handles, so you can clip faster.' Once he showed me how to do it, I started cutting real fast, I was a thread clipping fool, I could put out 600 pieces a day. I stayed on that job until they went out of business. After the war was over, they didn't need those jackets anymore.*

*In 1943, I was in Harlem, the war was winding down, they was still rationing food and other things. Me and two other women went looking for a job. We asked a man in a store, but he said he had house work to help his wife. The two girls didn't want house work. But I was desperate and said, yes. His wife's name was Florence too. They lived on 181st Street in the heights. They had two children, a girl and a boy. I stayed there with them until they outgrew their one-bedroom apartment and built a house in Jersey. I didn't go to Jersey. I left them a little while before they moved to Jersey. But they was nice people. I had met Eddie by then and left for Georgia to get married. I didn't tell them I was leaving either, just couldn't do it, so I just had my sister tell them when I left. Their names was Boris and Florence Zimeroth. I wonder what happened to them. You think you can find them on that book. What you call it face what...*

"Ask Pinky to do it for you. I don't know how to do it. But I like that story about how you met Daddee."

# TENNYBOOTS!

I had been in Harlem for a while now. Me and my friends from the block, Melvina and Doreatha would always go to the Savoy Manor to dance and have fun. It was a dance club where young people would meet and dance all the latest dances. Mel and Doreatha had grown up on 126th Street. They was still living with their parents. We would get dressed up and dance all night. I was from Louisiana and could dance that Zydeco. I had a great figure, a small, Coca-Cola waist, and big hips. And they loved to see me dance. One night we met these sailors in town from the Frederic Funston a Navy ship. Eddie was one of them. When we was leaving, he asked where we live. We didn't want to tell them our address, so we said we had to go because our parents wanted us home. The three of us jumped the turnstile and caught the train as it was about to leave the station. As the subway door was closing I shouted my phone number to the handsome sailor, MOnument 3-7822. It surprised me that he remembered. He soon called me and asked if he could come to visit me. Eddie was the cutest one in the bunch, and I was the ugliest girl I hung with of the three. Or they thought so anyway. I felt special he chose me.

Food was scarce, Eddie brought meat, rice, flour, sugar, and a pound of lard in a suitcase when he came to see me the first time. I told him I didn't want it. Fannie said, 'I want it, give it here.' And every time he was off, he would come to the house and spend time with us. Every time he would come, he would bring that suitcase full of food. It was good food coming from the base and Fannie was glad to get it.

Fannie really liked Eddie. They were born on the same day or a day apart, I can't remember exactly. She thought he would make a good husband for me. I liked that he was in the service. The people in Opelousas who had nice houses in town had husbands in the service and they would get fifty dollars a month allotment. So that was right up my alley. He asked me to marry him and I said yes. Planning for our marriage, I told Eddie not to take his salary, to let his money add up so we would have a couple of dollars when he got out. He did, I would support him and send him money from my jobs. I figure we could use the money we saved to get ourselves started out.

I got married in April 1944 in Athens, Georgia. Eddie took a blood test outside the Navy for our license in New York, but he had to go to the base for them to sign off on it. They give him hell for taking blood on the outside, rather than letting a Navy doctor take it. They refused to sign off on the blood test. We went to Georgia, where you didn't have to take no blood test to get married.

# TENNYBOOTS!

*On our wedding day, I had on a navy-blue dress and that dress was fitting me, with my nice figure. Eddie wore his navy-blue sailor suit. We looked good together. We got married in the judge's backyard in the town.*

*Just the family was there—his mother, Lola, and his brothers, Early, who we called, 'Flam,' and Jack, and his sisters, Lucy and Bea. They loved me. I was from New York. Oh, and Eddie's old girlfriend came, she had a son for him about two years old, and she came to the wedding. Sitting on the back steps. I can see her face. I felt so bad for her. Didn't even know he had a girlfriend with a son. When I found out the day before the wedding in Georgia, I told Eddie I shouldn't marry him. He should marry her. But everybody in Harlem expected us to get married. So, I went on with it. That was the first strike.*

*Eddie had bought me some gold rings. I wasn't sure they was real. I rubbed them sons-of-guns in the dirt in the backyard, and the damn brass rings turned white as snow. A gold ring wouldn't turn. A brass ring would turn. I was so mad at him. Years later he bought me some real gold rings, but I got married with brass. That was strike two.*

*Then we went back to his mother, Lola's house and had a little celebration. On our wedding night, Eddie's middle brother, Jack, had took a cowbell off a cow. Somehow, he had attached it to the springs of the bed, so that when me and Eddie got together that night everybody would hear the cowbell. We got on the bed and we heard a ding-a-ling, then Eddie moved again, and the bell went ding-a-ling again. Eddie said, 'Wait a minute!' Then, he looked under the mattress and saw there was the cowbell. Eddie gave them what they wanted. He motioned to me to jump on the bed, we went bouncing up and down on the bed and the cowbell ding-a-linged itself crazy. Then Eddie unfastened it and we really went to town as a married couple. The next morning, they swore they heard us cutting up on our marriage bed. We told them the joke was on them.*

*So now we had the wedding and the celebration and I'm on pins and needles just waiting for Eddie to give me the nice pile of money we had saved. He hadn't said a thing about it, so I asked, 'Eddie you want me to hold the money?' He said that he didn't have no money. That after he bought the rings and got his mother's car fixed, he didn't have nothing left. I wanted to whip his ass right then and there and throw his ass back in the service that day. I told him that wasn't his damn money to decide what to do with. That was our money. That was strike three, and the marriage hadn't even started good.*

# TENNYBOOTS!

We left Georgia after a day or so and came back to New York City. I went to my old job and showed the woman I had worked for my rings. She liked to broke my finger, turning the rings round and round to see if they was real gold. Then she said she didn't need me no more, cause I had left, and she had to get somebody else. And guess who she got—Susetta, my best friend from 126th Street. I found myself another job. Eddie's mother, Lola, had said that 'Baby' should have 31 days off: that all the boys in her hometown that came from the war rested for about a month and drew their salary. Eddie was her firstborn, and she still called him 'Baby.' 'Baby' this 'Baby' that. I told her that 'Baby' needed to act like a man and get hisself a job. I thought it but I bit my tongue and didn't say that, especially since 'Baby' had spent all our damn savings to fix her car.

And I didn't know until then that Eddie was planning on mustering out. I just knew he would stay in the Navy for bout a year, so we could get that fifty dollars each month. The nigger stayed in the service one month after we got married. I was sick of him. Strike Four. He had done gone above and beyond his strikes for me.

When we got home, I had him out there looking for a job first thing. He had a hard time finding a job at first. Then he found a job washing cars. We did pretty good, he had a bank account, and I had a bank account in the post office bank round the corner on 125th Street. He had his name on his and my name was on mine. What they say, once bitten, twice scared. He wasn't gon have no control over my money no more to fix folks cars with.

"Shy, Ma."

"Huh?"

"Shy, once bitten, twice shy. But scared works, I get the gist of it. You were not trusting him with your money again."

Mama laughed and continued:

When it rained, they couldn't work washing cars. All the boys would come to our house and play cards. Eddie got broke one time, and he didn't know I was on my way home. I caught him going to the post office to sneak some money to gamble. He had got to the window already, and I went in the post office behind him. I said nigger, what the hell you doing here. Are you here stealing your money, man you better get the hell out of here. He had to come

# TENNYBOOTS!

back home with no money. When the men asked, 'Eddie, you in this game?' He said, 'Noooo.' I admit I was hard on him, but he more than made up for it later.

Then the final straw was that when the marriage license came, I just gave it to him and he put it on the shelf. A while later, I looked at the license and I didn't know the nigger was five years younger than me. I was 24, and he was only 19 when we got married. And you know I wanted to leave him right then. I wanted to marry a man at least seven years older than me, cause my big sister's husband, Jerome, was seven years older than her. I believed that men was supposed to be older than their wife. Every time I had asked him his age, he lied and told me he was older than me. I should've known the nigger's skin was too smooth. Like a baby's behind. Shit, he was still a baby. No wonder his mother called him, 'Baby.' I felt like a big fool then. My husband was younger than my baby sister. That ended it for me. I never would've married him if I knew how old he was. I talked to Fannie about it, and she said, 'Florence it's clear he loves you, nobody haveta know how old he is. Just make the best of it.' I tried, but I never forgave him. Although I didn't leave him, Strike Five was the final one for me.

Her memories now floating firmly in the universe, our conversation meanders like the curves on Central Park Drive. We speak of the senior citizen center that she will not go to. We discuss Yolanda's bodega and building that houses it, that is sandwiched in by gentrified buildings, because as Mama says, perpetually mispronouncing Yolanda's name:

"The white people wanted *Aylanda* to sell, but she said no, her parents worked hard and left her that building. I remember, Mom and Pop sure did. But they sure boxed her in on each side. Like we useta say bout them old mules, she can't gee nor haw."

Done with being proud of Yolanda for standing up to the gentrifiers, the conversation rambles across Fifth Avenue and 116th Street, to the venue where I gave her 75th birthday party and how she wants no more parties. Then her mind flits to my good friend, Randy and my ex-husband, Ervin.

"I sure miss Randy. It was him and his sister, Bea that rented that place for my party, right?"

"Bea managed that building, and I rented it through her. She's okay, she lives uptown, I keep in touch with *Cousin* Bea."

"Poor Randy, he just died this year, right? He was so sad when you wouldn't marry him. He called me that day and said what does she want."

"Yeah, I remember, Ma. That was something. I got no proposals for years and then two proposals the same year—1999. As Zora Neale Hurston would say, 'some years ask questions and some years answer them.' [5] I accepted the wrong one. Maybe Randy would still be alive if I married him. I miss him too."

"What about old Ervin, you ever see him?"

"Nope, I never see Ervin. As long as he can make me out to be the villain he's good. I wish him no ill will."

"He still over there in Jersey?"

"I guess so, Ma. I told you I know nothing about Ervin's whereabouts."

"I'd sure like to see him."

"Well, I called him a few times and left a message that you wanted to see him. Just let sleeping dogs lie."

****

---

[5] From *Their Eyes Were Watching God*, by Zora Neale Hurston, J.B. Lippincott & Co.

# TENNYBOOTS!

# Chapter Eight

### Susetta. Fire.

  **S**usetta was the last of Mama's good friends to die. Speaking daily by phone for 67 years, Mama and Susetta had kept their friendship strong. Susetta was long-winded and Mama would complain that she said the same things "over and over again." While on the calls, Mama would often feign boredom, and make faces, and sometimes pretend she had some pressing need to end the conversation. Sometimes she enlisted us to interrupt her at the hour mark, faking an emergency. Susetta would call us rude and complain about the kids not letting Mama speak on the phone, but it was all orchestrated by Mama's design. But every day, she would either call her, or pick up the phone when Susetta called, and spend at least an hour or two visiting with her by phone. When she died a few years ago, Mama's longing for her was palpable and often. She would follow up her mention of her with an offer to tell the story of their fight, as though we couldn't remember Susetta apart from the fight. Beyond my sister and me, no one had a clue what Susetta looked like, but they all knew her from her daily calls; and there is no story of Mama without a story of Susetta monopolizing hours of Mama's time. I had mentioned her name in passing and triggered Mama's memories.

  "Old Susetta. How I miss her. I never thought I could miss those annoying phone calls. But I would give anything to hear her voice. All my friends are gone. Susetta was the last one. You remember the story don't you?"

# TENNYBOOTS!

The longing in her voice to tell it again is so great.

"Yes, I remember."

Saying, "I remember" never stopped Mama from going ahead with the story she had fixed in her mind, it acted more like a checkered flag on the racetrack that waved her on. I had allotted an hour for the call, so I sat back and listened to the story I had heard so many times before…

*Susetta was my best friend since the fight. But she talked too much on the phone. Every day the same old shit. Couldn't get her off the phone. Finally, I used to just say, yeah, yeah, yeah, Susetta…But my friend died on me. I can't believe she's dead. Oh boy, what a life! I don't know why God is leaving me here for so long. All my sisters gone. All my friends gone. He must have a reason.*

*We met when I first come to New York and was living on 126th Street. Me and Eddie was married for a couple of years and we didn't have children. All our friends was having a baby. Eddie come telling me, 'You gotta get me a baby I want a baby.' I said 'Where the hell you want me to get a baby from? I'm doing the thing to get a baby.' The next day I went to the doctor to find out why I couldn't have a baby. The doctor said, 'Mrs. Edwards, you are six weeks pregnant.' I was jumping for joy and went back to the block sticking out my stomach, I'm gonna have a baby, I'm gonna have a baby I was telling everybody. Me and Pecola was the last to get pregnant. She got so jealous and said, 'She just clowning she ain't having no baby.' Every morning I treated my belly like a million dollars. That was the happiest day of my life. After a while I had my baby, I named her Edith. There was a story on the radio and one of the actor's name was Edith. I said I would name my baby Edith if it was a girl, cause that sound like Eddie, and I named her Lynn after my mother, Malinda. We called her Edie—she was born when we was living in 365 West 126th Street.*

*I stayed with Fannie until I got married and my Edie was born. When old man Johnson and his wife moved out of 367, me, Eddie and Edie moved to their old apartment. An old Puerto Rican man owned that building. It didn't have no boiler. Everybody had to make they own heat. There was two apartments on each floor, one on each side, six floors in the building. No heat. We would buy coal to put in the coal heater; it would heat up the front room.*

# TENNYBOOTS!

*And then, if it got too cold we would light up the stove in the kitchen. Another couple moved in with me and Eddie for a while, my friend, Melvina, and Bobby, her husband. Their first son was born there. We had no privacy in that old railroad apartment, you walk through the rooms you see whoever was in the bed. Oh lord, what a life.*

*I remember I had bought the living room suite from 125th Street; had a little furniture store there, I paid about $200 on time for it. When I left 365, I took the living room suite with me to 367. Then Fannie had to get a living room suite. Boy, I fixed up that apartment so nice. People would come to see my place and say how nice it was.*

*After Mel and Bobby moved into their own apartment, I had my second baby, a girl, we named Gaynell, after the nurse in the hospital. Gaynell was my adventure child. Even before she was born. Everything with Edie had been beautiful. Me and Eddie was so happy to have our baby finally. I was 30 when Edie was born, so I was older than most of the Mothers on the block. We worked hard and I dressed her up like a princess. I had learned how to sew at home, so I sewed all of her clothes. I would dress her in cute pinafores, patent leather shoes on Sunday and white kidskin sandals during the summer. Edie was pretty and smart and walked early. Everyone on the block loved her. And Eddie just stuck his chest out he was so proud of her. Now, Gay, my middle daughter, was born with a blue birthmark under her right eye. People would pick at her and ask her who gave her a black eye. Gay called it a beauty mark.*

*A lot of the girls, Mel, her sister, Lucy, Dorethea, had grown up on the block. Not Susetta. She and her husband, Willie, and her brother-in-law, Lester, and his wife, Pecola had moved on the block around the same time that we did. I had been friends with Susetta, but it seems like since we was new to the block we was the ones that had to prove ourself. Not so much the men, but there was always something going with the women. Somebody in the building told Susetta that I had said something about her. She was determined to fight me. She told everybody on the block that when she saw me, she was gonna kick my ass. Now I was a coward. I had always been a coward. I didn't like to fight. Eddie used to tell our children to never back down from a fight cause it would happen sooner or later; but I used to tell my kids if you get into a fight, to run like hell. Susetta was tall and skinny and real black. I was short. In stocking feet, I barely stood 5 feet tall. But I didn't want to look like I was scared. The word was out on the block, I couldn't get out of the fight. Eddie told* me to just go about my business, but if she starts the fight with you, beat the hell outta her. Boy, I dreaded that day that was sure to come.

It was one of those hot days in the middle of summer of...let's see that must've been 1950——yeah, cause I was a month or two pregnant with Gay. Edie was only a year old and I would take her to Fannie's apartment while I went to work. Fannie lived on the 4$^{th}$ floor and I lived on the 6$^{th}$. Fannie's husband Mac was still working on the railroad, and Fannie had Jeanie, Myrna, Boo and Sunny to care for. I took Edie there in the morning and picked her up when I came home. I was working for Ms. Schwartzberg in the heights, so I would take the A train uptown a few stops to her apartment. On this day, I had just got home. I had picked up a bottle of milk from the corner store for Fannie's kids and Edie. Ms. Schwartzberg was very kind to me, so on days I did her work, I didn't get home so tired. She made sure that I stopped and took a break. She always offered me lunch, but all us girls who did housework knew not to eat lunch when you did days work because they could deduct the lunch from your pay. Them white folks was slick that way. I always politely said, no thank you when Mrs. Schwartzberg offered me lunch. Sometimes that lunch would be looking so good. Lox and whitefish, and they made this chopped chicken liver that I loved. But I would always say no thank you. I wasn't tired, but I was hungry. Being pregnant with Gay, I was even more hungry than usual. I had cooked the night before, and I couldn't wait to get home to eat.

There was a lot of people on the block, sitting on the stoops and standing round. We all had fans then but no air conditioners. When it was hot people would sit on the stoops. My brother-in-law Flam, and some other men, including Susetta's husband, Willie, was sitting across the street, playing cards. They had made them a table out of a board and they sat on those wooden milk crates. Flam looked up from playing cards, saw me and said, "Hi Sis." Flam was a kind man, he didn't have no children and at that time he did not have a wife. Later, he married my cousin Mert so that she could live in New York City. But his real love, his girlfriend's name was Alma. Poor Alma was a bad drunk. Like Cooter Brown, but a lady. She was nice but she was always pissy drunk. Usually, Alma was sitting around not too far from Flam. I didn't see her anywhere today. I said hi to Flam and then turned to climb up on the stoop.

Somebody in the crowd round the stoop said, "Florence, Susetta is looking for you." My heart liketa drop to my stomach, but I said brave-like, "She know where I live, if she looking for me let her come find me." Before the

# TENNYBOOTS!

*last word came out of my mouth, Susetta was coming down the stairs leaving the building. From the top step she was on and the bottom step I was on, and her height compared to my height, she looked like a big old black giant. In my head, I heard Eddie saying, "Don't back down Pie," (that's what he called me), "Fight like hell." But my heart was telling me to haul ass. Between my heart telling me to run and Eddie in my head telling me to fight, I couldn't move. I wanted to cry right there, but I couldn't. For what seemed like a long time, Susetta looked at me and I looked up at her. Look like she was growing right there in front of my eyes. I started backing off the stoop cause I didn't want her to have no advantage on me. She came down the stairs and came straight up to me.*

She said, "Come on, why don't you hit me, hit me." The crowd started to gather round. They had been promised a fight and they was waiting to see it.

I said, "No, I 'm not gonna hit you, you wanna fight, so you hit me first."

At that point I saw somebody pushing through to the front of the crowd. Flam came running over to me. I was so glad to see Flam.

Flam, said, "Ain't gon be no fight today."

People in the crowd was hollering "Let em fight, let em fight!"

Flam called out to Susetta's husband. "Willie, come get your wife, there ain't gon be no fight today."

I was so relieved. Then I heard Willie say, "Let em fight, they gon' fight anyway, so let em fight."

Flam insisted that he didn't want me in no fight, but the crowd was egging him on to let me fight, saying they gon fight anyway, let em fight now. With that, Flam moved back, took my milk out my hands and said, "Okay Sis, whup her ass."

*And boy I liketa faint right then and there. I didn't know nothing bout whipping nobody's ass. I ain't never had to fight in the street like that.*

# TENNYBOOTS!

*Back home in Opelousas we didn't fight like that. Momma didn't 'low it and our Pastor at Little Zion Baptist Church in Opelousas preached that only heathens would fight in the streets. We was poor, but godly.*

*What we didn't know was that Susetta had a knife. But thank God, my niece, Jeannie, Fannie's oldest daughter, wasn't more than about five years old, she started hollering "Mama, Aunt Pie, she got a knife, she got a knife."*

*Flam jumped into action and shook the knife outta Susetta's hand and pushed it at her husband, Willie, and said, "Now fight fair."*

*Susetta took the first swing with her long arms. I ducked, and she missed. Eddie had always told me, if somebody get one swing at you make sure they don't get another. That thought was rushing through my mind as I tried to decide what to do next. Like I say, I ain't no fighter. All of a sudden something took over and I started hitting Susetta with both my fists. My head was down and I was punching like Joe Louis did Max Schmeling. I was hoping Susetta would fall, but then we both fell to the ground. She was on top of me, straddling me like a horse.*

*I started praying "Our Father who art in heaven hallowed be thy name thy kingdom come thy will be done on earth as it is in heaven give us this day our daily bread..." three times, fast. Momma had always taught us that if you need God fast to say the Our Father prayers three times and He would come to your rescue. I had just started my second round of Our Fathers when I felt myself roll on top of Susetta. Now I was straddling her like a horse. I felt as if I was blindfolded, I really couldn't see what I was doing but somehow I turned over and got on top of her and I butted her head on the stoop. While I was still under her on the ground, I had grabbed the chain from my baby carriage that stayed parked by the stoop and wrapped it round my hand. When I turned over and got on top of her, I started hitting her in the head with the chain wrapped round my hand. I was fighting for my life.*

*I had paid a lot of money for that carriage for my first baby, Edie. It was the kind all the Jews had in the heights for their babies. Since I had children later than most of my friends, I had saved up my money to give my babies the best. Since we lived on the sixth floor in the tenement building and there wasn't no elevator, I would chain my carriage to the stoop and lock the chain with a lock. When I got to the building that day, I had unlocked the chain to bring the carriage with me to pick up Edie from my sister, Fannie.*

# TENNYBOOTS!

*When I got on top of Susetta I hit at her to keep her away from me. I can see it now as if in slow motion or something the chain hit her in the forehead. Bright red blood splattered everywhere. The crowd yelled out at the same time when the blood spurted out and moved back together in a dance motion like they didn't want the blood to splatter on them. Susetta fell back like a sack of potatoes. I went crazy then and was standing over her like a prizefighter daring her to get up.*

*"Git up, you want more, git up, I got more for you." I gotta laugh now cause I don't know where those words came from. I had lost my mind.*

*Her husband, Willie, ran over yelling, "Stop it, stop it."*

*Flam said, "No, you didn't want to stop it before, don't stop it now!"*

*Then all of a sudden, something snapped and I came back to my senses. For the first time, I saw and understood that the blood was coming from Susetta's head. I grabbed my face and covered my eyes and cried out, "Oh my God, what did I do?" Somebody had called the police. I got hot and weak. I remembered that I was pregnant and hungry. The screaming noise of the sirens just took away all of my thoughts. I was never so relieved to see Police Officer Pippin. He was our local cop on the beat, and he always stood in front of Knickerbocker Bar, where all of the men hung out. He knew all of us. The same people that was pushing Susetta up to fight me was now shouting, "Take her to jail, take her to jail."*

*Flam told Officer Pippin that I hadn't started the fight, but was coming from work and had to defend myself. Officer Pippin looked at Susetta, and then he looked at me. He told Susetta to go to the hospital and get a few stitches and he told me to go upstairs and get cleaned up before my husband came home and beat me for fighting in the streets. He yelled at Willie, Susetta's husband for egging her up to a fight. Boy, was I relieved, I locked the chain back on my carriage and I ran my ass upstairs.*

*Somebody from the block had called Eddie on his job and told him about the fight. Eddie was hot-tempered. He was a Edwards and they didn't take no tea for the fever when it came to family. News of the fight had traveled fast. Susetta had called her family from Jersey. By the time Eddie came home, the Jersey family was on the block too. They had guns and was shooting into the sky to let us know they had them. But Eddie had a gun too. He called his best friend, Luke, and there was Flam and some other guys. Eddie went to the roof and started shooting his gun. Word spread that Eddie and his friends had guns too. I was so scared. I said the Our Father prayer over and over again. We made a code for knocking on the door. Whoever was with us had to knock a certain way six times together in a certain rhythm——-boom boom, boom boom boom, boom, boom. We stayed up all night waiting for Susetta's family to make the first move. I knew that Eddie would not take the last. I cried, I prayed, I cried, I prayed. Fannie, came over to sit with us. She was good at calming me down. Finally, in the wee hours of the morning, the word came that the Jersey people had gone back to Jersey.*

*That following year on February 27, 1951, my second baby girl was born at Sydenham Hospital in Harlem. She had a blue-black mark under her eye in the exact place where I covered my eyes when the blood spurted from Susetta's head. Everybody said, I "marked" her.*

*I didn't have a name for her because I hoped she was a boy. Eddie wanted a boy to pair with Edie. The nurse asked me what I was going to name her. I said I didn't know. She told me to name her after her. I asked what was her name, and she told me Gaynell. That's how Gaynell got her name and her birthmark.*

*Months later, I was walking upstairs in Fan's building to take my babies to her house, when Susetta was coming downstairs. I was carrying a baby in each arm. She asked if I wanted her to carry one. I looked at her for a minute. I searched her face to see if she meant it; the scar from the fight was in the middle of her forehead like a Ash Wednesday mark. I then said, "Yeah, sure." She took Edie and carried her up one flight to my sister's apartment, then put her down. I was watching her though. I didn't trust her. I said, "Thank you." She went down and I went into Fannie's apartment. I told my sister what happened. Fan said that she had heard that Susetta was really sorry about the fight. When Susetta's children was babies, and before my children was born, me and Susetta was very close. Since I didn't have children and Susetta's husband wasn't working, every day I bought them a bottle of milk. Susetta later told me that she was sorry that she had let people push her up to fight me. We made up and we been good friends for the rest of our life.*

Mama's tone signaled the end of the story. Where the telling of the story had revived Susetta, I heard in her voice that Susetta's dying was again making her sad. I lingered on the phone for a few minutes more, without comment or interruption, and then finally said goodbye to leave Mama with her memories. She was lost in thought and put the phone back in its cradle without even saying good-bye.

Mama must have ruminated on Susetta all night because early the next morning she woke me up with more stories about Susetta. Mama admired Susetta for her bravery with white people. Susetta didn't hold back. Most of the stories that Susetta would share with Mama on their daily phone calls would be how she conquered the white man or woman where she worked or lived. Susetta had moved from Marble Hill projects to a Mitchell Lama cooperative building in Riverdale.[6]

"Ju, you up?"

"Hmm, now I am. What's up Ma? It's so early. You okay?"

"Yeah, I was just thinking some more about Susetta. I sure miss talking to her. Even though she talked too much. I still miss our conversations. Even though she said the same thing over and over again. All that shit she would talk about, I heard it all before"

"Okay, you want me to call you back when it gets later. It's not even 5.30 in the morning."

"Oh, my clock must be wrong. Is it day or night? I thought it was nighttime. Wasn't I just talking to you?"

"Uhhh, that was last night Ma. This is a new day."

"Oh shit. I musta been dreaming then. Was I talking to you bout Susetta?"

"Yes, Ma. You told me the whole story of the fight again."

"Ohh I did. I was thinking that I was dreaming that."

---

[6] Mitchell Lama is the name of the bill that established affordable, limited equity apartments for 25 years.

"Nope. No dreaming. It was very real."

"Oh. I was wondering if you know the story about how Susetta got in the *white people projects*. This is for my book, right? Add this to my story on Susetta. This is important."

"Ma, I think I heard it. But can it wait until I wake up good?"

"Oh right, right. You said it's morning. It's still dark out. And I been up such a long time. The girls ain't here. Or if they here, they don't say anything, they go and come and I'm here in my room with the door closed."

"Ma. Okay, just say that you are lonely and you want to talk. Are you afraid that you are home alone?

"No. Hell no. Why would I be scared to be here by myself? I'm always here by myself. They go bout they business. And I take care of myself. I ain't lonely. I talk to God. I talk to Momma, and Fan, and Mildred. Sometimes Gay too. And I talk to myself sometimes too."

"Okay, Ma. Do you answer yourself too? They say it's all right talking to yourself, but if you answer, you need help. I'm up now. Tell me the story, please."

"No. That's okay. You said it's too early. That's okay. Do you know how to get my television on? That lil gal had my remote and now I can't get my television working."

"Sorry, Ma. I know nothing about remotes and televisions. That's why I never have mine on. But, I'm up now, Ma. Refresh my memory. What did Susetta do to get into the *white people's projects*?"

I place the phone on speaker and get up to get the recorder from the armoire in my bedroom. Mama's voice is animated and begins speaking before I am set up.

*Well you know when we got our place in the projects in Harlem, Susetta wouldn't take just anything. She went and asked them to put her in the*

# TENNYBOOTS!

*projects where the white people went. They said nothing was available in the white people projects. Susetta said that she would wait. But they told her that if she didn't take what they offered her they would take her name off the list. Susetta would not let it go. Her people back in Georgia had money. So you couldn't treat her any old way. She, and a few other people, they made them put them in the projects with white people. I think they took em to court. So that's when she left 126th Street to move to Marble Hill, all the way up there on Broadway. That's how she got way up there in the white folks projects.*

*But before they left 126th Street, we was all good friends again. We used to laugh bout her brother-in-law, Lester, and his wife, Pecola. Lester didn't treat Pecola so good, and one day she call herself leaving him. Lester went and got her and made her come back home. Pecola had moved a trunk full of her stuff into Fannie's apartment. Lester made her go get the trunk all by herself. Me and Susetta would laugh about Pecola hauling that trunk back home like a mule. She was a sad sack. She never had kids that she wanted so bad. Then, part of the ceiling in her apartment fell on her head. She got a good settlement, but look like Lester took her money and bought himself a car, and she didn't even get to ride in it much, cause he had a girlfriend round the corner. He had a baby with that woman, but he wouldn't let Pecola go. Finally, they moved to Jersey.*

*Soon, Fan moved too. After Mac started to earn more money, he and Fan bought a house in Long Island. Well we all called it Long Island then, but it was Jamaica, Queens. Aunt Annie had already got my sister, Mildred, her husband, Jerome and they three children to move to Jamaica, Queens from Galveston, Texas. They lived only a few blocks from Fan and Mac. They was in walking distance. A lot of famous people like Count Basie lived in they neighborhood. They say Count Basie bought his house when it was still a all-white neighborhood. He was the first Black person to integrate that area. I think it was called Addisleigh Park.*[7]

"Ju, you remember when we was gonna buy that house near Fannie and Mildred? I went and put a $50 deposit on that house. It was nice."

---

[7] Covenants in deeds kept Blacks out of the neighborhood until a Suprpeme Court case in 1940s. Many prominent Blacks lived in the neighborhood. qns.com :Addisleigh Park a Thriving Tribute to Black History

# TENNYBOOTS!

"Do I remember it. I was so happy. It was one of those attached houses and it had a pink awning. I was already decorating my bedroom."

"Yeah, but shit, I thought about Eddie not working. And I had to pay for that house by myself. I went and got my money back…"

"Three times," I interject. "I so remember."

"Yeah. I couldn't make up my mind. Even though it was a new house, I saw how much Fan and Mildred had to work on they houses. Fan and Mac said they would help. And Mildred said maybe Jerome would help me. Jerome was good, but he wasn't that willing to help nobody. And Mac wasn't that good at fixing stuff round the house. So that was the second time I took my money back."

"And the third time, Ma?"

"Well I started thinking that I could easily pay my rent in the projects. I wasn't sure that I could always pay for a house. Y'all was still small. Fannie had Mac, and Mil had Jerome. I couldn't count on Eddie. And thank God I didn't cause once he left it would have been all on me. So I said shit, let me get my money back and keep my black ass in the projects where I knew I could pay the rent."

"Saddest day of my life, Ma. I cried my heart out. For years afterward, whenever we went to Aunt Fannie's I would drive down that block and look at the house with the pink awnings that was supposed to be ours. Such is life. Such is life. But you bought us a lot of things and that money could have paid for the house two times."

"Well hell, once you got grown nothing stopped you from buying your own."

"True that, Ma. True that. I bought the coop in Fordham Hill instead."

# TENNYBOOTS!

*Well, after a while, my baby sister, Nettie, came to stay with me. She met that old soldier, Freddie Tate, who was from Tennessee. She married him and was living with Momma at first. He was in the service and Nettie went to Tennessee to live with him. While she was living in Tennessee, Freddie abandoned her for another woman and she went home to Momma. He was a old dirty dog. Left Nettie in Tennessee with those two babies. I knew she didn't want to stay down there in Opelousas so I asked her to come to New York City to stay with me for a while to watch my babies. She brought Freddie and Edward with her and they all came to live with me and Eddie at 367. Nettie was always frisky and lively. She was small and cute. Everybody loved Nettie. We was shocked when she died of Leukemia in 1962. She was so young. Then, at the beginning of 1952, we had a terrible fire. We got burnt out of 367. I was coming from a day's work and there was a guy who lived in the building next to us, he and his wife was number runners. He was going in the subway and I was coming out.*

*He said, "You know you burnt out."*

*I said, Yeah, I'm so tired."*

*Then he said, "No your house is burnt out, you had a big fire up there!"*

*What he wanna say that for. I screamed bloody Jesus and ran to the building. The firemen was there. The trucks was blocking the street. I was hollering and trying to break into the building. They wouldn't let me in and I was screaming my babies are in there, let me in to get my babies. I had left Gay and Edie there with Nettie. They pulled me away and somebody told me that my sister had my babies cross the street. I couldn't hear them, and then somebody just led me cross the street and they showed me the babies. I just fell down in the street and grabbed my babies hollering, thank you Jesus. Thank you, Jesus.*

*Eddie didn't know until he come home that evening. I never saw him look so pitiful. After the fire, we drifted along; we went to different families who let us stay for a while. We stayed with Herman and Thelma, Edie's godparents for a time. We stayed with other friends. Then we went to live with Mercedes, my first cousin who we called, Mert. She lived in Harlem too, in the basement of Aunt Annie's building on 111th street. My aunt had fixed her an apartment there.*

# TENNYBOOTS!

"Ju, you remember that place Aunt Annie lived in don't you."

"Yep. On Lenox Avenue. Large apartment. We used to visit her when she made Gumbo. She would have a large pot full of Gumbo. Best I've ever had. Aunt Annie loved her some boxing. Or was it wrestling. She always had the wrestling match on and would holler and scream at the television. It was such a treat to go visit her. She lived on the first floor."

"Yeah she lived in that apartment for years. And it was funny that we moved across the street from her."

*One day we came back to the old block and Letha, a woman who lived in 365 told Eddie that they was building projects on 115th Street, so Eddie went and got the papers, put in a application and used that woman's address, cause we didn't even have a address. So, when they sent for us, she let us know. We had to go to the office and put our names down. When they got the building ready we moved in. We was some of the first families in that building. We must have bounced around for two or three months. I was never so happy to get a place. Nettie didn't get called cause you had to have a husband to move into the projects then. She was divorced but put in a application anyway, but they never called her.*

*Move-in day was the best day of our life. When we first moved in our rent was twenty-four dollars a month. And then it kept going up. We all went there and scrubbed down every room. It was new, but you didn't move into a place without cleaning it. I can see the old bucket and mop now. Me, Eddie and Mert, cleaned that place up. There was a store name Saks Quality Store—that's where we got all our furniture from. We bought a double four-legged Formica table and chair set for the kitchen. It was white and red. We got beds and another living room suite. We got it all on credit and every month we'd go and pay about $7 a month on the bill. We had a small credit book and every time you made a payment they would stamp the book.*

*Years later, Edward, Nettie's boy admitted to me that he and his brother, Freddie was playing with fire in the old coal heater when they heard Nettie coming and threw the paper under the heater. That's what caused the fire. To lose everything you got is the worst feeling. But we stuck together and we got through it. I give old Eddie credit, he was a trooper, he wouldn't rest until*

# TENNYBOOTS!

*we found someplace to live. People gave us clothes for the kids, and little by little we rebuilt and got back on our feet.*

*You was born the year we moved into that project apartment-building 20, apartment 9D. It was in the summer of 1952. You was born in November of that year. My next-door neighbor, Ann Salley, who was my best friend was pregnant too. Our babies was due round the same time. But Ann went in early, her baby, Betty was born on the last day of October and You was born two weeks later.*

*Our building was beautiful. We had elevators and heat. Two things we didn't have in 357. There was a lot of grass for the children to play in. There was parks and playgrounds. We lived on the ninth floor. There was ten apartments on each floor. We lived in the D apartment in the corner of the hallway, four families lived in that corner. We all had children. We came from different places but we all got along. Amos and Ansel in 9C was from West Palm Beach Florida. I was from Louisiana and Eddie from Georgia. Ann and Glain Salley in 9E was from South Carolina. Moonie and Toni Dean in 9B was from Puerto Rico I think. So was the family in 9F. The Swintons in 9A was from another part of South Carolina and I don't remember where the people down the hall was from. But we all got along good and we all looked out for each others children. Those was some good old days.*

****

# TENNYBOOTS!

## Chapter Nine

### Judy Ain't My Mother
### Gumbo n Pralines

Mama had been hankering to get her stories published in a book. She was always asking "When you gon write the book when you gon write the book?" She was already envisioning the fame she would have after I wrote "her" book—while I envisioned more headaches, let alone that I had no time to write it. Our short-lived, joint business enterprise of selling pralines daily, and Gumbo on Fridays, which lasted only one summer had worn me out, both mentally and physically. I wasn't about to go willingly into another joint venture with Mama so fast. Plus, I used my stories about Mama to release the stress that caring for Mama placed on me. I wasn't giving that up.

In the Pralines and Gumbo business, I had to supervise the Gumbo cooking, and I had to make batches of Pralines so that Mama would have a batch to take out with her every morning on the bench. She was enterprising and had quickly built up a clientele. Every evening she would pressure me, "Where my candy" "Where my candy?" Demands, not questions. I would have to make the candy after working all day and deliver them to her the next morning before going to my office. She even had a distributor, a neighborhood guy named, Waki. Mama had a special relationship with the young men in the community, they loved her and considered her one of the guys. She sat on that bench with old gangsters passed their prime, spending the afternoon getting lost in

# TENNYBOOTS!

their glorious tales of life in the fast lane; addicts for whom the thrill of the high had long ago faded and now were just one more load they had to carry; number players who kept hope alive by hitting a single, a combination or a bolita; hustlers whose business was deemed illegal by dint of who they were and not what they did, and a bunch of folks with regular lives. Mama did not discriminate. It was important to her to listen to them, encourage them, and take in their stories to add to the treasure trove of her own, maybe even imagining herself in them. Waki was one such man who spent time in Mama's sanctuary that doubled as a bench. He also worked as her distributor. He would get a batch of pralines for one dollar each—on credit from Mama—and then sell them on the avenues for two dollars. He would bring Mama back her dollar—or he was supposed to. Waki was a hustler. A lot of days Mama was short. Let's just say the transactions were funny sometimes. Mama refused to believe that her boy, Waki had taken advantage of her. It was much easier for her to believe that I had. When he got sick and died a few years later, she made me take her to visit him at the hospice and spoke lovingly of him at his funeral.

Then I had to deal with being on demand when and where Mama wanted the products. One day she wanted to sell Gumbo in the middle of the week, and on Friday too. I refused. She asked me to buy the ingredients, and I purposely did not.

Around noon, Ashley called me and said "Ju, do you know that Mama is making Gumbo. I just got finished telling her I think she should let you take care of that. You know that roasting pan that we used to roast turkeys in that is as old as Mama? Mama has slopped up some Gumbo in that roasting pan. I don't even know what she has in it. It smells good, but no, just no!. She has it on the seat of her walker with a ladle, and the spoons and bowls and napkins. She's waiting on a big old pot of rice that's almost done. I told her I was gonna call you…"

"Dammit. What did she put in the Gumbo? What ingredients, Ash?"

"That's the thing, I heard the door slam early this morning. I thought she was going out to sit on the bench. But when she came

# TENNYBOOTS!

back she had stew, beef, chicken and some other stuff and said that she was making Gumbo. I asked her if you knew. She mumbled something. But when I didn't see you nowhere in the picture, I said ah hell no. Something's up."

"Thanks, Ash, I'll call her."

I hung up with Ashley and called Mama. She didn't want to take the call so Ashley put her on speaker.

"Hey, Ma."

"What!"

"Why are you so short? What's up?"

"Hell, what you mean short, you short too. I know Ally (her nickname for Ashley) done told you I'm selling Gumbo. Yes, I am. I bought it with my money and I am selling it."

"Ma, sorry," I say laughing that Mama takes no wooden nickels—she can play the dozens as well as anyone. "I don't mean that you are short in stature or in height, I mean that you sound as though you are angry or something. I just called to say that you don't have the right pot to make the Gumbo in. Please hold off and——"

Mama threw the phone down. A cordless that I was trying out for her—I heard the clatter when it fell on the floor—and situated her just cooked pot of rice in the canvas bag on her walker. Spilling Gumbo down the hall and in the elevator, Mama pushed that wagon-spilling-Gumbo-roasting pan and rice out of the building, down the ramp, and set up shop on the bench, Ashley reported.

My concern was two-fold. I couldn't vouch for the cleanliness of the pot nor the contents of the gumbo. That old roasting pan hadn't been used in years. And Mama had those *cadillacs* in her eyes. What a disaster. I left my house, running the four blocks to the bench and the walker that now doubled as a Gumbo food truck. When I got there, Mama had a line of

# TENNYBOOTS!

customers buying her Gumbo. I can't lie, it smelled just like Louisiana brown Gumbo, but I wouldn't eat it, and didn't think the people she was selling it to should eat it either. Ashley was standing a ways from the bench about to have a meltdown. She's very protective of Mama and didn't want the neighbors talking about her and that roasting pan full of Gumbo that had left a trail of savory roux from the ninth floor to the bench. Mama was in full swing. She was dishing out her Gumbo and some of her friends were helping her with the napkins and collecting the money. I would have had to physically restrain Mama to stop her. And because Mama was very strong and always threatening to "bust a hole in a nigger" with her fists, I refrained. I joined Ashley far enough away from Mama to communicate our displeasure, but close enough to handle any repercussions. By the time the line of customers thinned out, Mama had worn herself out. I began to hear people complaining that the Gumbo tasted a little different. Worn out, but euphoric that she had gotten away with her caper, Mama sat there guarding that batch of roasting-pan Gumbo until the evening. Finally, someone coaxed her upstairs. I promised to bring the rest of the Gumbo upstairs but tossed it as soon as she got into the building. I don't recall whether she asked for the rest of it the next day. I saw none of the money she made from her sales and didn't ask her for it either. Whatever she earned that day—she had definitely earned.

And that was the other thing, I was fronting Mama the money for the ingredients and supplies. I thought giving her something to do would reduce her boredom. But Mama wanted all the revenue to go to her church. I told her any good business had to reinvest from the revenue. She didn't want to hear that and would fight with me about the money. Plus, she was selling some of her candies on credit and keeping track in her head. She never had as many dollars as I had sent candies. I would hear her sometimes stop someone and say, "Hey, hey, so and so, don't you owe me for the candies?" The person would say, "No Ma, I paid you." She would ask if they were sure, on it went. Sometimes she ruminated about so and so hadn't paid her. Then, I made a notebook to keep her accounts balanced. That didn't work either. She would scratch some notes in the book and then swear that it meant what it did not say. But every Sunday Mama had a stash of money to bring to the

## TENNYBOOTS!

church. When I asked why this money hadn't made it into the daily profits, she always had some lie ready on her lips. I provided her a pouch just for her sales money, but invariably, she would pull dollars out of her bra, her socks, and her shoes. If she got upstairs before I could get the money, she would stash it in several places and only disclose one stash.

Then on Fridays, she had taken orders all week for the Gumbo. I didn't go into my office on Fridays and she would come to my apartment the night before to assist me in making the Gumbo. Early the next morning, she would get her walker and walk the four blocks home to sit on the bench and hawk Gumbo sales. I had to be cook and delivery girl. If I were running behind, Mama would be angry and have people calling me demanding the Gumbo. When I would deliver to the bench, I would have to sort through the orders Mama had scribbled down in her shaky handwriting with a crowd standing around waiting for their Gumbo—and Mama looking angry. At the end of Gumbo Fridays, exhaustion held me down until Sunday. And Mama still wanted to act funny with the money and take all the profit to church without giving me the money that I had put out. Then we had to fight over that. In the end, her church got more than a thousand dollars. I was out of pocket and got nightmares. So, I wasn't about to release no book with Mama. Lesson learned. Instead, I told her about the Sunday Morning Mama stories and each Sunday I read them to her. I shared the comments with her. She got a kick out of that. Sometimes she took issue with what I had written. Especially if I called her stubborn. For god sakes, don't call her stubborn! I promised her I would hold on to what she had written and her tapes for a book for later. I asked her what would she say in a book where both she and I would get to tell our sides of this mother-daughter story. I told her she could say whatever she wanted and I would write it verbatim—exactly as she had dictated. The following is what Mama had to say:

*I'm feeling good now. God told me I'm gon be here a while longer and I need to let Judy live her life. Every Sunday she's hauling me to church and she can't go no place. I want to give her her freedom. I've kept her away from her things long enough. But if I say that to anybody, they gon think I'm crazy. I talk to God like I'm talking to a friend. I used to read my Bible all the time. But since I got*

# TENNYBOOTS!

these "cadillacs" in my eyes—I know they are cataracts but I like to call them "cadillacs"—I ain't been able to read. Didn't wear no glasses for 94 years then just like that I couldn't read nothing. Judy told me a Black woman doctor invented the machine that's gonna remove my "cadillacs." I told her I don't care who invented it, I just want them gone. So. I just sit and talk to God. And God answers.

    God speaks to me. Sometimes I don't tell nobody what those answers are—I keep them to myself. But Judy asked, so today I'm telling her. Judy is my baby daughter. I remember when she was born. I already had two girls and my husband wanted a boy. But I was older, I was 33 when Judy was born—a blessing they say, cause Mary was 33 when Christ was born.

    "Oh Pie, you gotta get me a boy, you gotta get me a boy," he was always pining for a boy. So, I tried to get him the boy, and we thought we had a boy until it was time to go to the hospital. And then my other two babies, Edie and Gay, told me to bring home a baby named 'Judy.' And I be damn, she came out a girl, and we named her Judy. Not Judith, just Judy. I had her in St. Clare's hospital down on 53rd Street and 8th Avenue. It was near where I worked at my night job, cleaning offices. It was a Catholic hospital, nothing but nuns in their white habits. My other two was born in Sydenham Hospital, used to be right there in Harlem, near where we lived.

    But Judy was always different, and it started with the hospital. The pain got so bad, cause Judy was my biggest baby, she weighed 8 lbs. Well, the pain got so bad I couldn't see straight. After a while, I thought those nuns was flying cause them white habits got to looking like wings. I wanted to get out of bed and jump from the window the pain was so bad. I just screamed, "Lord have mercy take this baby outta me." The priest walked by while I was hollering and ask the nurses, "Why don't y'all give that woman something." The nurses, the nuns in the white habits that look like they was flying said, "No, she's an old hat, this is her third baby, she'll be fine." Now it was easy for them to say that, not ne'er one of them had ever given birth or supposed to not have given birth—what the hell did they know.

    The baby finally came. We named her Judy and brought her home. Well, back then you had to stay in the hospital with a baby for a long time, almost a week! Nowadays they send you home so fast, make your head swim. From a lil thing, she always was my protector and my stickin' plaster. Like she was born old and wise. Wherever I go—she go. She once came to get me all the way in Whitestone, Queens where I was on my day job. Took two trains and a bus, and she wasn't even ten years old. I was working for some Jewish families then. There was a knock on the door. My mistress was there, and she said, "You expecting someone?" I looked at her like, me? I came to work, who would I be expecting. Sometimes them people we worked for liked to test you, you know. I always answered no. And when the door opened, it was Judy. I likedta faint. I said, "girl what you doing here, your Daddy outside, what happened?" Judy stood there smiling and said, "No he ain't here, I came by myself." Neither me, or my mistress believed her, but she kept saying she came by herself.

I was almost finished my work anyway and was fixin to leave bout the time she came. My mistress offered Judy some ice cream. I tried to signal to her to say no thank you. But Judy didn't catch the signal, and she said yes please. She sat at the counter eating the ice cream. Two reasons that I didn't want her to say yes. They had a old dog, a boxer named Duke, and she used to give him ice cream from that same ice cream dish they ate from—yuk. And two, I thought oh shit she gon charge me for that ice cream—but she didn't and I didn't tell Judy bout the dog eating from the dish till much later. Even though I was gagging every time she ate it and tried to convince her to toss it when the boss lady wasn't looking.

We got finished and sure nough Judy had come all the way from Harlem by herself on two subway trains and a bus. But she was to me like I was to my mother, I never left my Momma, and when I did, the sun bet not go down and I wasn't home. I'd made many a folk bring me back home to my Momma. I got christened when I was seven, and my Godmother had made me a organdy dress, purple on the top, pink on the bottom. I looked so pretty. She asked me if I wanted to spend a night; I said yeah. I was so excited. But when that sun went down I cried my ass off. She had to find somebody with a buggy to take me back home to Momma.

I would always think that Judy would be the one to take care of me when I got old. Gay died, and she couldn't take care of me, and Edie had knee problems and then she moved to North Carolina when she retired. She asked me to come at first, but she know I ain't going to no North Carolina, so ain't no use in asking me. I went to visit twice. That was enough. It's a nice place though, and she got plenty room. I ain't going on no more airplanes, they been dropping from the skies too much lately. And the last time we went, Judy took me on a long ass train ride. Thought we'd never get there. Judy left me with Edie and went traveling and I thought she had tricked me and wasn't coming back. So, I fixed them. I wouldn't do nothing Edie asked me to do. I wouldn't

# TENNYBOOTS!

change into my pajamas. I wouldn't eat until after Edie had sat her fat ass down. Then she had to get back up. And I didn't even want to change my clothes. Judy had packed up a suitcase full of pretty clothes and nice pajamas and I barely touched them. I figured if I didn't cooperate, Edie would complain to Judy and make her come back to get me. It worked cause Edie started calling Judy every day. I heard her complaining about me, but I made like I was sleep. I was never so glad to see Judy when she came back after a week and a half. I learned my lesson, I'm gon keep my black ass home from here on out.

I said I guess Judy will be the one to take care of me. But she's always telling me what to do. I can't stand that. Hell, who tells her what to do? And everybody, even the people at church say, "I'm gon call Judy, I'ma call Judy." I say, "Judy ain't my mother. You think I'm scared of her? I'm not scared of her. She's my daughter. I'm the mother."

And she gets on my nerve sometimes. Sometimes she gets on my nerve all the time. She thinks she knows so much. She's always trying to tell me right from wrong. Who tells her right from wrong? Plus, she's always late. And I like to be early. Judy will call and say, "I'm coming, I'm on my way" then you notice you sitting there for two hours. I doubt if she's even up yet. I can see her sitting at her dining room table on that computer. I be looking at the clock thinking hell I'm gon be late for Sunday School. And then when she get here she come in the parking lot jumping out the car, saying, "Ma, Come on." I be mad as hell but I gotta show her a good tone. Cause I used to give her hell when she come. And that didn't help, cause now she mad and I'm mad too. So now, I don't give her hell, but she know I be mad. And then she says, "Ma, are you late? Sunday School ain't even started yet."

But sometimes I get there, and they already did the prayer. I say "That's started ain't it?" Before she was getting me there too early, and we had to sit outside until they open the church. I just have to take it. Sometimes when I am sitting on the bench waiting for her I tell everybody, watch she ain't coming she ain't gon be here on time. Then when she comes, I say, "Oh, I see you made it." And she says, "I told you I was coming." But I say it nice-like, cause she take so long I mean I think she ain't gonna make it. I tell everybody to watch what happens.

She's been picking me up every morning, waiting for me every afternoon, every Sunday. I imagine that's a lot on her. She been devoting a lot of time to me. Maybe that's why she take so long. But now with these "cadillacs" in my eyes, I can't see the clock. I just feel the time and damn if ain't feel like she taking longer.

And if Judy think she my mother, Russell, my grandson, think he my father. Here he come, "Ma, do this, Ma, do that." Sometimes I say, "Boy, just leave me a-lone!" But he's a sweet boy. He come every day with some treats for me. "Ma you okay Ma. You need anything?" Sometimes I gotta straighten him out too.

At first, I was kinda sad cause I was getting old. You know in my mind I thought I was much younger. And it bothered me that I had to depend on other people sometimes. I am used to doing for myself. I ain't never depend on nobody. I been working from a baby in the cotton field to help my mother. Then one day I say hell, I ain't young, I AM old. Now remembering what I went thru, I am happy to be getting old. Well, not happy to get old, but happy I don't have to get out and work like I did. When God takes me home, I'll be ready. Now somebody in my family have to be the long liver of the family, it have to be Judy. Maybe Judy will be the long lived.

I wasn't used to people doing anything for me. I wanted to take care of myself. I always took care of myself. When I first got the walker to help me walk I was 90 years old. I remember walking out there where they play balls at, and Judy said "Mama why are you walking so slow?" I said, "I don't know Judy, something wrong somewhere." So, I beat that old leg and I prayed on it and I rubbed that concoction of the wintergreen alcohol with the pinecones in it on my leg, and it felt better, but I still couldn't walk that fast. It took me a long time to get from my house to the corner. That's my first memory of getting weaker. We went to the hospital and finally, they said I had a blood problem. My sister Nettie died from Leukemia, she was only 42 years old. I had this anemia they said. At first, I thought it was cancer and they just wasn't telling me, but it's not cancer. I'm scared of cancer—once they open you up that's it. I know a lot of people who died with cancer. Hell, most of my friends from the building died with cancer. I told my kids if they say I have cancer let me die with it. Don't open me up cause then it spread like wildfire.

When I started with my blood doctor, he was at Mt. Sinai. Nice guy, I can't think of his name. But then Mt. Sinai wouldn't take me no more. They ran my ass outta there when I went there. I was so shame. Judy said something bout the insurance. But they could've taken me. They do that to Black people.

# TENNYBOOTS!

*Then I came to St. Luke. Dr. Yoe become my doctor. I hate to get those transfusions. They claim they giving you the perfect match. All that is a bunch of hunky lunky. It's cat blood or water. And then I didn't want to go to the doctor no more. I had prayed. And the Bible say your days are marked. Your first day and your last day and you ain't gon go before your time. I had prayed for Him to heal me. And if you pray for healing, then you have to be obedient and have faith that it's gon be done. But every time I feel a lil weak then they wanna make me go to the doctor. Make me go to the doctor. When it's my time, that's it and not before. So, I don't go. And then that's a fight. I'm so sick of the doctors and I'm not sick. And I am sick of fighting about going to the doctor with Judy.*

*Once I thought they was gonna put me in a nursing home. They wanted to put me away cause I was sick. One day I went to church, and I was crying, I didn't want to go to a nursing home. I got up to testify, and I told the church, "My kids want to put me in a nursing home. I'm not old enough to go in no nursing home." One of the ladies in my church came over to me while I was testifying and put her arms around me and said, "Mother Edwards, you don't have to go in no nursing home I will take you home with me." I told her wait and let me see what happened. When my kids found out, they got so mad at me. They said I embarrassed them and that they never said that they was gon put me in a nursing home. But, I thought I heard Judy and Edie talking and saying, "I know what we can do with her, we can put her in a nursing home." I didn't want to leave my house and my building, and I knew somebody that was in the old folks' home. She was away from her people and I didn't want to be away from my people. Cause if I went to the old folks home I was gonna miss everybody and all my friends in my neighborhood. Stuff like that, I just didn't want to go. I didn't want to go to no old folks home. But they say they didn't say it. But somebody said it. Maybe the grandkids said it, I ain't crazy. But I'm still here, so they ain't put me in no home yet. I wasn't gonna go, anyway.*

*Sometimes my conversations with God feel like I'm hypnotized. And sometimes I am—how you say it—I call it "remanessing." Sometimes I be "remanessing" in my mind, and it seem so real. I have to ask my kids did I say that to them or if that happened. I once had this, well I don't know if it was a dream or not...see I miss my mother. I want to see her so bad. So, I had this whatever it was and I saw her, she was dressed in all white, a long white robe. But I couldn't see her face, only her feet cause her back was turned. She recognized me, but I didn't recognize her. But God spoke and said that she's in that number. And in that same dream, I saw God too. And guess what? I be* damn, but He's not white. He's a light-skinned Negro! He was wrapped though in swaddling clothing. You know, his arms too. I couldn't figure out why he was wrapped like that. It probably was a dream. But I'm not sure.

Judy gon say I'm stubborn. She always say that. I don't pay her no mind anymore. Everybody say that. I'm not stubborn. I know what I can and what I can't do. In my mind, I was trying not to be a problem, cause I knew that I could do things for myself. One time when I was sick, Judy had to do a lot for me. Now I was feeling better and I could do it myself and I felt bad that every Sunday morning I would occupy her. I started insisting that I didn't need no help. I take the bus myself. I go shopping by myself. I was doing everything. And then I was doing nothing. Ain't nothing gon happen to me. Sometimes I had to get real rough with them so I could do for myself. I ain't no baby.

I go to Bible Study and Prayer Service. My Pastor Reverend Williams used ta pick me up and bring me home sometimes. And then my Deacon. Dorothy—I call her Marie sometimes—she would pick me up and bring me home. When she couldn't Sister Hunter and her husband, Deacon Frasier, or Deacon Bell would. So I didn't need no help. I had enough people to pick me up and bring me home when Judy was acting funny.

And now I feel reborn. I really want Judy to go and live her life, cause I'm gonna be here for a while and I don't wanna use up all her time. I told her from now on wherever I have to go I can take the bus or a cab. She don't have to take me anymore. Even with these "cadillacs" on my eyes sometimes I see better. And once she gets them off, I'll be fine. I don't want to take her time and I ain't sick so I don't need nobody babying me. She used to tell me to take a cab. But why should I take a cab? They want seven dollars to ride to 125th Street. Those taxi cabs been cheating me every since I got to New York. I don't bother with them if I don't have to. Shit, I can save that money and take the bus. I know how to take a bus. But when I do that Judy get mad, "Why you didn't take the cab?" Oh boy, I ain't no baby.

****

## Chapter Ten

### Mama and Me: Stickin'Plaster

*Please God Please Don't Let Anything Happen to Mama*, were my incessant petitions to the God whom Mama had taught us to kneel by the side of the bed, bow our heads, clasp our hands, and pray to nightly. *The Lord's Prayer* and *Now I Lay Me Down to Sleep* were nighttime prayers designed to cleanse us of our sins, and keep evil at bay while we slept to ensure our waking each morning. But I didn't trust them to protect Mama when she left us to go to work. It required more specific prayer. Mama said God was everywhere and saw everything. To my childish mind that seemed to be a lot for one God, so I had to be certain what I needed was clear, concise and to the point. I said this prayer at Mama's back as soon as the door shut behind her and repeated it whenever I thought of her until she had safely returned at night. I didn't have to bow my head, or kneel, or clasp my hands to say this prayer. I could say it while jumping rope, or watching television and even while playing with friends. No one knew. Like a mantra, I just said it over and over again, to myself, and only sometimes aloud when it was urgent.

When I was too young to meet Mama at the train station on Lenox Avenue, I sat on the floor by the front door of our apartment 15 minutes to 10 each night and I would listen for her footsteps in the hallway as she got off the elevator. If she were just minutes late, my prayers became more fervent. I always imagined her sick or robbed or worse—dead. By the time she walked through

# TENNYBOOTS!

the door on those late nights, I would be folded into a ball, crying at the door which only frightened Mama. She would have to calm me down first to find out that nothing was wrong; that my worst imaginings had gotten the best of me—what I saw in my mind had fueled my tears. On those nights, a very patient Mama would sit on the floor next to me and reassure me that our very benevolent God would not take Mama away from her babies. This, I accepted as truth—until the next time she left home when my petitioning began anew.

At eight-years-old, I had permission to leave our apartment at 5 minutes to 10 each night, take the elevator down to the lobby and wait for Mama on the stoop in front of our building. My eyes stretched the night searching for Mama to appear. When her silhouette, illuminated by the streetlights, shone through the darkness, I ran through the parking lot to meet her.

"Judy, what are you doing here?" she would laugh and ask each time.

Knitting my fingers into the spaces between hers, finger over space, finger over space, until our hands were as one, we would swing arms as we walked towards the building. Ms. Neecie, who lived above the stoop in apartment 2F, was usually in her kitchen window around the time Mama came home from her night job. Some nights we had to settle for the comfort of her shadow; but other nights, she would call out to us in her gravelly voice: "I was watching her, I knew she was going to meet you." Mama would laugh and respond, "Yeah you know that's my *stickin' plaster*, she thinks she can protect me, but who's gonna protect her. *Stickin' plaster* is exactly what I was, nothing came between me and Mama.

The wooden turnstile gates in the subway would be my place to wait for Mama by the time I was ten years old. My eyes would dart back and forth searching the subway cars to try to spot Mama before the train stopped and she got off. If the police were not in the station, I would scoot under the turnstile and run to meet her on the platform. If it were raining, I would bring an umbrella for Mama and one for me. If it had gotten chilly, I'd bring her a jacket.

# TENNYBOOTS!

Weekends and holidays brought no relief from Mama working outside of our home, nor my petitions for her safety. Mama often left us home alone-with keys around our necks and a set of rules to follow—chief amongst them: not to open the door for anyone, not to allow boys in the house, and to stay off the telephone. Thus, we had no real tradition of celebrating holidays as a family because Mama was always working. We would eat the leftovers that Mama would bring home at night wrapped in aluminum foil and packed neatly by Mama into shopping bags. Roast beef, brisket, turkey, ham and other meats were plentiful. I learned to eat and love matzoh ball and borscht soups, gefilte fish, whitefish salad, chopped chicken liver, lox, noodle pudding, and stuffed cabbage when my friends were eating leftovers of turkey red rice, candied yams, mac and cheese, and stuffing. Sometimes, if she had enough time, Mama would cook our holiday meals early in the morning before she left to go to work for the families, but rarely.

My sisters and I always felt the *families* were thinking only of themselves and not of Mama when they asked her to work on the Christian holidays. But for Mama, the devout Christian, it didn't seem to matter. Work was work and an opportunity to earn a dollar. When she served the parties, she even got tips that she looked forward to. She would rely on Mr. Wallach's twenty-dollar tip and Mr. Lindenheimer's five-dollars. Mama would always agree to work, no matter our requests that she not. Mama's motto was a dollar earned is a dollar earned. We never got what she was trying to say, but they always paid Mama less that she deserved, and never fully compensated for her work, so I guess she meant that even a dollar made a difference.

Mama's fighting spirit did not extend to the white folks she worked for. In all the years she worked for the *families* although she complained often, she never allowed a cross word to escape her lips, except two times—once when she had to ward off the advances of the husband of a woman she worked for, who had a habit of stripping naked and serenading her as soon as his wife left the apartment. Mama said she cursed him and almost "burned his old stink penis off" one day when he interrupted her ironing with his naked ass. Shocked that she had the audacity to spurn his advances, and assured by the look in her eyes she was intent on singeing his meat with that iron, he called her a crazy black bitch, but he never approached her again—dressed or undressed.

The other time was when Mama worked up enough nerve to ask for a five-dollars a week raise. It was 1985, and she had continued to work for two sisters and a brother and their families as they became more and more affluent. Mama followed them, cleaning their homes, raising their children and catering at their parties, as they moved from the Heights in Manhattan, to Bayside and Whitestone, Queens, to the Upper East Side of Manhattan with summer homes in New Jersey and winter homes in Florida. Mama recognized that she was being taken advantage of working for the "same lousy thirty-dollars a week since they lived in Queens," she lamented. For the first time in her life, she had the courage to quit a job, to her "madam's" face, in her own voice. This time Mama had painted herself in a corner by telling everyone that she would ask for the raise on a day certain. Ms. Lindeheimer's denial was swift and cut like a razor. She told Mama that the food Mama brought home from the parties, and the hand-me-down clothing and used furniture they gave her, more than made up the difference for a five-dollar a week raise.

It had taken everything Mama had to muster up the courage to ask. And being denied, she quit on the spot, before she had done one iota of work; left the laundry unwashed, the beds unmade, gave the shocked woman her keys and slammed the door on her way out. Mama would later say that she didn't know who was more shocked—Ms. Lindenheimer or herself. The woman had not expected this and began shouting at Mama's back. Like Lot, Mama had said, she didn't look back, and walked out of their lives that day.

In 2017, the woman who had denied Mama the five-dollars a week raise was very sick and living in Florida, where she had retired. Like Mama, she was the last of her siblings alive. Her life hadn't turned out so swell. One of her sons had gotten into trouble and disgraced the family. The other son had divorced his wife. She called Mama at the same telephone number Mama had for 60 years. Mama was happy to hear from her and asked after this one and that one, genuinely interested in what had become of each of them. The

## TENNYBOOTS!

woman's voice was raspy and her breathing labored. She had emphysema and other health issues. She could not speak on the phone for long, but would not hang up before she told Mama that she wanted to send her something. Mama was eager to give her address. Long ago, the older sister had told Mama that she was in her Will. The sister had died early, and no one had ever contacted Mama about any bequests. Mama was faithful and never stopped believing that one day the inheritance would come. The request for her address raised Mama's hopes anew that thank God, at last she would get the pile of money that her benevolent madam had bequeathed her.

Sure enough, one week later, Mama received a plain white business-sized envelope in the mail. It was addressed it to "Mrs. Florence Edwards," in the shaky penmanship of a person whose hands had outlived their dexterity. The old woman had placed a dry check in the envelope with neither a note nor a card. The check was for just—fifty dollars. Disappointed that it was not her inheritance, but Mama accepted it anyway. She didn't trust me to deposit it and came with me to the bank to cash it. I was so annoyed with Mama for accepting that lousy fifty dollars. I wanted to rip it up and send it back to the woman by FEDEX Overnight mail. But Mama never met a dollar she didn't like, and that sentiment held true for the fifty-dollar check. The woman died one week to the day that Mama indorsed and cashed the check. Mama could be heard bragging on the bench, that "Old Lindenheimer couldn't die before she paid me that old five-dollar raise. God don't like ugly and he ain't too fond of pretty."

I know now that I was not Mama's favorite child. But as a child and for a long time thereafter I believed that I was: even as it was evident to almost everyone but me that my middle sister, Gaynell, was the absolute apple of her eye. My belief that I was her favorite was anchored in the time and ease in which we spent our early years together and the partnership we forged to raise my sister's kids when I was 15.

With Mama's help, I taught myself to read the funny papers at three-years-old. One of my earliest and fondest memories is sitting on the living room floor with Mama and my 2 sisters with

# TENNYBOOTS!

the funny papers carpeting the floor around us. On Sunday mornings, the paper man delivered the Sunday News, and the Milk Man brought fresh bottles of milk to our apartment door. I would race to the door to be the first to open it, and bring in the milk and paper; Mama following behind me. This was the only time they allowed me to open the door without asking who is it.

I would make myself a tall glass of chocolate milk in those metal tin cups that kept the milk ice cold. We always had some Bosco—in the jar with the bear's head wearing a red cap—the chocolate syrup that would turn plain milk into chocolate milk. I would drink a glass of milk with Bosco down so fast that a scraggly mustache of brown milk would form on my top lip. Because of the milk mustache, my father nicknamed me Mushy Mouth. (Sometimes he called me Shu Shu too, but I'm not sure how I got that nickname.)

I would then take the funnies section out of the paper for Mama and spread them on the floor in the living room. Mama loved to read the funnies: Blondie, Little Orphan Annie, Dick Tracy, and Brenda Starr were her favorites. I loved the bright colors in the funny papers and while sitting on the floor with Mama, I would tease out the words in the balloons that floated above the characters' heads. Mama didn't mind interrupting her reading to tell me what each word spelled. By that time, my sisters would join us reading their favorite comics and I would also pepper them with questions, "What do L-A-U-G-H spell?" They would answer until they tired of me, but by that time I had "read" Gasoline Alley or one of the other comics to my heart's content. I would then flip to the back of the newspaper where the advertisements were. There were always ads for a store that sold baby clothes and furniture. I would cut out the little white babies, and the advertised cribs and furniture and make pretend I was a babysitter of several white babies. Mama never discouraged my play, but she always told me, "No babysitter for you, you will get your education and be something better. I only went to 7th grade cause I didn't know my *maths*." She would then follow that up with simple addition and subtraction drills: how much is 2 and 2? 4 plus 4. My sisters would join in and that's how we spent many a Sunday morning when I was 3, drinking Bosco, learning to read the funnies and doing *maths*.

# TENNYBOOTS!

Other memories of my childhood are not so idyllic. DadDee is the way we pronounced our Father's name. It was a holdover from my older sister's tongue-tied pronunciation as a toddler—when we met him, she was already calling him DadDee, my middle sister and I followed suit. DadDee, like most of the fathers in the projects—beat down and oppressed daily, and unwilling or unable to be the men that they should have been for their families—used his plight as an excuse for getting drunk. Mostly, on Fridays he got drunk before he brought his paycheck home to Mama. We could expect a fight, like a ritual every Friday night. It was always the same. At about ten that night, Daddee would stumble into the apartment. I didn't have to see him I could tell by the way he fumbled with his keys at the door that he was drunk. As soon as he would get inside the apartment and slam the door without bothering to lock it, Mama would start. At first, I used to lock the door behind him. And then I realized that it was easier to have it unlocked in case we had to run next door for our neighbor, Ann Salley.

"Eddie, where's the money. Eddie, where's the money?"

"I ain't got no damn money," DadDee would say. His words slurred just enough to make Mama ask again as though his reply confused her.

To emphasize that he didn't have "no damn money" he would show how broke he was. His face contorted into drunken contempt for Mama asking about his money, his balance falling victim to the effects of too much wine—he drank something we called Sneaky Pete—he would stumble his way to the bathroom, flailing his arms, reaching for, missing, and then finally, connecting with, and turning his pockets inside out, exposing the yellowed muslin of his inner pocket to show Mama that for real, not one dollar was in his pockets. Mama always waited for the theatrics, not wanting to believe that DadDee really had no money, to start her wailing and flailing her own arms. And then the shenanigans would begin in earnest.

# TENNYBOOTS!

Mama would start hollering, "Eddie, Eddie gimme the money. Eddie, you know these children have to eat. Eddie, how am i going to pay the rent."

Getting nowhere with the hollering she would start pleading, "Please Eddie, where's the money? Eddie, where's the money?"

Her pleading always emboldened him and every Friday night, when he stumbled out of the bathroom to her pleading, he acted more ready to fight than when he went in. We learned later that the bathroom stop was to hide his bottle of wine in the hamper. Once his Sneaky Pete was secure, he was ready for the fight, and would come out of the bathroom antagonizing her.

"I said I ain't got no damn money. I spent it."

Mama would continue to rage at him for the rest of the night, often leading to physical fight. My sisters could go into our bedroom and ignore the Friday night fights. I could not. Worried that Mama would get hurt, I had to protect her and would run back and forth between the two of them trying to be a peacemaker.

"DadDee, DadDee, just ignore her don't say anything, just go to bed, she's stupid" I would whisper out of Mama's earshot, while he sat on the edge of his side of the bed struggling to take off his clothes. I would help him to take his shoes off and swing his legs up to the bed—sometimes almost causing him to roll in the other direction onto the floor. Usually, just as I got him tucked in, and I had pulled the covers up over his fully clothed body, Mama would start raging and yelling again.

I would run to her covering her mouth with my hand and pleading with her, "Mama, please don't say anything, please Mama, please."

But Mama was brave and to my dismay, would never back down.

# TENNYBOOTS!

"Don't cover my damn mouth. He's going to find some money tonight. I don't care where he finds it."

Even as a child I thought that was dumb of Mama to think money was going to materialize out of the air. It never did on those Friday nights.

And on it went until DadDee fell asleep——which was a good outcome—or he reared back up wanting to fight, like a horse spooked by a snake. At those times, I remained steady at Mama's side, making sure he didn't hit her or hurt her. One time I jumped on his back and another time Mama had the iron and I had the spray starch aerosol can to ward him off.

Then there were the weekend nights when he didn't come home at all. And Mama knew that he was sitting outside of Knickerbocker Bar with his girlfriend, Leila Mae. Leila Mae, from Alabama, had worked with Mama at her night job after Aunt Fannie left. When DadDee would pick Mama up from work with us in the car, he would also offer to bring Leila Mae home. Since Leila Mae lived in the Bronx, DadDee would drop us off at home, and continue to the Bronx to drop Leila Mae off. Somehow Mama found out he was doing more than dropping Leila Mae off; Mama and Leila Mae had a big argument at work and Leila Mae got fired because Mama had seniority. Whenever DadDee was out late on the weekends Mama figured he was out with Leila Mae. She was always trying to catch them *in the act.*

On those nights around one or two in the morning, Mama would get dressed to go find DadDee at the bar. I didn't want her to go alone, so I would jump into my woolen snowsuit with leggings and the matching bonnet hat, with strings attached, and go with her to Knickerbocker's to catch DadDee and Leila Mae in the act. We would splurge on a taxi—the only time Mama didn't fight about the fare. We'd jump out around the corner from the bar, on St. Nicholas Avenue looking for DadDee's car. Mama was quick and stealthy. From experience she knew that if DadDee saw her coming he would take off, "like a bat outta hell," she would say. We had to be invisible while she adjusted her night vision to find the black, 1957 Ford Fairlane 500, four-door, that without fail, DadDee

# TENNYBOOTS!

had parked near the bar. It wasn't that DadDee varied his routine, but his best friend, our *Uncle* Luke had the same car but with a soft top and only two doors, so Mama had to be careful to find the right car. One time we had pounced on Uncle Luke's car and caught him in the act—he was sitting in his car with a girlfriend and not his wife. Mama told his wife, but she said she wasn't about to go chasing behind his black ass.

When Mama was certain she had DadDee's car she would move with the precision of a bobcat to leap at the car and snatch open the door before DadDee or Leila Mae knew what hit them. Sometimes DadDee would try to take off. So I had to be a stickin' plaster for real and jump into the backseat. One time, DadDee took off and Mama was riding the hood. We could always count on Leila Mae to look up at Mama, jump out of the car and *haul ass*, as Mama liked to say when she was telling the story again and again. Sometimes Mama would take off after her, but most times she would start hitting on DadDee. Embarrassed, DadDee would start the car and drive like a fool all the way back to the parking lot in front of the building where we lived. Sometimes the fight would continue in the parking lot. But most times we would ride the elevator upstairs together, go into the apartment together and the fight would continue until both of them, sated by the ritual, fell asleep in different rooms. On those nights, me and Mama slept on the couch and DadDee always got their bedroom and the bed.

DadDee would leave for good before I turned ten. But not before I tried to kill him. It was on a Friday night and the ritual was repeated, but worse. This time, they had gotten into a tussle and Mama had grabbed and wrenched his penis and DadDee had bitten a small piece of meat out of her back. Mama was yelling and banging on the wall for our neighbor, Ann Salley, "Call the police, call the police." Ann Salley must have called them and then knocked on the door to break up the fight. When the police were banging on the door DadDee was in the bedroom nursing his wrenched penis and Mama was walking around with a small hole, down to the white meat, bleeding from her back. The police called the ambulance and Ann Salley offered to keep us girls, but I would not allow Mama to go to the hospitable by herself. By the time they got ready to leave, I had jumped into my snowsuit and was ready to

## TENNYBOOTS!

go. Mama, DadDee and I all went in the same ambulance to Sydenham Hospital. DadDee was on one side of the busy emergency room—lit up by large metal dome-like lamps hanging from the ceiling casting an eerie yellowish light on the sick and dying—and Mama and I were on the other side. The doctors were joking about who got the best of whom. Mama got a few stitches in her back and a bandage and DadDee got some X Rays and ice packs for his swollen penis. Mama was more perturbed about having put her hands on his "old stink penis" than the hole he had bitten out of her back. It was after midnight when *Uncle* Luke came and picked us up from Sydenham Hospital and brought us all back home.

Once home, DadDee beat a path to the bedroom and Mama and I retreated to our places on the living room couch. After getting undressed, I had to use the bathroom. DadDee hadn't fully hidden his bottle of Sneaky Pete, it was half sticking out of the hamper. Bleach and peroxide and rubbing alcohol were in the cabinet beneath the sink, I added them to the bottle of wine, along with some Mercurochrome from the medicine cabinet to retain the red color. Tightening the bottle, I was careful to put it back where he usually buried it among the dirty socks, underwear, and clothing in the midway the hamper. Mission accomplished, I went back to the couch and snuggled into the space Mama had left for me between the couch pillows and her warm body.

Saturday morning, I awoke to DadDee vomiting and shitting and Mama accusing him of having gotten some woman pregnant. "You done got some woman pregnant Eddie, that's why you throwing up like that." DadDee would jump off of the toilet to throw up and then jump back onto the toilet to shit. Mama—dressed only in the white full slip that she had worn to bed and was now sticking to her skin with static cling, the bandage beneath the thin adjustable straps of the slip had dried-up blood on it—was helping DadDee, and had a cool washcloth mopping his head and his mouth, at the same time as she was accusing him of getting some woman pregnant. I was so confused. Why was Mama helping him? DadDee was a sight with his hurt penis and now both his mouth and his butt were running too.

# TENNYBOOTS!

I went to our bedroom and tried to shut it all out with my sisters who were watching Saturday morning cartoons, and not at all bothered by the spectacle in the bathroom. I never liked cartoons. How many times could that rabbit bop somebody on their head? I mean at some point you had to know what was coming. *Father Knows Best, Dennis the Menace, The Mickey Mouse Club*—those were my shows. Nice parents, good kids, no fights. Yep. Those were my favorites. But I sat in the room with Edie and Gay watching them watch the silly cartoons and wondering why they found them so funny.

When things settled down, and I caught Mama by herself and I realized DadDee would not die that day, I asked Mama, "Why didn't DadDee die?"

"He's not gonna die. He got some old woman pregnant."

"But you always told us that if you drink bleach and peroxide and those chemicals in the bathroom that we would die. I put them in his Sneaky Pete last night and he didn't die."

Mama stopped in her tracks her eyes widened like three-cent Moon Pies from Ms. Cora's candy store. "You did what?"

I repeated what I had done and waited for her answer. She took me into the living room and we sat on the middle, curved section of the three-piece sectional couch. She looked me in the eyes and said, "Judy, you must promise me to never do that. No one would believe that a 4-year-old child did this and they would take me away and put me in jail. Do you understand?"

Scared to death that Mama could go to jail if DadDee were to die, I said my *Please God Please* prayer fervently, substituting DadDee's name where I had said Mama's and I even threw some *Our Father's* in there too because this was urgent.

DadDee didn't die at my hands. He lived to leave our home on his own accord, or Mama says she put him out. Either way, he didn't come back to live with us as a family. He went back to Athens, Georgia, to live with his mother for a while. After DadDee

# TENNYBOOTS!

left, I limited my role as Mama's protector to her goings and comings to and from work. The weekend ritual violence with DadDee was over. Mama would have to find the agency it gave her in other rituals.

Me and Mama were still good buddies. In my teenage years, we partnered to care for my sister's two children. When my daughter was born seven years later, Mama was invaluable in helping me to raise her. When I was struggling to pay a mortgage and private school for my daughter, and working two jobs, Mama bought me a new car and would pay my daughter's tuition when there were gaps in my cash flow. She didn't just do this for me. She also bought my older sister a car and helped her to care for her children. Mama was good like that to her children.

As the years grew long, Mama turned her attention toward the next generation, and the next generation, continuing to raise grandchildren and great-grandchildren. We were still close. But the God I had prayed to as a child spared her life and I no longer worried about her as much. When she turned 80, she got custody of her three-month-old great-grandchild. I helped her in various ways to raise that one, but kept my distance when it threatened to unravel. By the time Mama's need for help threw us back together again as a Baby Boomer and her aging mother, my daughter had grown into a fine adult, and I had my own grandchildren, a set of twins, Chloe and Elijah. Mama was so invested in the twins' birth, she prayed that God would just let her live to see them born. She was 85. They were the very first set of twins in our family and their birth brought Mama much joy. She maintained excellent health until her early 90s, then a diagnosis of a blood disease, Myelodysplastic Anemia, changed her life. As the disease weakened her, I became less of a daughter and more of a caregiver. It was a natural progression, we both accepted this as a given.

****

## Chapter Eleven

### Red Blood Cells

Mama has never cut a sympathetic figure. "Poor Ms." was never added as a prefix to her name in order to elicit pity for her predicament. Sitting on the bench outside her building—the remnants of Sunday's church curls spiraling in odd directions in her mane of white hair, and contrasting sharply with her black face—that she has always been a force to reckon with could not have been more obvious. The fact that Mama, in her four-feet ten-inch frame, continues to hold her own despite being in the *short rows* of her ninth decade, is evident to all.

But to be fair, none of the mothers who were Mama's peers in the projects were sympathetic figures either. They raised their kids and took care of their homes and families to the best of their abilities, without benefit or hindrance of a movement that told them they could have it all. When the toll of being Black women in mid-century Harlem became too much for them, they released the pressure in various ways. Some found solace in the bottle at night in the safety of their home, or cigarettes, or neighbors' husbands. Mama neither drank nor smoked—and I can't speak to neighbors' husbands—instead, she re-decorated and moved furniture around late into the wee hours of the night and early morning, completely rearranging or purging entire rooms before we awoke. Many mornings, my sisters and I awoke confused, in a newly arranged apartment. We learned to survey the trash each morning in order to rescue a toy, a sock or something we'd held dear because Mama deemed everything disposable. If it were not in its proper place it was tossed.

Obsessive-compulsiveness aside, Mama had a real flair for interior decorating. Our apartment was always ahead of its time and fashionably decorated. Had there been a model apartment for the projects, no doubt apartment 9A, where we moved from 9D, would have been it!

As a result of decades of working all day and moving furniture all night, Mama was strong as an ox and hadn't shriveled up much in the way that old folks do. She also doesn't take much crap and can give just as good as she gets. Fighting a good fight invigorates Mama, just like her Friday night rituals with DadDee and her compulsive room clearing and redecorating did. It's her agency. She bristles at any suggestions that run counter to how she wants to do things. She fights to do things her way. It's this Mama who, when this was written, shook off the cocoon of a long winter and welcomed Spring in rare form.

Around ten years ago, when she was just about to turn 90, Mama was diagnosed with Myelodysplastic Anemia, (MDA), a disease that hinders the ability of the bone marrow to produce healthy red blood cells. Her treatment, due to her age, has been periodic blood transfusions or iron infusions or iron pills when her blood hemoglobin count dips below a certain level. Mama hates hospitals and doctors. She got her first real physical at 75; I can see her now, almost skipping to the bus stop, happy and relieved to be in good health. The effects of aging and MDA have made her dependent upon others, hospitals, and doctors and it has also physically weakened her and restricts her independence.

Because Mama tends to wait until her red blood count is so low that she is taken to the hospital by ambulance, the transfusions are mostly performed during a hospital stay. At a count of five hemoglobin, she is still standing and claiming that she is feeling "fine" to the amazement of her doctor. Any emergency hospital visit can turn into unexpected problems and several have. One time she was septic, another time, a Urinary Tract Infection (UTI) caused her to be delusional for a few days. The disease, old age, or both, has weakened her legs, and towards the end of her 90th year, she was given a prescription for a rollator (walker) to assist her walking. She hated that thing and resisted it for as long as she could. She preferred to grab onto chairs, walls, doors, anything that did not broadcast her infirmity. Once she gave into it, the walker restored her independence.

Long ago, I promised Mama that I would always take care of her. I always intended to make good on my promise, but I really didn't know how difficult some days could be. Mama's mother lived in Opelousas, Louisiana and we only got to see her a few times. Our father's mother was estranged from us, so I had no real-life examples from Mama of taking care of older people.

When caring for Mama became daunting, I started complaining to anyone who would listen. No matter the listener, the results were mostly the same. The once sympathetic listener's eyes would glaze over and the listener would seem as though they needed to be anywhere other than listening to me. Or I received a quick nod, an "I know," and a dubious segue into another topic. Although some of my listeners sympathized with me, no one wanted to hear my constant complaints day-in, day-out, about my mother no less. Complaining about an elderly Black mother is *blasphemous* and makes people uncomfortable—I was not honoring her if I was complaining about her. And then there were the Blessed Bunch—This is blessed that's blessed. No matter my complaint about Mama, the Blessed Bunch's retort would not change: You are blessed to have your mother, and in her right mind, blah blah blah. I didn't want to hear that. Blessed, I countered, didn't feel this way, and if it did, it certainly wasn't something to aspire to. Gradually, conditioned by their comments I resolved to keep my complaints to myself—unless I just couldn't help myself. Bottled up like Mama's old pressure cooker with the broken release valve, for the first time in my life my blood pressure spiked. I was at my office in Flushing, Queens, and felt too dizzy to drive home. The Chinese prayer group that was meeting at my office in Flushing had just assembled. They offered to pray for me. The supplication went up in a beautiful lilting Mandarin. When they were done, my colleague translated that the prayer leader had reported that I was very black in the prayers. My daughter and grandchildren came through the door before I could respond. We went straight to St. Luke's hospital, where I had spent what felt like years with Mama in emergency rooms, and now I was the one sitting on the gurney awaiting my fate. My twice-taken blood pressure, from each arm, remained very high. The doctor prescribed my first-ever medication and suggested that I remain overnight for observation. Not wanting to, but afraid to go home, and encouraged by my daughter and grandchildren, I relented and stayed the night in a hospital for the first time in my life except for when I gave birth to my only child. For the first time I knew how it felt to be Mama and myself at the same time. My daughter and grandchildren were concerned about by welfare; I wanted to go home, but didn't want to act as Mama had so many times with me, so I gave in easily.

Once in a while, Mama acknowledges the toll my caring for her takes on me. When that happens, she will call me and say either she dreamed it, or the Lord told her to let me have my time, that I have been good and done my part, but since she's gonna be here a bit longer, she needs to free me up. But the epiphany is often short-lived. When I speak to her later, she invariably has a list of things she needs for me to do, or that she needs from the store and gets impatient that I have not delivered on them already. So, no matter what the *Lord* tells her, or what she dreams, I don't see myself getting that break until she's dead. Some days I am okay with this. A lot of days I am not.

Publicly and honestly chronicling our journey leaves me vulnerable. Black children are notorious for being very loyal to and protective of their parents. Aging Black parents achieve deity status in the eyes of the community. Much respect is given for Black elders' wisdom and having survived to old age despite the never-ending struggle of being Black in America. So, to speak ill of a living parent who has attained advanced age is frowned upon in our community—even if it's true. I have shocked many a caregiver friend when I've asked about their elderly parents. They usually give a respectable response, but with a telltale grimace that I immediately recognize. I then say, "I know, it rhymes with witch." I can't tell you how relieved they are to be given an opportunity to complain about the elderly parent, whose actions and antics rhymes with witch. It is liberating!

Even as an adult, I still crave Mama's approval and adoration. No matter how old I am—I am her child, and a natural desire for a child to please her parents is irrefutable; it cannot be wished away based on a parent's ill-treatment. It is extremely rare that I receive either. In my head, I recoil from the lack of acknowledgment but something deep inside of me compels me to continue. Some days I wish that I were strong enough to walk away. We have a large family and I presume that someone would step in. Instead, every single day, I lie to myself and keep going. I am often worn out, depressed and discouraged as this mind-body split is my reality whether or not I admit it.

Whatever family roles and dynamics that were left unresolved when I left Mama to become an adult with my own family, flare up again. I am charged with making life-altering decisions for her and limiting her independence in myriad ways in order to keep her safe. The old ways that we related to each other during a different time in our lives, whether good or bad, replicate themselves; except now, Mama feels disempowered and vulnerable and I feel burdened and unappreciated.

A nursing home was out of the question. Black folks, like other ethnicities, Latinx and Chinese, come to mind, also have the added burden of a tradition of caring for our aged in their homes and not in nursing homes, unless there is a serious medical necessity. Any mention of a nursing home would send Mama into a tizzy, so I could not even consider one as an option until medical necessity required it.

Mama's relationships with our large extended family often aggravate what I try to do for her. Someone is always in Mama's ear telling her that I am not doing something right. Mama basks in the attention and is also known to carry stories back and forth. The chaos this causes is an ongoing burden for me. Even when I've tried to extricate myself from the drama—it still finds its way back to me as though there is an unmovable target on my back, chest, and head. Mama's personality is such that she rages at the people who do the most for her and praise those who do the least. This has also made me angry, but with age, I've become nimble and employ a deftness where I avoid stepping on some minefields in our relationship.

Our story is not unique. Mama was able and did articulate her needs, wants and displeasure at my actions. She was still as she said "…in my right mind." Mama's voice in this book represents the voice of the aged living out their lives with help, and care from their children, grandchildren, and other people. I daily walked a tightrope between ignoring Mama's shots fired at me or calling her on it. The paradox is that I frustrated her. She told herself that but for me, she would be more independent. But she knew, that but for me she could not be more independent. Her frustration combined with feelings of powerlessness lead to her abusing me. Mama knew all too well which buttons to push. Admittedly, I am easily offended by Mama's jabs at me, and I am not as big a person as I would like to be: Turning the other cheek for me sometimes feels a lot like getting slapped twice, it stings! In a perfect world someone else should have attended to Mama's old age; and I would have been the nice daughter who would come to visit. But life had other plans and here we are bumbling and fumbling and making each other miserable at times.

****

# TENNYBOOTS!

## Chapter Twelve

### Sunday Morning Mama Ain't Carrying No Load

Dammit I did it again. I had promised Mama that I was coming and now I wasn't going to make it. I worked later than I had intended. It was cold. I was tired and knew that I wouldn't find a parking spot, plus my time would be limited so I was calling her to say I wasn't coming. Ashley, who lives with her, told me she'd been waiting. I knew I was due some tongue-lashing, or worse. The more I anticipated Mama's response, the more aggravated I became. The aggravation was made of equal parts beating myself up for making the promise and not keeping it, and the reality that with so much on my plate, I could not do everything. On any given day, I would disappoint someone. My muscles had tensed, and I was subconsciously willing myself to breathe, just breathe.

"Hey Ma"

"Ju, you not coming, huh?"

I was stuttering my explanation and then just blurted out, "No," when she interrupted, "That's okay baby, it's cold and late, I'm sure you want to get home."

Who is this Mama? Relieved, I relaxed and apologized profusely, promising to come to get her early on Friday to hang out with me.

# TENNYBOOTS!

She didn't want or need my apologies today, and we hung up easy-like.

"Love you."

"Love you back, Ma."

This is not the Mama of even a few weeks ago. That Mama would have been spitting fire by now. That Mama would have said something like, "I've been waiting for you all day, I need some—insert potato chips, food, seeds, Pepsi, etc.—you shouldn't have said you were coming if you weren't going to come."

Friday morning, I get up, and as promised, call her.

"Ju, I was waiting for your call. You ready."

I tell her I am and will pick her up in about an hour. She has finally agreed to get her hair done, and the plan is that I drop her off and pick her up because there is snow on the ground; she recalls falling on the ice years ago and the neighborhood boys having a hard time picking her up and that the boys have grown up and moved away, so if she falls on the ice she may be on her own. I marvel at all the thought and energy that goes into making such a simple decision of whether to go to the salon on her own.

I pick her up from in front of her building. She is waiting at the entrance to the parking lot. She seems a bit tired, and she winces as we do our routine that has her put her front leg in and squat to a seated position, while I push her onto the seat. She grabs onto the passenger handle and hoists herself in, and that way we can make it in a finite number of steps. I collapse the walker and put it on the back seat; she always carries a bag on the handle. Sometimes the bag is one of those black plastic Arab bodega bags, but today it's a dingy gray canvas bag advertising *Harlem Tours*, owned and operated by a neighborhood youth, now an adult, one of Mama's fans. She's had the bag for a while, I make a mental note to take it off and wash it next time. I look into the bag out of curiosity. Mama has a half roll of toilet paper—she complains of her nose running; a cracked, plastic, hand mirror to make sure her

# TENNYBOOTS!

face is clean; a spoon wrapped in a napkin, some old mail, a small jar of Vaseline without a top on it, a few loose dollar bills and an old potato chip bag. I place the canvas bag on the back seat, pile the layers of her down coat into the car, and put the seat belt on her. Thinking of Sara's routine with her, I plant a noisy kiss on her cheek. She laughs.

"My knees are trying to get stiff on me, I told them they better not, I've been beating them and moving my legs back and forth, they ain't gon get stiff on me, no sir! When you get a chance, get me some of that wintergreen alcohol. I gotta find some pine cones and I can make a jar of that old potion I used to make. That worked good."

I bring her to Clara's, the Dominican hair salon. I help her to get out of the car and onto the sidewalk. She walks into Clara's where the women always welcome her as though they've missed her. As she's signing her name in the book, using her walker as a dance partner, she starts doing a shake-your-booty dance, magnified by the large coat she is wearing. They laugh and ask her where has she been.

She tells them, "I'm still here God don't want me yet, I hope He ain't forget about me."

They laugh again and fawn over her. She's in her element now. I tell her I will come back two hours later. In the car, I had to give her money to pay for her hair and a tip, because paying for it myself made her seem like a baby. I had learned my lesson after doing so one time, which made her angry with me for a week. I had stuck the money in the bag on her walker, so that she could get to it easily enough.

An hour and a half later, Ashley, is calling me from Mama's home phone.

"Mama's here, she says she waited for you but you didn't come so she came home."

# TENNYBOOTS!

"Shit, I'm waiting outside for her, tell her to come downstairs."

Mama comes back down with her white hair flying in the cold wind. She just got her hair washed she should know better. Her hands are white-knuckled and ashy, gripping the handlebars of the walker. No gloves, no hat. But I don't want to ruin our day by fussing with her.

"Where's your hat?"

"I don't wear no hat."

Reaching into her canvas *Harlem Tours* bag to get her hat and put it on her head, I tell her it really is too cold not to wear a hat on freshly washed hair. She doesn't mind this time. And she's apologetic about coming home on her own and says, I figured I would save you a trip back so I left and came home. I get her settled back in the car in our two-step routine and we head downtown to pick up my grandchildren, the twins, from school.

As we ride downtown, Mama is orienting herself, a habit she has picked up in recent years. If she knows where she is, she still has a grip on reality.

"This the East River, right? Where's the Triborough Bridge? Remember when that bridge was twenty-five cents? How much is it now?"

"It's $7.50 one way."

"Aww that's highway robbery, $7.50—how can they make people pay that much money? Hmmmph! Remember when I had that '69 Plymouth and had that accident right before the bridge?"

"I remember."

"Yeah, those was the good old days, I would drive out to Bayside, do that work at the Bowman's; on Thursdays I'd go to Whitestone to work at the Lindenheimers, then I'd make it back home, cook dinner, and then head on down to my night job. Me and Fannie. I sure miss Fannie… This is the East River, right?" "What is that bridge there? "

"It's the 59th Street Bridge."

"Oh right, right, that's the free bridge. I never took that one. It's been a long time since I been down this way," she says, and then catches herself.

"But wait, you brought me down here, not too long ago right?"

"It's been a while."

I didn't want to discourage her so I was easy on her self-correction. Mama is in rare form today. She says she feels great, and she's not letting anything bring her down. When her conversation meanders from herself and things, it always turns to people. Ashley and her sister, Asia are always low-lying fruit for Mama's ribbing. The 70 years between them in attitudes are sometimes too much for Mama to swallow.

"Them girls don't never wear no clothes. They prance around showing they naked ass, I say put some clothes on, I know your ass *yallow*, but it ain't no looking glass. Then they want me to eat the food they cook. I say no thanks, I make my own. They ain't giving me no naked ass food."

She laughs, a hearty laugh—with no conscious awareness that her revulsion grows out of our Ancestors' pain whose naked bodies were pinched and prodded and raped and branded without their choosing—self-satisfied that her Victorian notions of propriety rightly trumps their Gen X lack of decorum. I marvel at her being so reviled by nudity that it's a daily complaint, or maybe, preoccupation with her.

"Seriously, why you think they don't put clothes on they ass?"

"Ma, nudity is not bad. A lot of people wear no clothes in their own homes. You gotta give the private parts some air, sometimes."

"You! You too. You don't wear no clothes at home either. Hell, and I been eating your food?"

I am doubled over laughing while keeping my eye on the road ahead. I already know not to say anything that Mama can change my words and take back to the girls, or anything that will convince her that she cannot eat my food either.

"When we was young we would never run around like that. Momma and Aunt Bessie, they made our clothes. Aunt Bessie had a sewing machine cause we was too poor to have one. They worked the fields in the day, and Aunt Bessie was the washwoman, and later Momma was the cook. So late into the night, they would stay up sewing our clothes using the old kerosene lamp for light. They would buy a few yards of that old yellow cotton, it sold for bout a nickel a yard, and they would cut it out and make us those big old bloomers."

Mama is cracking herself up remembering the big bloomers.

"Boy, those bloomers was big, but they'd wrap our ass. We didn't have to worry 'bout running round naked."

I think of the irony that big yellow bloomers gave them a sense of security that they did not have against any white man who desired what those bloomers were hiding, but gave them agency to believe it was so, nevertheless.

We are almost at school to pick up my grandchildren now. It's a citywide talented and gifted school. It's a decent education for the kids, but it's all the way down in Alphabet City on the Lower East Side, a good six miles from their home. We have to coordinate bringing them to school and picking them up because it's too far for free school bus service and paid service costs $3500 per child for the year. I drive them down to school and my daughter or their dad pick them up, or we hire someone to pick them up, or place them in after-school classes at the school, which easily run a few thousand dollars each semester. The forced flexibility in my schedule to be available for Mama helps in navigating the grandchildren back and forth to school.

"You know Ju, I was worrying bout everything and then I said why worry. I don't have to hustle out to work, I got a roof over my head, I pay my bills, what am I worrying about."

My eyes meet her eyes in the rearview mirror and I validate that she has no need to worry.

"The only thing though, I'm bored."

She says this with a palpable sadness for people, long gone. It's a yearning, even more than sadness. A yearning for the way things used to be. Yearning for a job, a yearning for her younger self. Yearning for her birth family. Earthly things cannot fill the boredom she speaks of. But I am nothing, if not a repertoire of solutions. My reply was inadequate, lame even, but I did not want to leave that space between her boredom, sadness and her yearning, empty.

"Why don't you go to a senior center?"

Before the words are out of my mouth, she says,

"No, that's the thing I don't wanna be bothered with no old people. The lady at the hairdresser said, 'Why don't you come out to our center?' They have a party every week. I smiled at her and said okay, but I said to myself, shit, I ain't gon look in no faces of old people."

"That is the problem, Ma. You are bored but don't want to do anything other than Bible class on Wednesdays, Church on Sundays and sitting on the bench in good weather."

"Hell, when I go places, people are always saying, 'lemme help you, lemme help you,' some of them look older than me; I think hell, you look like you need help yourself. I just don't want all those people tryna help me, they think cause you old, you need

# TENNYBOOTS!

help, I don't need no help, I can do for myself, and I don't want to be bothered with a bunch of old people. "

We both laugh at that, and the conversation ends because we are at the school.

I leave Mama double-parked in the car and run to pick up the kids. They are glad to see *Big Momma* in the car.

My grandson gets in and says, "Hi Big Momma, I didn't know you were coming."

She tells him how he's gotten so big and that he's handsome *now*, emphasizing the "now," and she remembers when he was born. On the drive uptown, she is telling them the story of when they were born. Some parts of the story that she didn't actually experience, she has now given herself a role. I chuckle to myself. The children are listening raptly and are peppering her with questions.

Just as I am thinking about how she wanted to live to see them born, she tells the kids, "I kept praying, asking God to let me live just to see these twins. I was so excited cause we never had twins in our family, y'all are the first."

Chloe, the girl—a numbers and years person—asks, "how old were you when we were born Big Momma?"

And then before Big Momma answers, Chloe has subtracted her age from Big Momma's and says, "Big Momma, you were 84, and our mom and dad were 30."

Mama's voice rises in a question and says, "Oh I was?" relieved that Chloe had figured out the answer to the question.

"Yeah, well, I asked God to let me live to see y'all born and to see Sara grow up. Sara's a big girl now, I can go now."

Elijah, saddened by the thought of Mama dying, says, "Nooo Big Momma, we don't want you to die yet."

# TENNYBOOTS!

Mama promises him she won't die that God told her she will live until 103.

Chloe quickly adds the years and says, "Oh we will be 19 then."

We are back on the Franklin Delano Roosevelt Drive now heading uptown. Chloe is interested in the mechanics of how Big Mama will make it to 103.

Mama answers, "I feel good now, I don't want for nothing I am just easing on down the road."

In that way that twins know each other's minds, at once and without a cue, they both start singing, "Don't you carry nothing that might be a load, just ease on down the road."

Mama and I join in singing "…ease on down the road" we all laugh at the merriment, and continue singing ease on down the road, which is exactly what Mama is doing this week.

****

# TENNYBOOTS!

## Chapter Thirteen

### Sunday Morning Mama Brings in A New Year

I had already written Mama's Sunday Morning chronicles for the week when a different version pushed through my spirit. I'm going to blame it on a dark night, and the eclipse of the moon, but the account I had already written, seemed unimportant by my reflections on the end of another year with Mama. As I began to write tonight, years' worth of pent-up emotions came tumbling out, and I am overwhelmed by the depth and variety. I am at once all the conflicting feelings of the past few years. I am crying. Some days have been hard. Some days turned into nights and seemed endless. Nights turned into weeks that morphed into months, and months all blurred together to form years. But as we come to the end of this year, looking back is sharpening my vision, and that keen vision is strengthening my resolve.

The Sunday Morning Mama stories have helped to release my frustrations by putting my feelings and Mama's antics down on paper. Removing the stories from my psyche gives me distance. In the distance I can see that it's more than a sum of the parts. I can follow the journey—a journey back to love. The chronicling of two Black women, a mother and a daughter, 33 years apart in age, and more than a generation of differences, traveling, as many Black women have before, along a hot, dusty road. Mama and I both kicked up a lot of dust this year trying to figure out our individual paths on this shared journey. But we've made it to another year.

# TENNYBOOTS!

Each year, the dynamics of taking care of an elderly Mama changes. The Mama I cared for at 92 is not the Mama I deal with today. She changes with the difficulties she has to overcome. I have no experience being a daughter to a mother, whose fierce desire to remain independent sometimes dwarfs her ability to do so. As if living Dylan's words, Mama is intent on raging against the dying of the light.[8] She is determined that death will not find her complicit. My problem was that I believed that if not complicit, she should at least be accommodating. Accommodating for her age, accommodating for her station in life, accommodating for her condition. My constant childhood prayer for God not to let anything happen to Mama had failed to anticipate this result. Thankful is a hard thing to be when feeling burdened and overwhelmed.

I stopped by her apartment on the day after Christmas. A brouhaha between her and her twenty-something-year-old roommates has tumbled into hurt feelings, and apologies—not given, and also not accepted. But at least things are quiet. Mama has worn herself out from raising hell this week; she can give as well as she takes. She lay across her bed in a deep sleep, her burgundy Christmas slippers, a gift from one of the girls, still on her feet. I call her name, and she doesn't answer. I call again and she still doesn't answer. In the ritual reserved for those who care for a sick or elderly person, I study her chest for a sign of her breath to ensure that she is still living. I run my fingers across her cheek, as one would caress a baby or a lover. Her cheeks have almost no fat on them now, and I am surprised how easily I can feel the contours of the bony structure of her jaw. But the skin, smooth and ebony-colored, is still soft. Her mane of white hair has flattened to one side of her head as though she's been asleep for a while. I blow her hair and just like that she wakes up, and this time she is wearing a smile.

"Ju, I waited for you for so long I thought maybe you wasn't coming."

---

[8] Dylan Thomas: Do Not Go Gentle Into That Good Night

# TENNYBOOTS!

The way Mama experiences time now is odd. As soon as she hears something, it travels way back in time, as though her brain has processed the same sensations over and over for so long that it no longer needs a reference place to store the information. It jettisons it back somewhere far into the recesses of her mind, instead of placing the information in some proximate queue where she can easily access it. As a result, time for her flies, literally, well not literally, but it moves really fast. And that has been the source of much friction between us.

It doesn't help that Mama's worship of time is directly proportional to my disrespect of it. Time is relative. I am task-centered and am late a good amount of time. Mama would get so frustrated waiting for me to visit, or do something that she swore I had promised to do a long time ago when it was only maybe an hour ago. If she were outside sitting on the bench, she would enlist everyone she knew to call me at ten-minute intervals, indignantly telling me that "Ms. Florence is waiting on you." Mama had sat and complained so much about me, that when drove up, her face would be fixed in a frown and her fellow bench sitters would roll their eyes, and mutter about how I left Mama waiting like that. Mama's friends never took kindly to what they deemed Mama's mistreatment—whether or not it was true. If Mama said it, they believed it, and acted on it towards me.

Then one day Mama explained to me how she experienced time. I explained how it really happened and how it made me feel when she complained about me to everyone. I told her I would do better, and she promised that she would be more patient. I told her I understood. This was a rare moment of Mama being able to hear what I was saying. Typically, even the sound of my voice gets on her nerves if I am not saying what she wants me to here. Her complaints about me have gotten better, but as a result, she is never sure whether it has really been a long time, or if that's the way she is experiencing it. But tonight, she is right, I told her that I was coming over earlier in the day, but because I spend my free time sandwiched between Mama and my twin grandchildren, the day got away from me, and it's another weekend I have had no time at all to myself. It is nighttime and I am just now getting to see her. I confirm her impression that I took a long time. And I apologize. For some reason, it comforts her.

She begins the conversation, the same way she has all week, referring to the great-grandchildren who live with her.

"You know they are moving right? I don't care, I told them we can all get along if they follow my rules, if not..."

The bruised egos of the past week have the girls threatening to move out and Mama is preparing herself to not feel the hurt by saying that she doesn't care. She doesn't care because she can take care of herself, which is true only sometimes. She is feeling better than ever, she says, because those doctors were making her sick. She is, in her own opinion, stronger, her eyes see better, her legs are stable, she can do her own work and keep her place neat and clean, and she will be fine. On and on it goes until she convinces herself that she doesn't care.

This time I do not participate in my listening. I fake body language to make her think I am listening. I have heard the same story at least three times a day since last week. I cock my head when she looks in my direction, press my lips together and push them outward to show fake emotion, and nod my head perfunctorily. But I say nothing. She notices but is too proud to acknowledge my lack of engagement. She chooses instead to bask in the neutral peace of non-committal rather than have me voice an opinion that differs from hers, which to her would mean that I am taking sides. I sigh and tell myself that I am so tired of hearing it because the thing is that she cares. Actually, she cares too much. But somewhere during her life, showing that she cares, was not a luxury she allowed herself to take. Instead, she defaults to strong and stubborn, which is really the exterior hardened shell of caring and vulnerable.

Mama's life never gave her the luxury of self-reflection. Mama raised three girls alone -- who begged her to never go on welfare because they identified welfare kids in school by big signs that they held up and everyone knew who they were. (A lie my sisters had concocted.) She sometimes worked up to three jobs a day to spare us the embarrassment she had known from poverty

# TENNYBOOTS!

and lack. When my aunt died of Leukemia at 42, Mama took in her three boys and raised them as her own. After that, Mama and I raised my sister's children, Pinky and Russell. And Mama raised my sister's grandchildren as her own grandchildren. At 80 years old she gained custody of a 3-month-old great-granddaughter. She buried my sister, her middle child when she died at 45 years old. And she has now buried her mother, step-father, all of her sisters, and their husbands, her husband, nieces, nephews, and her best friends.

She worked until she was 82, because it was the only thing she had ever done, and for her, not to work, was to not have value. She started a candy business making pralines as her sharecropping mother did before her, at 93, to support her church, and would still be doing it, if she hadn't worn me out. In all that living, it was Mama's independence and stubborn will that were constant. It was her temple, her familiar, her agency—that which kept her going when other people had already given up.

She will never acknowledge being wrong, and she will not apologize when she says or does hurtful things to people. I can't excuse it. I am learning not to emulate her.

By writing the *Sunday Morning Mama* stories every week, I have forced myself to reflect on the whole person, and find other ways of seeing Mama. Seeing her, not just as Mama -- but as the little girl who became the woman, who became the person she had to be to survive -- has me trying to transform my love for her into acceptance of the whole person, not just the Mama I need her to be to make my life easier right now. These are goals I aspire to. My need to manage the input, as much as possible in order to direct the outcome, increases her proclivity to resist. But if I can't make caring for Mama doable to the point where I have some semblance of my own life, which includes being 100% present for my grandchildren, as Mama has been for hers -- then my life is not worth living. By God's grace, and our Ancestors might, we come to the end of 2013, Mama and me, still traveling along that road. I am determined to forge ahead.

By now Mama has finished her story about not caring that the girls will move out. I rejoin the conversation, and we talk and laugh about other things. I get ready to leave. She has enjoyed the visit and me. I kiss her on the third eye, with compassion and love, hoping that she can feel it, that it will lighten her burden, and get her to admit that she cares.

"Love you, Ju."

"I love you Ma."

That's how I left her on the next-to-last day of 2013 -- feeling strong and independent and trying to convince herself that she doesn't care. Her 94th year is going out with a bang. 2014 we're coming.

****

# TENNYBOOTS!

## Chapter Fourteen

### All the Sentimental Reasons

Two weeks of Christmas and New Year holidays, polar vortexes, snow, and ice has kept Mama cooped up in her apartment. The day before the polar vortex here in Harlem, she wanted extra cash, so I dropped it off in the morning before the snowstorm on my way downtown. I called her in the afternoon before the storm hit to check on her.

Before I could say hello, she cranked out, "I'm starving ain't nothing to eat here!"

"Ma you can't be starving!"

"The hell I ain't."

"Ma, I've told you about working me to death when you have others at your disposal. Hell, next to you I am the oldest one. Send someone to the store. Anyway, I know you still have groceries from what I brought you last week. I will bring you some food for the snowstorm before I go in tonight"

Perhaps prodded by the guilt of working me to death, she remembers that she has a can of skinless and boneless sardines, and she hangs up the phone to eat them with some crackers. On my way back uptown, I stopped at the supermarket near her apartment and bought her three of each- meat, cookies, yogurt, fruit, chips and a six-pack of Pepsi and dropped it off at her apartment. I only stay a

# TENNYBOOTS!

moment as the snow has reached blizzard conditions. When I left her apartment, Mama and the great, great, grandbabies (the fifth generation) were fighting over the chocolate chip cookies. It took me one hour to walk four city blocks. The snow was coming in horizontally at an inch an hour.

The buses had stopped running and there was no way home except to walk. The mounds of snow had taken on a life of their own. All I could see ahead of me and behind me were snowdrifts appearing strategically poised to prevent me from taking a straight route home. Dusk had come quickly and paired with the blinding blizzard snow, I lost all sense of direction a mere four blocks from home. My heartbeat quickened, my head began to hurt, and I felt like running. But the snow wouldn't allow me. My breath was coming in short, quick bursts, and I was feeling faint. I had to get my bearings. I searched for landmarks and followed them slowly home. A ten-minute trip took an hour, and I finally made it home.

From day-to-day, I couldn't tell which Mama I would get. Yesterday had been such a good day. I had called Mama and asked her if she wanted to go for a ride.

"Yeah, I think I'd like that."

When I got to her block, she was waiting for me on the stoop. She was down the ramp before I could open the door.

"Whoa! Moving kind of fast Mama."

"I'm feeling good today, got my '57 Ford with me!"

We both laughed at the reference to the car that DadDee had. We drove around for a few hours. I took her on my errands and we picked up her coat from the dry cleaner. We stopped to pick up my grandchildren from their piano lessons and took my daughter, Cricket on her errands.

"I got a taste for some neck bones over rice from that place where you take me on Sundays."

# TENNYBOOTS!

"Umm, I don't remember getting neck bones from Jacobs. I…"

"Oh yes, you did. You remember. That place where you get my food from on Sundays."

"All right, I'll see."

I went to *Jacobs* and sure enough, there were some neck bones on the hot table. I scooped up some white rice and dished some neck bones over it, paid the man and returned to the car. Next, she wanted some doughnuts. We drove to the donut shop on 145th Street where they were always fresh and got her two jelly doughnuts. The jelly donuts reminded her of Wilson's, a now-closed bakery, on 125th Street that sold donuts ever.

"They had the best jelly doughnuts, I used to buy them by the dozen."

Driving around in the rain, Mama's eyes are often closed now as if to get a better glimpse inward at the stories she tells of almost a century past. My nine—years-old grandchildren love her storytelling, egg her on, and ask her questions. She was giving us snippets of stories, most of which we've heard before, but some are new. She speaks of Grandma Lindy, her mother, always getting sick and this one time falling in the gully, and Mama stepping over her thinking it's a pig rather than her mother, until much later when she looks for her mother in the field and her aunt tells her that Lindy had never made it there that day. Mama went running and retracing her steps hollering Momma, Momma. When she got to the gully, her Momma had groaned, and she realized that it was her mother that she had stepped over, not a pig. She ran and got her Aunt Bessie, hollering, "Baaayaa" the name they called her, all the way back to her Aunt who was toiling in the field, about a country mile away. Mama and her Aunt Bessie ran back to the place Mama had seen her mother and got Grandma Lindy out of the gully and home where they gave her medicine, for her headache and gas, and put her to bed.

# TENNYBOOTS!

My grandkids pepper Mama with questions about the story, laughing first behind their hands, then outright when Mama laughs wildly too at the thought of her stepping over her mother's back, thinking she was a pig. They have heard the story of Mama's pet pig Suki before, so one of them asks if the pig were Suki.

"Hell no, the pig was Momma," Mama says laughing hysterically from the memory as much as from the attention.

We all laugh easily.

"What a life..." Mama muses.

Enamored with her audience and basking in being the center of attention, Mama quickly segues into another story. The kids are still egging her on and encouraging her, and Mama assures them she has "Lots of stories."

With her eyes shut on the present, the stories tumble out easily, one after another. She told the story of working in the field at the big house, hoeing her row and her sick mother's row too. Of getting baptized in the new church pool and not in the swamp at Reverend L.C. Simon's church. And about how she was always bringing something home to her mother, who would hold the thing in her hand the whole time she was gone until she got back home to her Momma, and how the thing would be pulverized when she opened her hand, but her Momma would still take it, and eat it, and be thankful for it. She told of her coming to New York for the first time to work for five dollars a week so she could send three dollars home to her Momma for medicine. Between her stories, she would open her eyes to orient herself in the moment.

*"That's my church over there, isn't it? Is that Nat Cole singing? He was one of the best! They have Deals here? Now that threw me. When did they put one there? These white folks said they were gon move back to Harlem. Shit, they here."*

When we pass Lenox Avenue and 115th Street, still demonstrating to herself mostly that she is in her right mind, she

# TENNYBOOTS!

asks, "Remember that Mom and Pop store that used to be on this corner?"

"Yes, you mean Mr. Jimmie's, or when the Jewish couple had it—the Morrison's or something like that," I respond.

*"Yes, Jimmy, the colored guy, and his wife. He was nice, but that wife wouldn't smile a lick. I would get off the subway from my night job, stop there and buy some bread and milk and stuff on credit."*

"Credit," I ask, surprised I never heard that before. "You bought things on credit?"

That brings me back to all the times I had gone to Mr. Jimmie's store and had stood in the line, snaked back to the door, waiting my turn behind someone who was buying on credit. They held up the line because they had to have their purchases written in a soft-sided, tan, composition book, hanging by a worn piece of twine from the cord of the old phone hanging on the wall. If they weren't making a purchase on credit, then they were settling up a debt they owed from that book. I felt such a sense of pride that because of Mama's work ethic, we never had to feel the shame of waiting to record our purchases in the old composition notebook that meant you could not afford what you were buying. But now, I am feeling so many emotions: shame, anger, and, mostly sadness, which brings me back in time to a similar feeling of sadness, anger, and shame.

All of our young lives—like Dagmar and her sisters in "I Remember Mama" based on the memoir, *Mama's Bank Account*—we were sustained knowing that Mama had a bank account for emergencies.[9] Mama was fastidious about saving some of her earnings each week for an emergency. When she first got to New York, she saved two dollars a week at the Post Office Bank on 125th Street. When she got married, she opened an account with Jackie Robinson's bank, Freedom National. When Carver Bank, the second independently owned African American bank opened in Harlem, she took us there to open a bank account. It was a big deal.

---

[9] *Mama's Bank Account* by Kathryn Forbes (Harvest /HBJ Book)

# TENNYBOOTS!

We got all dressed up to get Mama's bank account at Carver. They gave us great tasting lollipops—the short, thick ones with loops for sticks—not at all like the ones we bought for a penny apiece, at Ms. Cora's candy store. But we left with much more—we left with the confidence and security that we were *somebody* because Mama had a bank account. We promised Mama that we would be good kids and behave ourselves if she continued to work two jobs, because it was so important to have that bank account. That was our bargain.

Work many jobs, she did. Mama would finish her day-job cleaning apartments for the *families,* come home to cook us dinner, while watching soap operas: *The Edge of Night* and *The Guiding Light.* At 5:00 P.M. she would leave us to go to her office cleaning job until 10:00 P.M., five nights a week. When we had the 1957 Ford Fairlane 500, (which for some reason had a hole in the floor under the mat in the back seat, that led to the street, which, three little girls sometimes used as a potty), DadDee would pick us up at 9:30 P.M. and drive through Central Park to pick Mama up from work. The gospel music station would blare Mahalia Jackson and other icons, while Daddee rounded the curves on Central Park Drive at 90 m.p.h. When we no longer had a car, Mama would take the IRT Subway Line from 50$^{th}$ street uptown to Harlem.

Then in 1963, the year I turned eleven, Mama's sister, Nettie, died of Leukemia. She was only 42, and she left three boys. Mama took them in to live with us. Daddee had already left, and Mama was taking care three girls, and our three cousins all by herself.

My middle sister, Gaynell, and my cousin, Cornell were graduating from 6$^{th}$ grade that June and they both needed all-white outfits. Social Security survivor's benefits of $37.50 per child, per month, for my aunt's children, were slow in coming. Because we had the boys in the house, Mama had to cut down on her work hours. Mama had been dipping into her savings trying to make ends meet. Caring for three girls and three boys, 12, 16 and 17, and robbing Peter to pay Paul had caught up to Mama. One Saturday morning Mama woke us up rolling back and forth on the floor between the kitchen sink and cabinets, crying out in anguish

# TENNYBOOTS!

because she did not have enough money to get the graduation outfits and to pay the bills.

Sitting on the floor close by, wiping her tears trying to comfort her and make everything all right, my 11-year-old self suggested we use the money in the bank account because this was an emergency. Mama got up from the floor and gathered my sisters and me around her—at the old chrome and Formica kitchen table with the red hearts on either end—and told us, much like the mother in *I Remember Mama* told her girls—that there was no money in the bank account. I wanted to be brave, I really did. Mama had always called me wise, and I was Mama's self-appointed savior. I always had the answer for everything—I had once healed myself with my own-made medicine after we had our tonsils removed in 1955. But in that moment, a sad, small child is all that I was and I could not for the life of me, hold back the tears or the feeling of betrayal.

Mama had not kept her end of the bargain. It wasn't fair. I remember feeling faint, and right then and there, I bawled my 11-year-old eyes out. That bank account was as much ours as it was Mama's. We had kept our end of the bargain. My anxiety about being poor and stuck on welfare fueled my despair. My sisters, who could be indifferent to family drama, looked scared. And that frightened me even more. Gaynell, my middle sister, who was always writing her name on anything—the wall, her arms, the ironing board cover, her legs, books, pictures, 45 rpm record labels and 78 rpm album jackets—took her pen she always had, and started punching holes in the red hearts of the vinyl covering of the chairs that perfectly matched the Formica table. Edie, who could be aloof and able to stay above the fray, busied herself by looking anywhere but at Mama. Once when DadDee picked up his girlfriend, Leila Mae, in our car, and I told Mama, when Mama asked Edie about it, Edie said she saw nothing because she was looking out of the window the whole time. Gay just flat out lied to protect DadDee. Seeing their reactions now made me more upset. Mama was already beside herself because we had no money, but letting us down and seeing our reaction devastated her and she began to cry even harder.

## TENNYBOOTS!

We got beyond that day somehow. Gay and Cornell graduated in all white outfits. And I don't remember us not eating. Eventually Mama built up her savings and got us new accounts at Carver Savings Bank. The thought of Mama having used credit back then to buy food for us instantly conjures up memories of that day and makes me sad again. Save for that one time, Mama never let us know how poor we were. We were secure because Mama was secure.

My reminiscing ends in time to pay attention to Mama, who is back in the present now, telling more stories. She's cracking jokes, and she's talking about her exploits with her housemates. Mama laughs at how wily she believes herself to be with the girls. I laugh. My daughter and the grandkids laugh. Sam Cooke is playing on the CD in the car. Mama is patting her foot and doing the sit-down dance to the music in her seat.

"How I loved Sam Cooke, it hurt me when that woman killed him. We all knew that was a set up," she muses to no one in particular.

We ride and listen some more to Sam Cooke sing his heart out. Self-determination against old age is Mama's mantra today, she's not going to allow herself to look old.

"When I see myself going down, I say oh hell no, I push myself up, I sit in the rocking chair and push my back against the back of the chair, I will not walk all bent over. That's why I keep wondering about my mind, what happened, I was out of it for a while, wasn't I? But even that, I ain't gonna let that get me down either, I just keep pressing on, and rolling with the punches. I used to worry bout it, but I ain't gone wear myself down worrying bout whether I'm in my right mind."

I assure her that she looks great, she's in her right mind and that she's my hero. She smiles. Today Mama is easy to love. Too easy. Not sure if it's the melancholy mood I'm in or what, but I love her today for all the sentimental reasons. For all that she endured. For all that she put up with. For the credit that she got and settled on payday. For the Carver Bank account, she didn't have anymore.

## TENNYBOOTS!

For getting old with such self-determination and independence. For all the clichés she embraces: raging against the dying light; pressed to the wall but fighting back; embracing the ever-changing dawns, and for her fierce determination to yank herself back to the here and now. Today I love Mama with action and intent.

****

## Chapter Fifteen

### New Pants Suit

Last night, before I went to bed, I called and asked Mama if she were going to church. She had been iffy at first and then she declared emphatically that she was not going.

"Ma are you sure? Do you want to just decide in the morning?"

"It's too cold, it's snowing, Nah, I ain't going. I am *not* going."

Last night, I went to bed confident that I could sleep in. It's nearing 7:10 a.m. and I'm enjoying sleeping in when Mama calls.

"Ju, you sleep? I decided I am going to church. I can take the bus if you sleep."

Instead of saying that she changed her mind and now she will go to church, she makes her case.

"Ju, I will take the bus."

Slowly waking up to what she is saying, all I can say is, "Ma," when she gets really loud, talking over me.

"Yeah, I can do it, I'm *gonna* do it."

# TENNYBOOTS!

She knows I won't allow her to take the bus in this cold and snow. Walking with a walker in the snow is a recipe for a fall. She fell once when she first got the walker and was ashamed that the neighborhood boys had to pick her up. If I suggest that she takes a cab, she will swear that she has no money; and if she has money, she will not take the cab, anyway. Pissed, I get up to get ready to go get her.

Mama has been in a strange mood all week. She's been fighting with the girls, and she is brooding. Mama is a difficult person to live with. It's because like a chameleon she's forever changing. One day, she feels one way and the next day she changes her mind. She will change her mind based on something someone told her, or her pride, or her recent determination to set things right. The flip side of this is that often I have caught Mama and the girls sitting in her room having a good old time. They confide in her all sorts of things that I never have, and she tells them stories about when she was young and frisky. When it works, it's magical. Across 70-90 years Mama and the fourth and fifth-generation are sharing and caring and having a great time doing so.

Mama also loves gossip. And is good at quickly sharing it. You know it's coming when she prefaces a conversation with, "I didn't know…" Sometimes she tells so much so quickly that she runs out of people to tell and winds up sharing the story with the person who initially told her not to tell anyone. She is also judgmental and quick to give her opinion about how she believes something is to be done. I am beating around the bush here, but suffice it to say that Mama can stir up, defend, and keep a lot of shit going.

As a result, someone is always thinking Mama is saying more than she should have said; or showing favoritism; or should have kept her mouth closed about something. It leads to very confusing dynamics in the family. But it also accounts for Mama's sharp wit in her late 90s. Taunting her antagonist and *playing the dozens* is not beneath her. Taking the high road means defeat to her. Some of her zingers are brilliant, even if they are not nice.

# TENNYBOOTS!

I used to wade into the middle of the fights between Mama and the great-grands. If it were the girls living with her, and Mama would insist that she wanted them to move out, I'd defend Mama and tell the girls they had to leave. Mama would then change her mind and talk about me, saying that it was her apartment and that only she decided who stayed with her—not Judy. It didn't take me long to extricate myself from the midst of their problems. But I'd still get telephone calls in the middle of the night to referee some disagreement that they've had. I didn't get up and go over there anymore, and sometimes I'd turn the phone off. I learned that they all lived until the morning. When I really started listening to both sides—a lot of times Mama had either started the fight, or was equally at fault.

Everyone calls me when they feel that Mama is out of line, being stubborn, or won't do something she needs to do. My role as Mama-enforcer exacerbates my relationship with Mama and the family. I've learned to mind my business unless it's unavoidable. But I am still a moving target for Mama or our family, depending on which side I come down on.

This week has been eventful. NYCHA botched up a repair job on Mama's stove, and it sparked a small fire in the kitchen. One neighbor called to tell me about it and I dropped everything and ran over there. Apparently it had happened before, and the girls thought Mama was to blame; but this time it happened all on its own, and Mama, thrilled to prove that she was capable and had not started either this one, or the previous stove fire, said, "I stayed in my room, far from it, so they couldn't blame me." I was dumbfounded. That is not the response I'd expected. But Mama is *not speaking* to the girls so once she realized the fire was not a problem, she remained in her room. Also, the stove fire gives her fodder to complain about an elderly maintenance man who needs to retire.

"That old man from housing changed the burners, and he's old as me. I know he don't know what he doing. I asked him how long you gon work. He said, 'I'm gon work as long as I can.' I told him, well your *can* done come and gone, your *can* is over baby, been over. He been here long as this project, what he gone do die, not

# TENNYBOOTS!

take a vacation, just die? Walking round here like a double-over old man. Time for you to take a vacation, do something. You see all that snow, used to be a time I had to get out in all that, I don't miss that. He better get hip."

Her complaints about the maintenance man diverts her attention from the topic of not speaking to girls. I don't ask what happened. The problem—and the good thing—is that I never get the whole story. Mama tells me it was nothing and another time she says it's a full-blown fight. Like a snowball rolling down a hill, the story grows in the telling. Having been on the other side of that with Mama, I know full well her propensity to wax the hyperbole, to not tell the whole story, to even lie, and also never to be at fault. I figure somewhere in the middle is what has really happened. So, this week she is not speaking to her housemates, and she seems to enjoy the ways she has found to not speak.

"When she asks me anything I just wiggle my fingers," she says, showing me with her fingers beckoning. "One wiggle means yes, and two wiggles mean no, that way, I am not speaking to her."

"God give me strength!"

I laugh at how petty this is. Mama believes I am laughing at how clever she is and we both laugh together, albeit each for a different reason. I ask her, as I've asked before, if she wants them to move, or if she wants to move to a senior citizen apartment. Her answer is always the same: "No." And that's the catch-22. Mama wants things to be different, but she doesn't want to do the work to make it different. And she doesn't want to face the consequences. And just maybe, despite all of her kvetching and complaining, she doesn't want to be alone. She enjoys the lively company of the young people, and the little one, Ryder, adores Mama, they are great friends and each other's biggest supporters. As I always do, I remind Mama that she is welcome to come to live with me. But we both remember all too well how a couple of years ago she moved in with me. She had visitors running in and out of my apartment; and got angry because I would not allow a 15-year-old to move in with us. I had already softened and allowed the 15-year-old to spend each Saturday night, against my better judgment. After a few months, she left in a huff, balancing a stuff, and pushing her belongings on her walker. I had to catch up with her and give a ride. I was thrilled that she was leaving and sweetened the pot by making over her old bedroom. We both remember.

Mama quickly says, "No, I can handle it."

I called her yesterday to see if I should pick her up to go to a party for one of the 5$^{th}$ generation. She refused to come to the phone several times pretending to be asleep. When I finally got her on the telephone, she came to the phone with her offense intact, braying like a donkey.

"I'm not going. I don't want to go! I just don't want to go."

"Hey Sweetie, how are you? You've been sleeping a lot today, I just wanted to check on you," I purred into the phone.

"I ain't going, I don't feel like going."

"Oh, I don't care if you don't go, I am just checking on you because they've said you were sleeping a few times when I called you."

Relieved that I was not telling her she should go to the birthday party, she eased up.

"No, I just don't want to go. Let them go and then I will have the house to myself. My living room is a garage and a plantation."

I thought Mama had mispronounced some words but then she clarified.

"Well, there's that big pink Barbie car parked in there; and now there's a dollhouse in there from Christmas! A garage and a plantation right here in my living room."

I howled. I laughed so hard it broke the ice and made her laugh too. Concerned that her blood count might be low, I asked her why was she sleeping so much. Did she feel tired?

# TENNYBOOTS!

"I wasn't sleep. Every time they would call me, I would close my eyes and pretend to be sleep because I didn't want nobody tryna make me go to the party."

"Ma, ain't nobody can make you do anything, you forget who you are?"

So, on the heels of a strange week for Mama, her saying she wasn't going to church and now she is, is keeping with the mood she has nursed all week.

I get to her building and she comes out with Sara, the 17-year-old who has held favorite grandchild status for the fourth living generation, since she was three months old. I am always happy to see Sara on Sunday mornings, because Sara will collapse the walker, put it in the car, push Mama up into her seat, buckle her in, and she always plants a kiss on her, which is cute. I don't even get out of the car when I see Sara.

Mama is wearing her big, brown, down-filled coat. All week, in her funky mood, when I could get her on the telephone and remind her that she needed to get her hair done, she had refused. On Saturday night, I had suggested that she put a roller or two in her hair in case she decided to go to church. She had thrown back to me, "If I feel like it." This morning, her naturally beautiful, white hair is kind of yellow and stringy, sticking out of a red knitted skull cap. I look down at her feet to check to see if she is wearing boots. She is wearing a pair of khaki jeans rolled up with a cuff the length of my forearm. This is the Mama who refuses to allow me to buy her a pantsuit because she will not wear pants to church.

Mama's refusal to wear pants to church runs deep. Only a proper silk stocking would do when we were young. She has worn stockings and dresses or suits to church as long as I can remember. If it's Sunday it's stockings, and so it has been for the 65 years that I have known her. Every Saturday we used to go to the stocking store to purchase a pair of Red Fox silk nylons, kept in tissue paper, in flat rectangular shaped white boxes, stacked on top of each other on dusty, over stuffed shelves. The shop was narrow and had a full assortment of undergarments hanging from clotheslines, and

# TENNYBOOTS!

sticking out of strange places. I always marveled at how the Jewish shopkeeper knew exactly what was in each box, even though there didn't appear to be any labels on them. I would stand with Mama in front of the old wood-framed glass counter—the wood had been painted white so many times it was a pale yellow—waiting for the shopkeeper to get it wrong. But not once, in all that standing and waiting, did the shopkeeper not conjure up the very thing Mama asked for. Like magic, she would reach for a box, remove its lid, part the tissue paper, and voila, she would hold up the shimmering nylons in both hands for Mama to inspect. Sometimes a fine black seam covered the fold and followed the outline of the nylon in the shape of a woman's leg, sometimes there were no seams. Mama had worn her first pair of nylon stockings during the Great Depression, when Aunt Annie had gotten her a rationed pair, for a nickel. Since then, the Saturday ritual was to purchase the nylons for Sunday Morning church. During the 60s, when nylon stockings gave way to pantyhose, the ritual changed. The lingerie store was replaced by the bodega that sold racks of pantyhose, from the jobber, who made a pretty penny off of them. French Coffee, queen size, big enough to get pulled up in the full-length girdle, Mama still wore, and still be comfortable. Off white pantyhose for Missionary First Sundays, and that was it. She never wore fishnet, or opaque, or any of the fancy ones with bling. My pushing pants suits on her will be one more surrender of her autonomy.

"Ma, maybe one of the velour warm-up suits would have been a better choice," I say, careful to not sound too judgmental.

Interrupting me, she says, "Oh it's okay, I'm warm, nobody is gonna see my pants!"

When we get to the church, Sara hops out and helps her out. Years ago, when Sara was only a baby the church people used to call them "the old lady and the baby" but the baby is now bigger than the old lady. I bring Sunday morning breakfast to my grandchildren. They come down to the back door to pick up the breakfast and then I am on my way to K&G, a discount clothing store on Eighth Avenue, around the corner from her church, to buy Mama a dressy pantsuit so at least she will have something decent if she wears pants again.

# TENNYBOOTS!

I stop dead in my tracks to check myself to see if I am imposing my will on Mama by buying her a pantsuit she says she doesn't want. Am I doing this for her, or am I doing this for me? I think about how until I was five years old and my sisters were six and eight, Mama changed our clothing twice a day. We had white kid leather shoes that she polished each morning with *Griffin All White Shoe Polish* and then buffed them with an old weathered rag to a high glossy shine. In the afternoon, we wore black patent leather shoes; or a pair of red oxfords similarly polished and buffed using *Griffin's Oxblood Leather Wax*. We also wore dresses, which Mama had made for us, sticking out over crinolines, and white cotton socks with the square toe and green line across the front. And this was how we dressed every day until I was five.

One day we pleaded with Mama to buy us a pair of dungarees. All the kids were wearing them. She finally relented and took us to Blumstein's Department Store on 125th Street (famous for having women elevator operators, who wore white cotton gloves; infamous for only hiring Black women whose complexion could pass the paper bag test) and bought us all a pair of dungarees. She also bought us striped polo shirts. We stopped at Harry's Buster Brown Shoes around the corner from our house. Mama bought each of us a pair of PF Flyers sneakers. Mine were red, Gay and Edie got blue with the white rubber tip at the toe. The sneakers had a circle tag in the heel. The tag was a picture of a winking Buster Brown wearing a red beret, and his dog, Tige, sporting a maniacal grin. I am unsure if it was the winking Buster Brown or the maniacal Tige, but wearing PF Flyers made you run faster and jump higher than anyone on the block.

We begged Mama to let us wear our new sneakers home from the store. I can see the shoe store now: there were pastel colored vinyl covered seats with metal arms, attached in a row, back to back with another row on the other side. They always had a lot of those low stools where the salespeople sat and pulled the shoes on your feet, and those black and metal Brannock Devices to measure your feet and determine shoe size scattered around. We always raced to beat each other to the stools to pretend we were the shoe salespeople, all demanding at the same time that Mama put her foot in the device so that each of us could determine her shoe size.

# TENNYBOOTS!

We would get a balloon, a comic book, and a lollipop with each purchase of shoes. When we had our shoes and were going home, Mama crossed us across 115th Street from the north side of the street to the south side and let us go.

"On your mark, get set, go," we yelled and raced each other up 115th Street, jumping higher and running faster than we had ever done before.

When we got to our building Mama took us upstairs, and we put on our dungarees and polo shirts. Those dungarees were stiff and scratchy, not at all like I thought they would feel, but we went outside, and sat right in the dirt by the stoop, and in our five, six, and eight-year-old glee, we shouted for everyone, to "Look at us, we are getting dirty!"

Mama's stories about being ridiculed are deep wounds still. I decide that I *am* buying the pantsuit. I am buying it for Mama, and I am buying it for me. She needs it and I never want her to feel that way again, or be ridiculed for what she is wearing, even if she doesn't realize that she is susceptible. And that get-up she is wearing today is ridicule-worthy for sure.

When Sara calls to say that they are ready to be picked up, I am right around the corner. I drive around and they get into the car, Sara puts Mama in again, no kiss this time. I tell her I bought her a pantsuit, but I have to shorten the pants. She protests a little.

"I told you not to spend your money. I don't want one. I'm not gonna wear it."

"It's not my money, it's yours, and I am spending it on you," "I say.

She gives in quickly today, she's not up for any more fights, and is more concerned with telling me about her struggles in keeping time straight.

"Now I know I am not crazy, but the sermon the preacher preached, I heard it before."

# TENNYBOOTS!

    I'm not in the mood to listen today, so I hand Sara my phone and let her videotape Mama struggling to make sense of how she is experiencing time. When she stops, I take the phone and put the recording away for another day. It satisfies Mama that what she had to say was important enough to be recorded. We go to *Jacobs* to get her Sunday dinner. She wants doughnuts too, so we get her a few, and then I drop her and Sara off at home. I keep the suit to hem the pants. Next Sunday if it's as bitter cold as it has been she will wear the pantsuit if I have to dress her myself.

****

## Chapter Sixteen

### Ballerina and Mind Pictures

Picked Mama up for church this morning and she's wearing the pantsuit I altered last night. She and Sara are waiting in front of her building. She looks good and warm. Sara puts her in the car quickly and we pull off.

"What did you eat this morning Ma?"

"Um... Um... I ain't had nothing to eat."

"Why didn't you eat? I bought you waffles, yogurt, you have bacon, you've been waiting for me since seven this morning, you had time to eat. Sara, you too, why didn't you make something to eat? "

"Aw, it's okay, I'll go to McDonald's and get a mash potato."

"Mc Donald's don't have any mash potatoes, Mama"

"No, she means Hash Browns," Sara clarifies, laughing.

"Ash browns, hash brown, whatever they are. Y'all know what I'm talking about. Sara know."

The snow hasn't been shoveled from the street to the church so Sara and I hold onto to her until she gets firmly planted on the sidewalk. The walker is useless now until she gets on firm ground. We get into the church building, and Mama is sashaying like a child in Easter clothes.

"Ju, you ain't gon take my picture today, look at my pantsuit."

I usually post her picture with her Sunday Morning Mama Stories. She models her pantsuit, glad to be warm and chic today. I take the picture while she models the suit.

Last night, I went to her apartment to alter her pants. She told me to cut off eight inches, but I was certain that was not correct. I show her the pantsuit and she loves it; She tried on the jacket and ran her hand over the fabric.

"Oooh, it feels so silky," she crooned, drawing out the word silky to convey the feeling of luxury.

"Ju, stop spending so much money on me. The people at church say I want to be like Mother Edwards, when I get old, she dresses her behind off. They all want to be like me. Hell, I say, it's not to my credit, my daughter buys me all these clothes."

"It's your money. May as well spend it on you,"

She tries on the pants and comments on the nice quality of the material. Years ago, she used to sew very well and she taught me how to sew when I was ten years old. She knows fine fabrics.

The two and five-year-olds, Ryder and Riley, are dancing around Mama as she tries on the pants as though they are playing look who's here Punchanella, Punchanella—and Mama is Punchanella in the shoe.

"Mama, Mama, what's that, whatchoo doing?" the little one asks in a crackling singsong little girl voice.

"Trying on these new pants Judy bought me."

# TENNYBOOTS!

I've brought my sewing tin containing straight pins and needles and spools of thread with me. I'm pinning a hem in Mama's pants and keeping the kids from playing with the straight pins at the same time. They are fascinated by the shine of the pins and the way they seem to disappear into each other when they roll around the plastic case they are in. I hold onto the case and shake it for them, knowing if I give it to them to hold that the pins will be all over the floor in minutes. I motion to Mama to take the pants off. She falls back onto the bed raising both her legs so I can pull the pants off. The two-year-old sees this and throws herself onto the bed the way that Mama does, and also raises both her legs. I pretend to take her invisible pants off as well. I check out the pinned hem in the pants, and sure enough, Mama needed at least eight inches altered. She is shorter than five feet now, despite the 5'1" she always used to put on her driver's license. Old age has definitely shrunk her a few more inches.

I am hemming the pants, squinting, to thread needles, pulling the straight pins out of the fabric and holding onto them between my lips, while the two girls are asking, "What's this, what's that, what are you doing?" I tell them that I am sewing.

The five-year-old says very matter-of-factly, with all the poise of a five-year-old trying to be fifteen, "Oh my Mom's a designer, and she's very good, she sews pockets."

But for the pins I'm holding tightly in my lips, I would have burst out laughing at the "pockets." Instead, I manage a chuckle and make a mental note to tell her Mom that she is a famous pocket designer. Mama has dozed off so I am the sole audience for the girls, Riley and Ryder, the two-year-old who identifies as a ballerina. She is sporting her favorite tutu that she refuses to take off even to get it washed. She is twirling around singing ballerina songs, and demanding that we stop and take notice. I stop and watch her as she pirouettes sloppily, unable to balance on one foot the way she believes any self-respecting ballerina should. Her two-footed landing looks more like a sumo wrestler stance than an arabesque, but I applaud her attempts and resume my hemming of Mama's pants. Her face lights up with self-satisfaction.

# TENNYBOOTS!

Both Riley and Ryder are also asking me to sing songs. We start singing nursery rhymes and Mama wakes up energized by the merriment pulsing through the room. Mama initiates Miss Mary Mack, twenty-four buttons up and down her back... clapping as off-beat as she has for four generations of kids. I pair her up with the *ballerina*, and me and Ryder clap furiously to Mary Mack, Mack, Mack, dressed in black, black, black... We move on from Mary Mack and the 24 buttons up and down her back to Ring Around the Rosie, when Mama says, "that's the song we was singing when I was a little girl at that party and they made fun of me, calling me tenny boots.

I steel myself for Mama's bad feelings about being called tenny boots, but tonight, almost one hundred years removed from that time, neither ridicule nor poverty, nor the memory stings tonight, and she laughs through her stories of her stepfather's lack of experience and his antics as a poor sharecropping farmer.

*Pa Steve was the worst farmer. His mother, M'Hannah, had a house out in the country near where we were living, but they house completely burned down to the ground. There wasn't no fire trucks or hydrants in the country, we only had wells; and the little bit of water wasn't helping so they let it burn out. M'Hannah's son brought her to the town part to live in a new house. That's where Papa Steve was raised. He didn't know nothing bout no farming, but he tried. We had a wood stove and everybody could go chop wood and get it chopped nice like, and pile it up on they porch or in the kitchen and all they had to do was put a log in the burning stove. Not Pa Steve, he would cut a big old piece of wood as long as I am, like a tree. He would push one part in the stove and the other part would be blocking your way, you can't pass to get around the stove, cause it's cutting you off it's so long. And poor Momma would say, 'Steve, can you make this shorter, what you gotta make it so long for?' He'd say, 'Lindy, you do it yourself if you can make it shorter.' Every morning he'd get up, and we had an old dog, and him and that dog would go round to bout three neighbors to get some coffee, cause we ain't had none. No sugar, nothing. He'd go to one neighbor, drank a cup of coffee, go to another neighbor drank another cup.*

We can't catch our breath from laughing so hard about Papa Steve and the old dog and his mooching coffee off the

# TENNYBOOTS!

neighbors. The kids sensing fun join in laughing loudly too, which causes Mama to laugh more.

"Ma, how far would Papa Steve walk for free coffee?"

*Oh, about two or three city blocks. The only house we was close to was Aunt Bessie's house. That's where I used to run down every night Momma would get sick, hollering A-u-n-t Beees-sie. I would run cross the fields, jumping cross snakes calling Aunt Bessie, Momma's sick. Momma would be dying on the floor, least I thought she was dying. I done jumped cross many a snake, no shoes on my feet, just running and loping like a horse, guputa guputa, guputa. And there was a snake called a blue runner, he could stand on his tail and he could whistle like a person. When he was whistling, he'd be running your ass. I done outrun a blue runner many a day, hollering Aunt Bessie, the snake running me. Oh, what a life!*

Mama is whistling like the blue runner while she is telling the story, which fascinates the *ballerina*. So now the *ballerina* is also trying to whistle like a snake but succeeding only in blowing spit on her sister. The five-year-old, pushing her away twists up her face in disgust and says, "Gross!" The *ballerina* caught off guard, plops onto the floor and gets right back up as though we had attached her to a bungee cord. Mama yells at the five-year-old for pushing her, but I defend the five-year-old because at the same height as the *ballerina* most of the whistling spit was landing smack dab in her face. Bad feelings averted, the girls and I resume our places as Mama's captive audience.

Mama is emboldened by our attention and is still whistling and telling us how many times she has outrun a blue runner. We are all laughing so hard at the memories. I dare not interrupt because she is deep in memory lane and this may be the first time these fifth-generation children have heard these stories. She's still sitting up near the edge of the bed, but her eyes are closed now as if getting a better view of the pictures running across her mind. As she speaks, her hand crossed against her breast, she is rocking back and forth on the bed, leading with her shoulders, creating a matching rhythm for the story.

# TENNYBOOTS!

The *ballerina* tries to pry Mama's eyes open, asking in a whiny, two-year-old voice, "Mama whyse your eyes closed now?"

The five-year-old, unsure as to what is going on, is looking at me with an arched eyebrow, shaking her head and pouting her lips as though we, she and I, are in cahoots against the two of them—the old whistling woman, rocking rhythmically to her voice, with her eyes closed, telling a never-ending story, and the spitting *ballerina* in the well-worn tutu, trying to pry open the old woman's eyes. I point the needle I have in my hand, with a good length of black thread dangling from it, like an index finger, at my temple and make air circles with it. The five-year-old gap-tooth giggles her pleasure that I've confirmed what she's been thinking—that both she and I find the two of them *loca en la cabeza*.[10] I am still hemming the pants while enjoying Mama, the girls, and the stories. It's not that late and Mama senses that she can take advantage of her captive audience for a while longer so she launches into another story.

*We were the poorest family on the plantation cause Pa Steve was no farmer. When you were in the fields you had to off bear the rows, so that you didn't have so much to work. Pa Steve would try to off bear the row. The rows were bout a block long, to plant cotton and corn. You had to hoe the row and put clean dirt around the roots of it so it wouldn't sprout up. Otherwise the row would be that wide (here she gestures with her hands) and grass would be on it. You took your plow and mule to off bear it to get some of that grass off so when you hoe it you have a little piece to do. It would be easy for you. Pa Steve would off bear the damn row and look like it a get wider. Look like he added grass to the row...*

Mama stops talking because she is cracking her own self up with the story. We are both doubled over laughing.

*Fannie would have to take the plow, had one mule on the old plow, she'd wrap that strap round her neck and say, git up, git up, and she would plow it and get as close to the cotton or corn as she could, so when we hoed it we would only have a little to hoe. Fannie was a gentle soul, but was good as any man in the field. She could really work that field. But when Pa Steve did it, you*

---

[10] Spanish for Crazy in the Head

# TENNYBOOTS!

*would have to hoe a whole yard to plow, I could lay down and have a picnic on his grass.*

*Sometimes it was very hard though. We all had to be out in the fields every day, when daylight hit. There was a overseer guy, Big John Prescott, a Black man who would ride a big horse. We would take Momma out to the field with a blanket. We would stand Momma up on the hoe, and when he passed he would see her in the field. Then we would let Momma lay down on the blanket in the field cause she was sick. At 3:00 P.M. he would come back. And we would prop her up again on the hoe. That's the way we kept them from knowing that Momma wasn't working. I would hoe her field and my field and I was only bout twelve or leven...*

Mama pauses here for a minute, visibly saddened by thoughts of her always-sick mother, then muses to herself.

*It was just us five girls, Pa Steve, who wasn't no farmer, and Momma who was sickly. Most of the families had a lot of kids. Aunt Bessie had eight children and a few sons, so she was better off than we was. We couldn't even keep a box of Arm and Hammer baking soda for Momma when she was sick. Mama was always belching rrrrrrrrrrrr, Then she would feel better. Lotsa times we couldn't even make cornmeal. When we couldn't make cornmeal, we had to make cush.* [11] *Sometimes the meal had them worms in it. But we wouldn't know until we put the milk on top of it and the worms popped up. I wouldn't eat that cause I'm fraid ta death of a worm. I'll tangle with a snake and try to outrun one, but I'll run a mile from just the sight of a worm. They'd be skimming the worms from the milk. Mama would have to take me to the barn and milk the cow and skeet some of that milk in my mouth. Or I would be under that cow sucking his teet.*

*There was this fruit called maypops, and I loved maypops, look something like a plum. And I would go to get the maypops and had to watch for the snakes. They liked maypops too. Sometimes we would go into the boss man's watermelon patch and eat the melon. I remember we would go sit in the boss man's patch, bust the watermelon with our fists and have a good time. We had a lot of fun. That was fun now that I think of it. We was poor, but we had some fun too. But we sure worked hard...*

---

[11] A meal enslaved people made from cornbread derived from the Senegambia food called Kusha

# TENNYBOOTS!

Mama's voice sounds strained now, as the reality of the hard work is palpable.

"I know now why I see some people be talking to themselves and be laughing. They not crazy, they enjoying those stories in they mind."

And that's what Mama's doing, she's enjoying the stories in her mind. That we are present in the room, just gives her an opportunity to speak them aloud. She takes a swig of her soda and has to give the *ballerina* a swig too. She offers the five-year-old some, knowing full well that she won't take any. As if on cue, the five-year-old scrunches up her face in disgust and shakes her head vehemently, no.

"I knew that one wouldn't take it, she won't take nothing if I touch it. And sometimes she wants it so bad," complains Mama.

To appease Mama, I remind the five-year-old to say no thank you and now she's a bit unsure whether our pact is broken and is tentative with saying no thank you. I wink at her—reassured, she mumbles a "No thank you." I finish hemming the pants and start to put my supplies away. Mama doesn't get the cue and launches right in to another story. I'm tired of the stories now and am ready to leave, but Mama is in such good spirits, I tarry until she is done.

*Now Aunt Bessie had a business, she would take in the white people's laundry. I was just thinking, we useta boil them clothes. I say what the hell was we boiling them clothes for. Aunt Bessie had a sewing machine and she had a iron. We all had soothing irons, those old heavy irons. You had to heat it up from the fire. But Aunt Bessie had a gas iron. You would shoot the gas up in the iron and you would light it with a match and it burns and it heats. We called it a gas iron. She used that. She would take in laundry. Boy them white people shirts would be so white when she finished with them. Aunt Bessie could iron, man, she would iron those clothes, fold them up. Then the white folks would come out and get them, they'd ride out there in their car. Aunt Hattie used to do that too. We ain't' never had enough water to wash clothes for nobody else. Everybody had a well and a pump but us. Every time we would dig a well it would go dry. That gully was our well. We drank out of that lil gully, that's*

# TENNYBOOTS!

*why now I be thinking bout it and all that shit and water that would go through the fields and we drank out of it, make me want to vomit. Yuk! Then a mind say, hell you still living it didn't hurt you none. What don't kill you make you fatter, right?*

"Stronger, Ma. How did you get water if you had no well?"

*We had gallon buckets, we would go and scoop it up from the gully and bring it to the house and put it on the table. Sometimes we would get some water from some of the neighbors who had a well and a pump. And that would be clean water. I drank a lot of that old gully water. Dog shit in the fields, the water would stream down when it rained, but at that time to me, it was cool fresh water. But even if we had a well, Momma wasn't gonna do no clothes. Momma was sick all the time, and it was enough for my oldest sister to wash all the clothes for us. Then we would hang them on the fence or the bushes outside to dry. When they dried, we would fold them up and put them in the press, but they wouldn't stay in the press for long cause we only had a few clothes.*

"A press?" I ask, "What's a press?"

*You know a closet made of wood where all the clothes would go, something like a chiffarobe. A lot of time we didn't have kerosene to put in the lamps and we would have to sleep in the dark. There was times when Pa Steve would be mad at Momma and would be looking to fight. Momma would hide and would tell us where she was. One time, Momma done told me she was under the table and said don't tell him where she was. It was pitch dark, we ain't had no oil in the lamp. Somebody came up to me and I thought it was Fannie, I said don't tell him, Momma's sleeping under the table. Pa Steve said, 'All right.' I said oh no, then I yelled, 'Momma run.' Momma hauled ass from under that table and he never got her that night. By the morning he had forgot why he was mad.*

The *ballerina* who has been flitting in and out of the room, still doing endless sloppy pirouettes, and stealing Mama's cookies, now gets tired of Mama telling stories and demands that Mama opens her eyes right now and watch her *do a ballerina*. Mama obliges her and opens her eyes. We all watch while the *ballerina* twirls around again and again. Mama, eyes open, now sees that I am ready to go and brings her musings back to the present. She asks about the mayor and his wife.

# TENNYBOOTS!

"She's Black right, with braids?"

"Locs."

"Oh, he isn't the one who was cheating is he?"

"Nope, the cheater didn't win."

The girls' Mom calls them to eat dinner. I lay out Mama's clothes for Sunday morning, pack up my black sewing tin can with the flower painted on the lid that one time had been filled with cheap, but good chocolate chip cookies, from a stationary mail order supply business, and get ready to leave.

"I'll probably press the hem down flat," Mama says as she's walking me to the door.

"That's a good idea."

"Thank you Ju, even though I don't say it, I appreciate all you do. Love you, Ju."

"Love you Ma, I know you do."

****

# TENNYBOOTS!

## Chapter Seventeen

### Bored Impatient and Talking Loud

I can hear her even when she is not saying it. "These *cadillacs* gotta come off my eyes Ju. I can't see." I even answer her in my mind: "Yes Ma, we will try again to get them done." Now that Spring is approaching we need to get back to the business of getting Mama seeing clearly again. There is not a day that goes by that she doesn't bring up the problem of the *cadillacs* in her eyes, as though it were a brand new problem. She's not at all blind, there's just a list of things she cannot see, but it hasn't curtailed her independence.

We were almost there. After four trips to the Manhattan Eye and Ear Hospital, we had an appointment in hand for outpatient cataract surgery when we reached a hiccup. Mama's hematologist cautioned that he would only approve if it were performed in-patient, because of the possibility that she could bleed and need a transfusion, or risk losing her eyesight. In front of the hematologist, I slowly repeated the doctor's caveat to Mama to make sure she understood, emphasizing the potential consequences of blindness in the eye when she fixed her eyes on the doctor and said, "Hell, I can't see now so what's the difference?" Dr. Yoe is from Nepal and has a good bedside manner with Mama. He has fun with her. He laughed and said, "I guess you're right, you can't see now and you couldn't see then, so let's get it done."

We were having a hard time finding a doctor who had privileges at the same hospital as Dr. Yoe, so I put it off, promising

# TENNYBOOTS!

to start again in the Spring. Before making this appointment, I asked Mama if this was what she wanted. She yelled, "Yeah, I can't see, I gotta do it." This appointment is the first step in removing the *cadillacs* from Mama's 97-year-old eyes.

I call Mama in the morning to remind her we will see Dr. Yoe today, but not until late this afternoon I tell her, "So don't be expecting me until later."

She says okay. At 3:00 P.M. I call her and tell her to meet me downstairs. She hesitated, bordering on a stutter, a telltale sign that a problem was brewing and she didn't know how to tell me.

Then she blurts out, "They left this baby here with me and I have to wait for her father. I'm sure he's coming now. Her mother just called and said he's on his way."

So sick of having to bear the brunt of Mama putting everyone ahead of my precious time, I want to yell, but hearing the hesitation in her voice, I tell her it's okay; we have time, take care of that and when he comes, go downstairs and wait in the lobby. She seems relieved that I don't admonish her for agreeing to babysit Ryder knowing we have an important appointment. I leave home to go pick her up and when I drive into the parking lot in front of her building, a neighbor says, "Judy she's in the lobby waiting on you."

"Story of my life," I reply.

"Flo-rence, Mama, I am here," I call from the car. Her white hair is the first thing to emerge from the lobby, pulling her walker and her body behind it.

"Ju, where you at? Ju, that's you? I'm coming."

"Right here Ma, just come all the way down the ramp, I am right here," I yell back to her. I am loathed to leave the car, even for a minute. In the way that the poor are taxed for everything, I have known an overzealous tow truck driver to swoop into the parking lot, hook up your car and not unhook it unless you pay $250 on the spot. I am always caught between guarding the car and

# TENNYBOOTS!

helping Mama from the building. Her independence here is a godsend.

But here we go. Mama has this thing about dog shit. Or maybe shit in general. I'm thinking back to her reasons for never ever going to a beach again from when we were little. She told us she was chin-deep in the water when "Some shit floated by, right past my mouth and that was all she wrote, I ain't been in a pool or beach since." This shit phobia now manifests itself in her fear of stepping in it. As I meet her at the bottom of the ramp and pull on the front of her walker, she becomes testy.

"Wait, dammit, don't let me step in no dog shit!"

"Ma, really, would I really pull you through dog shit and then let you sit in the car with it on your feet?"

"I know but they let the dogs shit all over. You may miss some."

The irony that I, with decent eyesight, will miss the dog shit that she, adorned with cataracts will see, escapes her. I give up and in checking her feet for the dog shit; I notice that she is wearing the same fake uggs that I am wearing. I bought two pairs; one for her and one for me, and now we both look like we are wearing fuzzy slippers outside. I will disguise mine as soon as I get into the car. She climbs into the car without waiting for me to set her up.

"Gimme a push, don't let my ass fall out," she says.

She didn't get her outfit quite right today, but I bite my tongue and say nothing about the way she looks. I push her into the seat, click her seat belt, and load her walker into the back seat. I take a quick look into the canvas bag swinging off the handle of the walker. Today there's a banana peel, some toilet tissue, an empty potato chip bag, a comb, and her cracked, plastic mirror. Before I pull off, I pull the legs of my pants out of my boots and let them fall over the top so that we do not look like Bobbsey twins.

# TENNYBOOTS!

Once in the car, Mama says, "I don't know if was dreaming or what. Did I tell you they left the baby upstairs and I had to wait for her father to come?"

I nod my head. I figure she's about to make up a lie for having agreed to keep the baby. I'm gonna let it slide.

"Well, there ain't no baby there, she went to school. That must've been a dream. I called her and she didn't come, then I went and looked in all the rooms, and she ain't there."

What the... I stopped the car at the next corner and called Ashley to make sure Mama was dreaming. Once she confirmed that Ryder was indeed at school and was not left home with Mama, we continued on Dr. Yoe's office. I told Mama again in slow and plain language that today's visit was to her hematologist. It was not the eye doctor, but we have to get clearance from him so that we can go to the next step.

"Do you understand?" I asked her.

"Yep, I understand."

It was our lucky day. There was a parking spot on the opposite side of the street from the doctor's office. Pointing to a building on the wrong side of the street, Mama asked if that was the doctor's office. I told her no it was across the street. I got her out of the car and then got the walker out, but the wind was picking up. We were both too eager for Spring weather to arrive and had shed our heavy winter coats with its first signs. Mama would not allow me to get her a wheelchair although it would have made more sense on days like today when we needed to move quickly over a distance. I had taken to having her sit on the walker and I would push it holding onto the handles, while Mama held her feet up from dragging. Because the walker is really not to be used for pushing someone, and it has a huge red warning sign to that effect on the seat, one bump in the road and the walker and Mama would topple backward and the person pushing would fall over her. It had happened once with me, a couple of times with Russell and once with Pinky. Mama knew how to fall safely, she would holler, "Whoa don't let my ass fall," and hold her head up so as not to hit the ground. Once had been enough for me so I was extra careful and pushing her while she sat on the walker required my full attention, and all my mental and physical processes to be on high alert. I had to survey the street or sidewalk ahead for depressions or potholes and keep my feet aligned on the outer edges of the walker while pushing, all the while prepared to prevent a fall before it happened. If anyone looked twice at Mama riding on the walker, embarrassed, she would blame me and say that, of course, she wanted to walk, but I made her ride. The truth is some days she had more energy than others. And some days expediency demanded that she sat her butt down so we could quickly get where we were going. Today was one of those days. Some days she waited to see if I would ask her to sit. Other days like today, she plopped herself on the seat as soon as I got it out of the car. On those days I knew that she felt tired.

As soon as I set the walker on the sidewalk, she planted herself on it. I didn't want to ask her to get out, but we had to get across the street. I struggled to bump first one wheel down the curb and then the other all while balancing Mama. I managed, but not without a lot of effort and maneuvering. Plus, today was more Winter than Spring. I had thrown her furry hood over her head when we started to cross the street and it plopped over her eyes. Unaware of the precariousness of our position, and how hard I was trying to keep her from falling, Mama began squirming and complaining about her hood being on her head.

"Shit, I can't see."

"Shit, you claim you can't see anyway, so just let me lead you, stop resisting."

"Hell, I can see something without this hood on my head," she laughed, pushing the hood back to expose her old eyes yellowed with age, clouded with *cadillacs,* and now running water from the cold.

Mama had sat heavily onto the walker seat with all of her weight and was maneuvering her head to keep the furry hood from hiding the view from her cataract-clouded eyes. Silently, I wished her to be still. Her moving around like that made it harder for me to push her. Crossing in the middle of the block juggling the walker, the cars, Mama's antics, and the wind that had my bare hands freezing on the aluminum handles like a tongue on a frozen pole, I cursed Mama's vanity that would not allow her to use a wheelchair. I had once rescued a small, almost new, wheelchair from the trash for days like this when Mama was either too tired to walk or we had to get somewhere in a hurry. But Mama had concocted and executed a plan for Ashley to dispose of it by complaining that it was "in the way." When I noticed that it was missing, Mama blamed Ashley, and Ashley blamed Mama.

By the time we got to the old brass doors of the building, closed to keep the winter-like weather out, we both started pushing on them at the same time, eager to get inside where it was warm. Thankfully, the doorman came right out to help Mama navigate the stairs. I was winded and cold but guided her to the balustrade, also brass, but worn to a green patina from too many hands like Mama's grabbing onto the whole darn thing. Mama pulled herself up the five marble steps holding onto the banister in a vise-like grip, while I climbed behind her, one baby step at a time because of my arthritic knee, to guard against her falling. I was thankful that the doorman carried her walker to the landing. Mama reached the landing the same time I did, grabbed her walker and steadied herself. She would not allow herself to be pushed into the doctor's office.

"Which way Ju?"

"That way," pointing down the hall to the right. Twelve flickering bulbs in a huge candelabra on the wall, each one casting its own ominous shadow, provides the only light in the lobby. Mama took the lead as I followed behind her. She seemed eager to see Dr. Yoe. Ever since I told her that I made the appointment, she had been preparing herself. Three times already she told me that she was looking forward to a fight. She had seen it in her dream: Dr. Yoe and all the ladies at the front desk were going to ask her where she'd been, and how come it took her so long to come in. She had planned to tell them that what Dr. Yoe was doing wasn't helping her, she was sure of it now. As she and her walker covered the distance of the long dimly lit hallway, wielding her walker like a chariot, she had the air of a prizefighter walking to the ring for a championship bout. She was about to spar with Dr. Yoe and she was giddy with anticipation.

Classic, solo practitioner doctor's offices in retrofitted apartments on the ground floor of stately old pre-war apartment buildings are peculiar to New York City and a throwback to an era long gone. Dr. Yoe's office is typical in that way. An apartment door with small plaque announcing the doctor's name is all that differentiates the office from the rest of the first-floor residential apartments. Mama reaches the door before me, turns the knob and pushes herself and her walker into the waiting room, a former foyer with beautiful old oak floors; the intricate inlay is now oddly down the middle of what was once the edge of a room, made larger to accommodate the doctor's needs.

Mama must have forgotten what it's like at this office on Fridays. This practice has outgrown this apartment, and people have filled all 16 of the chairs in the waiting room, the triple ottoman in the middle, the empty spaces along the wall near the door and in front of the open window where the secretaries and office manager are situated. As soon as she sees the crowded waiting room, the gladiator spirit disappears and in its place is 4 feet 10 inches of a small and old Mama, sighing loudly and trying to bulldoze her walker through the crowd like a plow without a mule. Just then a man is called into the examining room. He gets up and I quickly position Mama in his seat, placing her walker in front of her knees like a television snack table. The doctors wife, who doubles as office manager greets us warmly and says, "Miss Florence, where've you been?" The recognition and personal greeting revive the gladiator spirit and Mama lobs her already-rehearsed answer into the crowded room, drawing a smile from the doctor's wife cum office manager.

Dr. Yoe, is also an oncologist and most of the patients are here for chemotherapy treatments. Friday is a good day for chemotherapy because they have the weekend to recover. Typically, I make Mama's Friday appointments later in the afternoon so we can avoid the crowd. We came a little earlier today, and the crowd is just beginning to thin out. Mama's spirits nosedived once again, and she slumped against the wall in her seat, already bored and regretting that she is here.

I've never been able to make Mama understand that most of the people in this office have cancer. Cancer and Alzheimer's are two words that absolutely spook her, so I avoid saying either as much as possible. And because she doesn't know, I always feel that she is irreverent of the tremendous fight these patients are waging. She is usually pleasant but in a self-indulgent kind of way that makes me uncomfortable.

Like now, she says loudly to the room and not really to me, "Ju, I need some water." A woman standing near the water cooler pours her a Dixie cup full and brings it to her. She drinks it quickly and holds the cup in her hand, not knowing exactly what to do with it. I thank the woman, taking care to say what a nice thing it was to do, as I take the cup from Mama and stuff it in the gray canvas bag that's always hanging on her walker; it's too much to navigate the waiting room crowd to get to the trash can. Another man gets the coveted three months appointment and leaves, vacating a space along the wall, right beside Mama. I flip her walker around from in front of her knees, place it alongside the wall, and wedge myself onto its hard, plastic seat. This seat is not for wide loads, and my hips are flush to the aluminum poles, so I am not all that comfortable. I've brought two books to read and I've just opened one and started reading when Mama began to fill the space between her and me and the room with chatter. Nothing new, nothing even important, just inane chatter. So that I don't appear to be rude to an old lady, I close my book and allow myself to be engaged by her "Remember when." questions. A man across the room with gray locs keeps glancing in our direction. I can't tell whether he is annoyed by us or find us pleasing. I tell Mama to speak a little lower and I answer all of her questions. Sighing loudly between her chatter, she is complaining about waiting.

Annoyed by the spectacle, I ask her, "For god sakes, what is the matter, Mama?"

"Bored, just bored," she says as she blows air between her lips being careful not to dislodge her loosely fitting false teeth.

I swear Mama has had that one set of dentures for 60 years now. Years ago, she refused to get another set because those were so comfortable. The fit is loose though, and she refuses to use any of the "sure grip" dental adhesives because she claims that sometimes they fasten her teeth to her gums too well and she can't remove them for days. I've suggested that she needs only to use a little dab and that wouldn't happen, but she doesn't so here we are with Mama blowing air and holding her teeth at the same damn time. She blows, plops, and twists in her seat until I ask her again, what is wrong.

Now I'm annoyed and about to become aggravated. I'm sitting here with her, she won't allow me to read the book; the office is crowded and too warm, and too full of sick people with terminal illnesses, and Mama is talking *loud* and flopping in her seat like a fish out of water.

I ask her, "Bored with what, what is there to be bored of here? We are waiting to see the doctor."

"I know but y'all don't understand."

"What *don't* we understand?"

"I'm not sick, I don't need to be here."

"Well, let's leave then."

"No, I need to be here cause I want my eyes done, but I am not sick."

Then shut the hell up and let me read my book until we see Dr. Yoe, is what I want to say. But I refrained.

Every single day Mama complains that she is bored. Some days I can indulge her but other days it's too much. She doesn't want any solutions she just wants to say it. At one time she was a superb seamstress, she made our clothes and taught me how to sew.

# TENNYBOOTS!

She was also an excellent knitter. She once knitted a V-neck, All American, cable-stitched sweater that was as fine as any I've seen. She taught me how to knit and helped me with the many sweaters I made for my daughter during her elementary school years. Mama could ride a two-wheel bicycle backward, sitting on the handlebars, a feat she showed us when she and DadDee bought us our first English Racer bicycles and showed their prowess on them, in the parking lot in front of the building.

She also was an interior decorator by nature. She decorated our apartment way beyond what anyone in the projects could have imagined. And she changed the décor often, so often actually that we had a running joke that we were thankful we weren't blind because we would go to bed at night and wake up the next morning to find the entire apartment changed. When every window in our building had regulation brownish-yellow shades on the windows, the kind that could only be replaced if you brought your shade roller stick to the management office, we had Venetian blinds. When Venetian blinds became too common and always dusty, we had custom scalloped, colored shades with awning-striped, canopy, kitchen curtains.

Once Mama began to work two and three jobs each day, she gave up her hobbies and by the time she got sick, the only things she did with any regularity was to watch television really loud and nonstop, attend Bible class, read her Bible and sit outside on the bench. Now with the *cadillacs* on her eyes reading her Bible was out. She never wants to go to a senior citizen center and cannot really pick up her hobbies. So there she sits, bored of things she cannot name, and lonely for people long gone, and feeling that she is not as old as others make her out to be. But she is.

I look over at Mama slumped in the chair, leaning against the wall with her eyes closed and looking disgusted. I get disgusted too. Then I am reminded of a philosopher who said that boredom is the awareness of time passing. I wonder about Mama. And whether this thing she calls boredom that causes her so much angst is really her being acutely aware that time is passing and she is hurtling closer to her end. What if Mama is not really bored at all but afraid that the end will come and catch her not yet ready to go.

# TENNYBOOTS!

We've talked of her dying. She always says that she is ready when her time comes. But sitting home waiting, day in and day out, not working, not being busy, not being needed, must be as torturous for her as a death row inmate counting the days to execution.

Now I am chagrined by this epiphany. I wake her easily with my pen and paper in my hand and ask her to tell me more of her stories. Immediately her countenance changes, her face lights up and she relates one of her ancient stories that are never very far away from her consciousness. I ask her how to spell "Couteau" and the teacher's name, "Solete" and she spells without hesitation. In the waiting room where cancer is king and where so many are acutely aware of time, I help Mama spend it feeling useful and relevant.

"I got some stories, don't I?"

"Yes, you do. You are our family Griot. In Africa, the Griot is most important to the family. In the oral tradition, they learn all the family stories and tell them, again and again, ensuring that the families' history is passed down to the generations. You are our Griot, we are very fortunate to have you for so long. I am thankful that you have so many stories. I love you, Ma."

Her pleasure at being so important is visible. Shortly after she began to relax Dr. Yoe calls her into the examination room. He is happy to see her.

"Where've you been," he asks.

"I've been home, I'm not sick. I just need to get my eyes done."

"So you want them done, right? I explain to you again what can happen. But you want them done, right? "

"Of course, I want them done, I can't see. I need to get these *cadillacs* off my eyes so I can see. Otherwise, I can't live with em."

"Okay, let me see how your blood work looks," he says.

# TENNYBOOTS!

He likes Mama. He tells her she looks good all she needs to do is dye her white hair. Mama says, "No way, everyone loves my hair." She stirs up memories of his great-grandmother, and he tells us a long and poignant story about how his great-grandmother always said that he had good hands, and she would always send for him when he was a little boy to massage her. She had over 50 great-grandchildren but he was her favorite. When she was near death at 96, not recognizing anyone, he had gone to see her and began to massage her when she looked into his eyes and called his name. Out of all of her children, grandchildren, and great-grandchildren, she remembered his name. It was a special story, and he was happy to share it with Mama.

The blood work comes back, Mama's hemoglobin count is good but her red blood cells are lower than he likes. He asks if she would prefer an iron infusion or transfusion. He recalls that the last time she got an iron infusion it didn't do much, but also that sometimes she has an allergic reaction to the blood transfusion. We leave the choice to Mama, and she says, "Give me the one that makes me better faster. Not that it works anyway, but whatever gets me to the next step to get my eyes done." Dr. Yoe laughs at her and tells his assistant to make the appointment for the transfusion. The office for the transfusion is now closed, so the assistant promises to call me next week with the appointment date.

We leave the office the same way we came. Back down the dimly lit hall to the lobby, candelabra bulbs flickering and casting ominous shadows——but not for us today. The news is good. Mama will get her eyes done. Back to the steps with the brass balustrades. Mama takes the left side of the steps so she can hold on with her left hand and I don't know why because she's right-handed. The same doorman is there, and he is kind to carry the walker down the steps for us this time. When we get out of the building onto the sidewalk, darkness has rolled up Cathedral Parkway, and it is even colder since the sun has gone down. Mama asks if I can make a U-turn and pick her up on this side of the street. Gladly, I agree. I should have thought of it myself. I place her securely against the building, out of the wind and pull her hood down over her head. She's seated on the walker again. I cross the street and get in the car, make the U-turn and stop right in front of where I planted her.

Her eyes are running water from the cold. I pile her into the car. She is moving stiffly in the cold and it takes a step longer to get her all piled in. She asks if I can get her some fried chicken and french fries from that place near Clara's, her hair salon. I tell her anything her little heart desires. She laughs. I decide to get me a Florence Burger from Ottomanelli's, which is across the street from the chicken place Mama likes. I stop on Fifth Avenue and park at a hydrant in front of Ottomanelli's and call in an order for a Florence Burger-a burger with tomato and cheese and lettuce and waffle fries.

"Did you say Florence Burger?" Mama asked.

"Yep!"

"Florence, like my name? Well, I'll be damn who would name a burger after me?"

"Well, not really you, but after the city, Florence, in Italy. But we can pretend they named it after you."

"Bad as Momma. I asked her why you named me Florence. Nobody I know have that name. Momma said she named me after Dr. Young's wife, Florence. Momma used to work for Dr. Young, cooking at his house. And his wife was Ms. Florence. When she told me that, I said you named me after a white woman, no wonder nobody else have that name. Momma said ain't nothing wrong with being named after a white woman. All my life, I only met two other women named Florence."

"Well, it fits you, Ms. Flo."

"I guess, but people have really butchered it up. Ann used to call me, 'Flonce.' How I miss Ann... I miss her so bad. Me and Ann was good buddies. We was pregnant at the same time with you and Betty. But Betty was born about a few days before you."

"Two weeks. She misses you too," I said, being silly. Mama laughed, and I left the car to go get my Florence Burger and her chicken, fries and a Pepsi Cola.

When we pull up in the parking lot of her building, she asks me to call upstairs and ask the girls to unlock the door so she doesn't have to figure out which lock is on. I do as she asks. I get her walker out of the trunk and position it at the door which she has already opened, cleared the seat and is standing at the door. I walk with her to the ramp, being sure to tell her I am watching out for dog shit. I pull her hood onto her head because it is even colder, and she's not wearing a hat; she yells that she can't see. We laugh and I pull it back some from covering her eyes. When we get into the lobby, I hang her chicken breast and french fries bag on the handle of her walker. I put the Pepsi-Cola in her gray canvas bag on the other handle. We wait for the elevator, as I keep a lookout at the car. When the elevator comes, I push nine, and she maneuvers her walker into the elevator. No longer a chariot, cause Mama's no longer a gladiator—it's more like a shopping cart now, and she—a tired old lady pushing it home. She knows the routine. I stand in the lobby until the elevator stops on nine. She calls down that she has 'reached.' I then run back to the car, illegally parked with the hazard lights blinking, dodging the tow truck driver known to swoop down and hook up a car in minutes levying a $250 fine. I call her when I think she is in her bedroom to make sure she is safe. She answers the phone on the fourth ring.

"I made it. Thanks, Ju, I'm gon eat my food and go to bed. Was the car alright?"

"Yup, everything was okay. Don't eat too much Ma, you don't want your stomach to hurt."

"I'm not, I'm gon save some for tomorrow. Love you."

"Love you Ma, goodnight."

I crossed my fingers and hoped that Mama didn't eat too much and get one of those bad stomach aches that she often gets. It was too cold and I was too tired to be running back over to her place tonight. Lately, she hadn't called me, relying on the girls to get her through. Thank God for the girls, they made some things easier for me.

****

# TENNYBOOTS!

## Chapter Eighteen

### Mt. Sinai Takes Her Back

As luck would have it, on Monday night Dr. Yoe's office calls me to say they have made the appointment for Mama's eyes for tomorrow, Tuesday at 1:00 P.M. and if I don't take that appointment I will have to bring her back to his office, something about a three-day lapse in time for the referral. I hang up and change all of my plans for Tuesday when they call back and change the time to 10:00 A.M for the eye doctor and 1:00 P.M. for the transfusion. I call Mama and tell her to be ready by 9:30 in the morning and I will pick her up.

Once again, neither of us had dressed well enough to ward off the raw cold of the early April morning, where the promise of spring had waned. But at least we both had worn hats and gloves this time. And I had a scarf that I placed around Mama's neck. Battling the wind and sore knees this morning, Mama ambled. I suggested that Mama sit on the walker and I push.

"If it will be faster" she quickly agreed and backed her rump to square with the seat of the walker.

"Hope I don't fall," she said without anger or malice as she plopped down hard on the cold plastic seat.

"If you fall, I fall," I said, and we both laughed.

# TENNYBOOTS!

Backpack on my back, I pushed Mama and her walker into the wind. She held her feet up just enough that they didn't drag, and I pushed while positioning my feet on either side of her dangling feet and the wheels, so as not to trip her or me. Poised just so, we headed to the bus stop. I had not driven because of the dearth of parking near the hospital.

Just as we hit Fifth Avenue, one bus passes and then another. Just our luck it's our bus. It's the M1 bus, the worst line in the city. The bus originates in Harlem. We miss both of them and will have to wait at least another ten minutes. We got to Fifth Avenue and had to cross from the south side to the north side of the street. Gentrification had caused the old bus stop we had for over 50 years to be moved. The bus stop had been directly in front of 1390 Fifth Avenue, a building in the projects on the corner of 115th and Fifth Avenue. But when million-dollar condos were built at 1400 Fifth Avenue, they moved the bus stop to directly in front of that building. Now, angered about the injustice and annoyed with the M1 that sends two busses at the same time which causes a 10-minute wait for the next, I push Mama across the street with much effort. The elderly people in the projects need the bus stop to be closer to them, more so than the wealthy condo owners—with a gym in their building to keep them fit enough to walk, or run if they are afraid, one-half block across the street. We get to the crosswalk ramp and the ground is not level so I have to get Mama to stand up in order to get the walker up the ramp.

"Ma stand up a minute and get on the curb."

"Is right here, okay, Ju?"

"Okay. sit back down now."

Mama eases up and then plops back down heavily as I hold the walker steady. I began pushing again until we finally reach the bus stop. We are both happy to have refuge from the wind and the cold in the shelter of the bus stop.

"Where is this?" Mama asks, orienting herself like a GPS gone awry.

# TENNYBOOTS!

"Fifth Avenue, between 115th and 116th."

She taps on the advertising kiosk anchoring the bus shelter and asks, "What that say?"

I purposely don't answer, knowing that she wants to try to see if her eyes can read the words.

"New-York-School" she teases out the words on the sign.

"No, Sports Club," I correct her.

"Oh, I got the New York, then I saw the S, these old eyes, sure hope we can get them done. Are they gonna do it today?"

"Nope, not today, and I don't know what will happen but we are starting over and time will tell," I say not wanting her to get her hopes up and then dashed with disappointment, because the truth is I don't know what the doctor will say.

"Okay, cause I need these eyes done, I can't go on like this."

"I know Ma. I know."

The raw chill of the morning slices right through me. I hate feeling cold. I stand in the street hoping for a bus running early, and when I don't see the bus I look for a cab. Just as I hail one, I see the bus turning the corner. I tell the cab to go on and I ready Mama to get on the bus. I didn't know it then, but we had bonded against the cold and hustle, and the rest of the day would be easy.

The last time we made a trip to the doctor on the bus, I wanted to kill her. She was nasty and full of attitude. She went sashaying ahead of me and I was so angry with her that morning I thought if she had fallen it would serve her right. Then I had to ask God and the Ancestors for forgiveness for even thinking that way. Mama could get me so riled up. But thank goodness today was much easier.

Mama is low key and easily led today. She says she is tired; there's none of the antics of the last two doctors' visits. No filling

# TENNYBOOTS!

the gap between us with empty chatter; no trash talking, no twisting and turning—her eyes are closed while she waits. She moves easily from one room to another without complaint. She allows them to probe and measure her eyes without flinching.

I can smell the urine from her soaked underwear every time she sits down. "Pissing like a goat," she had said when I met up with her that morning. I have to be very sensitive about telling her of the urine smell, even when she asks. If I say yeah I can smell it, she's very defensive and will tell me that I can't smell it. Unless it's unbearable, I keep my mouth shut and my nose too. I asked her if she wanted to get it checked by the doctor a few times, she said no, she had padded herself well and changed often. I am about to suggest that she goes into the bathroom and change the pads when they call her to another room. The technicians are gracious and do not let on if they are getting a whiff of the goat piss.

I like the eye doctor. He thinks that she could take the cataract surgery with no problem. Her surgery is scheduled and we are out of the clinic by 10:30.

We leave the eye clinic and I push Mama over to the cancer clinic on Fifth Avenue. We take the elevator up to four. We are early, which is good. They take her right away and draw blood to match the type. This usually takes two hours. I get Mama comfortable on the sofas in the waiting room. I have a travel pillow in my backpack and a small blanket. I prop up her head and cover her with her coat and the blanket. I leave her this way while I go to the deli on Madison Avenue to get her bacon, lettuce and tomato, sandwich, wafer cookies and a bottle of Pepsi Cola. When I return, Mama is sound asleep. I wake her and she eats half her sandwich and sips some Pepsi. Two hours later they have the two pints of blood for the transfusion. They assign her a room and a bed. I ask the nurse to help her to change her Depends before she begins the transfusion and she does. The nurse finds a vein easily today and Mama is all set to receive two pints of blood. She's given a prophylactic Benadryl so there's no reaction and I ask them to set the intake to slow. When the Benadryl takes effect and Mama gets loopy, I leave. They estimate that she will not be ready to go home until at least 6:30 in the evening. I will return to get her then. I tell

Mama that I am leaving. She's high off the Benadryl and says bye pleasantly, and I am gone. Today was a good day.

When I pick her up, Mama is in high spirits. Her energy level is up and her color is good.

"I feel like new money, Ju," she says when she sees me entering the room.

"Good," I say. "Let's get you dressed and blow this joint."

The car is downstairs parked on a meter. We get her dressed quickly and get ready to leave. The nurses are all saying goodbye. I ask Mama if she wants a ride on the seat of the walker.

"No way—I can walk." Then she turns and says to the nurses lest they believe that she is dependent, "She's always trying to baby me."

On the elevator going down, she says, "Ju, I feel so good. When do I get my eyes done?"

"April," I say. "Next Month."

"I will sure be glad."

"Me too, Mama. Me too."

The cataract surgery went without a hitch. One eye is done in April and the other in May. Mama comes through with flying colors. She can see again. I finally realize the toll her poor eyesight was taking on me, and her. Now that she can see, she's more independent again, and I don't have to do so much for her.

She is so happy to have her eyesight back. She is 96 and had never used eyeglasses. Everything is new again for her. She talks about how she is now seeing people she'd been talking to and she sure didn't know they looked like they did.

"Stop right there Mama," I laughed. "And be thankful." She didn't protest this time.

# TENNYBOOTS!

****

## Chapter Nineteen

### Shawnee Yellow Rubber Bracelet as North Star

"Hey Ma," I say when Mama answers the phone on the second ring this morning.

"Ju, you know I found myself."

"Ma, I didn't know I lost you."

She cracks up laughing and says, "Y'all don't understand. I've been traveling in my mind, didn't know where I was. Susetta died *this* year, right? But I kept thinking it was a long time ago... but you know how I found myself this morning? When I looked at the yellow bracelet, I said wait a minute I just got this bracelet in the Summer..."

And so it goes. Each time her *Polaris* is different—a song, a saying, a memory of a person, place or thing that jars her mind, and leads her into this moment, into this place and time.

This morning her *North Star* was the yellow rubber bracelet from Shawnee Village that she wore during the week we spent in the Pocono Mountains. It's a trip she looks forward to each year. The bracelet has been on her arm since then—jewelry, along with the trendy rubber band bracelet my granddaughter, Chloe, made her for her 95th birthday. The bracelets complement costume jewelry rings on her fingers.

Today the yellow rubber bracelet, Mama's *North Star*, is illuminating the way through nearly one hundred years of living, stacked up as memories, all threatening to dislodge and tumble in upon a Mama *raging hard against the dying of the light.* [12]

It wasn't always this way. Until a few years ago, Mama had no discernible changes in her cognitive ability. In order to avoid regular doctor appointments, Mama swears that the *cat blood* in the transfusions she gets for her anemia makes her sick, or she's waiting on the healing she asked God for. She avoids the doctor like the plague—until her red blood count is so low that she has to be taken to a hospital by ambulance. Yet, it chagrins her at being taken out in an ambulance and she usually pleads with us not to make the call. Powerless at the point where we do call, Mama has devised ways to be taken by an ambulance that is less demoralizing for her. The housing projects where she has lived for as long as I am old has ten buildings that are fourteen stories each. Everyone knows her. When the ambulance sits in front of her building with the red lights blinking, and the paramedics roll her out on a gurney, or in a wheelchair, everyone crowds around asking if she is okay.

"Ms. Florence," "Flo," "Mama, are you okay?" "Praying for you Mama," they say.

When this happens, she has two routines she employs: One is her Redd Foxx shtick.[13] Making a grand spectacle of the whole ordeal, waiving broadly and exclaiming that this is the *big one* and she won't be back. This creates a crowd of followers admonishing her to be strong and think positive. I do not understand why she does this. I don't know if it's because she wants to predict her own death to be the heroine of her own ordeal—where everyone will say, that Ms. Florence knew when it was her time, she called it—or, she believes it distracts from the humiliation of being carried out on a gurney.

---

[12] Dylan, *id.*
[13] Comedic genius Redd Foxx was an actor on *Sanford and Son* sitcom.

# TENNYBOOTS!

At other times Mama either *is* or pretends to be totally out of it when people are asking if she's alright. After she receives the transfusions and has recovered, she tells me that she heard every single person but didn't want to be bothered. Sometimes she even mimics what they were saying: "Sweetie, sweetie, are you okay?" The truth is probably that a lot of times, she is really out of it. Whatever reasons Mama has for employing these machinations, the melodramatic ambulance runs to the hospital, due solely to her mulish refusal to see her hematologist regularly, leaves me drained.

Typically, the way it happens is that I get a call from someone. If it happens outside, her friends, Linda, Ms. Frasier or Wanda all have my cell number and will call me. If it happens at church, Sister Hunter, or Deacon Williams, or even the Pastor, Reverend Williams, will call me. If it happens while she is home, either the girls or my nephew will call me. I have to drop whatever I am doing and run to meet her, either at her apartment or in the emergency room of St. Luke's Hospital. The worst times are when I am downtown and have to fight twin evils of traffic and anxiety to get to the hospital before... At Mama's age, death was always the elephant in the room. Even when we didn't mention it, for fear of drawing it in, every time there was a hospital run, the potential that this could really be the *big one* loomed large.

I would lose another workday getting to Mama; and we'd spend another night in an emergency room waiting for a bed so that Mama could be admitted. At St. Luke's, the wait can be as long as 24 hours, the average is 12-15 hours. But at Mt. Sinai's Hospital, a large teaching hospital that is very prominent in New York City, the wait—akin to a scene in Mash with gurneys foot to head, spilling out all of the rooms—is generally 72 hours for a bed. Typically, after about a pint or two of blood, Mama is back to her old self, and then pleads to go home. Sometimes her doctor allows her to leave and sometimes she has to stay another night. Sometimes she stays for several days, then she's discharged and all is fine. Until the next time.

Except for this one time. Mama had just turned 93, and we had to make a hospital run. This time her body temperature was very low. She had to be warmed up with huge plastic bags that had

# TENNYBOOTS!

Mama looking like she was stuffed in a box with packing pouches; and either the transfusion went in too quickly, or she had an allergic reaction to the blood they gave her. She was shaking and jumping, and her chest was hurting and they thought she had sepsis. The doctor started describing a terminal state and asked if they should resuscitate. Mama has been clear that when it's her time to die, to let her go because she is ready, so I expressed her wishes and watched with more than a little trepidation, as the doctor scrawled a big DNR in red sharpie on her chart.

Mama's condition was not good. Grandchildren and great grand-children came and went. I sat an all-night vigil with her, relieved for a few hours when my daughter, and then my nephew, Russell, came to take my place. Slowly, Mama began to feel better as time passed. We were still in the emergency room the next morning initially awaiting an Intensive Care Unit room so they could monitor her. As her condition improved, they opted for a regular room on the ward. But Mama didn't seem quite herself to me. She finally got a bed around 10:00 A.M. in the morning. I followed her as they transported her to the room, running to keep up with the transporter who must've gotten paid per patient, because he was moving like a NASCAR race car driver across the hospital halls. Out of breath when we got to the room, I was happy to plop in a chair in the hall while they got her situated.

These hospital visits are always a crapshoot medically, and also because you never know the condition of the roommate. Mama's roommates have run the gamut: there have been those who screamed night and day; people who moaned all the time; people who talked nonstop; people whose relatives started fights with the staff and security had to be called; and sometimes, when we were very lucky, she got nice people, or rarely, a room to herself. This time, due to the protocol for sepsis patients, she got a room to herself.

As the transfused blood circulated through Mama's veins and improved her hemoglobin and platelets count, she began feeling medically better. Feeling better meant that she could begin her routine of complaining about being in the hospital and wanting to go home. She bugs the hell out of the doctors to discharge her.

# TENNYBOOTS!

Her pleas are unrelenting: when can I go home, Doc, when can I go home. Her pleas, this time having fallen on deaf ears, the doctors were being cautious, Mama was not being sprung so fast. After she settled into her room, I finally got to leave the hospital, some 30 hours after we came. Since it was early morning, I walked through Morningside Park to my apartment on the Harlem side of the park.

I dallied at the bottom of the steps near the pond that had been the site of huge protests against Columbia University by Students for a Democratic Society and Students For African Studies that ignited student uprisings around the world. Columbia had dug a huge crater in the park where they had planned to build a new gymnasium. The protests stopped the construction, and the beautiful pond filled in the eyesore of the crater. None of the past is evident now. [14]

The telephone call for Mama's discharge doesn't come until two days later. On the day she was to be released from the hospital, both Mama and the doctor called me to apprise me of the good news. Still exhausted from the last four days at the hospital, I take my ever-loving, sweet time getting there, not arriving until 7:30 that evening. Mama was enraged and raked me over with questions without allowing for answers. I didn't respond.

"You didn't get the call?"

"I been dressed. I dressed myself."

"My phone was under the bed. How did it get there?"

"Where my house from here?"

"I dressed myself. I'm ready let's go."

Mama had gotten herself ready all right. I had left her clothing, a tan warm-up suit. A blouse and socks in the plastic bag in her closet. But she had the landline telephone from the hospital—a tan, push-button institution type—packed to go in the

---

[14] NYC That Never Was: A Gym In Morningside Park Sparks 1968 Columbia University Protests and Shutdown, by Samantha Sokol untappedcities.com

basket of her walker; and the long, coiled wire that attaches the receiver to the telephone base was wrapped around her waist, with the receiver dangling from her hip like some trendy chain belt popular in the 60s.

Something was off. I had started towards Mama to prepare her to leave, but stopped in my tracks when I noticed the chain belt telephone dangling from her waist. Reclining from my waist and stretching my neck, while pulling my shoulders back, I locked my eyes on Mama to get a better look at what I thought I was seeing. In the weird ways a mind can conjure up the strangest things at the right time, I thought of Ms. Clavell from Madeline, turning on the light at the orphanage and exclaiming, "Something is not right."

"Ma, where are you going with that phone?"

"That's my phone," she argued, raising her voice with indignation that comes from having to constantly answer stupid questions. "Where you think I am going with it, I am going home."

"The hell you aren't," I thought to myself. "Not if you think that phone is yours," I said aloud, more to myself than to her.

I knew better than to argue with her. She followed up that proclamation with some random conversation that made no sense. My heart sank. I felt flush and weak and wanted to throw up; panic in the guise of angry mobs trampling each other accosted my whole entire being. Something was wrong, really wrong. I instructed Mama to stay put while I fled from her room. She looked at me suspiciously. Pushing back dry heaves, I stopped at the nurses' station on my way to the bathroom and requested to see the doctor who had signed Mama's discharge papers. After washing my face and trying to gain some composure, I returned to the nursing station. I was not going back into the room with Mama. I stood at the nursing station until they located the doctor, spending the time imagining a dozen scenarios of what was wrong with Mama—all of them severe. Mama in that condition changed everything. The doctor finally came, and surprisingly, Mama had not followed me out of her room. The doctor was a young African American woman, not Mama's regular doctor. I told the doctor that something was very wrong. She tried to assure me that Mama was fine.

I told her "Mama is *not* fine; the emphasis on NOT. She's acting like she has Dementia or Alzheimer's. She is not fine. This is not the way I brought her here. This is not her baseline, or whatever the term is. I cannot bring her home acting like this. "

Stone cold fear prevented me from letting up. I requested that she rescind the discharge and keep Mama until she got better. I was pleading with the doctor. She must have heard the despair in my voice. She relented and agreed to keep her one more night. She said that medically Mama was fine and they had to discharge her tomorrow. Only somewhat relieved, yet scared stiff, I went back into Mama's room and told her that she had to stay another day.

She wailed, "Nooooooo." "I am going home whether or not you take me." "Where Frasier, Frasier was here. She can take me."

The bravado soon faded to plain old disappointment and she started to cry. "No Ju. I can't stay here another day. Take me home, Ju, please take me home."

Frightened and fearful, I felt awful that I was leaving Mama. But I was more scared than concerned about how Mama felt at not going home. I got the coiled telephone wire unwrapped from her waist and told her that I had to go. I could help her get undressed if she wanted me to, or the nurse could do it. Her choice. Resigned that she would not be going home, she fell back on her bed and said, "Okay" quietly. I knew I disappointed her. But I was afraid and uneasy and knew I could not bring her home like that.

Overnight, Mama had lost her mind. What the hell!

"This changed everything. I could not bring her home in that condition," I told myself while getting her undressed.

As soon as I could get out of that hospital, I left. I was confused and distracted. A dark cloak of despair settled over me

# TENNYBOOTS!

just as darkness was settling over the city. Me and the darkness were one. In my despair, I took a certain amount of comfort from the night. I did not have to face anyone until the sun rose again. Although I wanted to and I needed so badly, I could not cry. Mama in this state changed everything. Racing thoughts filled my head: What do I do, how do I do it. I could not stay at home to care for Mama. I had to work. Was it Alzheimer's? Dementia? Was it caused by the Sepsis? Mama had mentioned that Ms. Frasier, her good friend from the building had visited her. I couldn't be sure if Mama was talking out of her head. Halfway down the block, I stopped and cowered in the alleyway of the Church of The Grotto, and I called Ms. Frasier. She confirmed that she had been at the hospital earlier to visit Mama and that she had brought her a bag of snacks. Ms. Frasier also agreed that Mama had been acting strange. She recounted the same story, that Mama was wearing the telephone around her waist and refused to take it off.

No comfort derived from my conversation with Ms. Frasier, panicking, and forgetting all about my 60-year-old knees, I ran. Out of that hospital to Morningside Park, and down the 89 stairs near the pond. I was running from the fear that Mama had lost her mind, and whatever danger may have been lurking on the dark stairs in the park. I did not stop until I got to my stoop, across the street from the park. The adrenalin released from both fear and running was petering out; I sat on the stoop and allowed the exhaustion to occupy my mind with hollow thoughts. I didn't fight it. I just sat there relieved to have zero thoughts. After a while, I climbed the stoop, took the elevator up to my 4th-floor apartment and let myself in; but I don't remember any of that. At some point, I called my sister, Edie, in North Carolina, my nephew, Russell, and my daughter, Cricket, and told them about Mama's mental state. I needed to share the weight of the news. I turned off my phone and tried to sleep, but with my eyes closed, all I kept seeing was Mama, with that telephone dangling from her damn waist, arguing that it belonged there. Tired and weary, but unwilling to entertain the images my sleep would conjure up, I drew the bedroom drapes to shut out even the light from the streetlamps, and sat on the edge of my bed the entire night, savoring the quietude of darkness, unprepared for what the new day would herald.

# TENNYBOOTS!

When I finally opened the room darkening drapes, the bright sunlight of the new day mocked my desire to hide out forever. I left home quickly, en route to the hospital to face my fate; the sun's scornful rays added a heaviness to the weight I carried on my shoulders. On step 67 of the 89 stairs that I had to climb in the park to reach the hospital on the Columbia University side of Harlem, the stale taste of baby aspirin residue in my mouth—that I had chewed during the night to preempt a heart attack or stroke—was a bitter reminder that I had forgotten to take my blood pressure medication. Dammit. I sat on the steps to decide whether to go home to get my medicine or to continue on to the hospital. The feral cat colony that lived on the precipice above the pond was lying about, their bellies full, having eaten cans of food dropped off by so many do-gooders. They were not even wary of me, so accustomed they were to human interaction. Breaking my stride, and not just reacting, gave me time to consider my next move. Also, there was something soothing in watching the feral cat colony laze around in the morning's sun on a brisk, but not cold, winter's day. The cats were neither concerned nor preoccupied with tomorrow. I longed for that level of peace. "Why in the hell was I rushing to the hospital? They weren't expecting me until later. Mama hadn't even called."

Decision made, I descended the steps that I had just climbed, stopped at the pond at the very bottom, and watched its many turtles vying for space on the rocks in order to bask in the warmth of the sun. Water is comforting to me, and standing at the pond watching the turtles poke through where the ice had melted, the sunlight no longer felt so contemptuous of me. I left the pond, slowly taking the long path home. Once there, I took my medication—a blood pressure pill—a proper shower, brushed my teeth and combed my hair. It had been a long five days. I opened my laptop to check my emails and finish some work that was overdue. Mama could wait. She was being cared for and they would not put her out. I turned my phone off again, and waited until the evening to pick her up from the hospital. If I had to deal with an unstable Mama, it had to be on my terms. I hadn't managed to hold back the dawn, but God damn it, I was prepared to manage it.

# TENNYBOOTS!

Before the sun went down, I left my apartment to go get Mama. It was interesting that she still hadn't called, but I pushed that out of my mind so as not to make something out of it. The setting sun felt benevolent as I walked around the park, up the hill this time instead of taking the stairs. When I got to the hospital and up to 9West, the floor Mama was on, I bumped into the young doctor who was making her rounds. She recognized me and pulled me over. The doctor told me they had run some tests and that Mama had a Urinary Tract Infection (UTI); and that sometimes in elderly people, UTIs could make them confused for a period. She had anticipated my question and assured me that she had given Mama antibiotics and was sending her home with a prescription. When the infection cleared, she said that the behavior would subside.

Relieved that there was a diagnosis and an end in sight, but concerned for what lay ahead until the infection cleared, I braved seeing Mama face-to-face. She was glad to see me, but not trusting me to take her home this time either, she asked, "Well, are we leaving?"

I nodded my head and got her things out of the closet. After I had her dressed to leave, I took Mama downstairs to get a cab. As soon as I got her home, I called my nephew and my daughter. In the time that we left the hospital and had gotten home, Mama was full-on delirious. She was making no sense and saying all types of silly things. It hurt me to see Mama this way. It had reduced this fiercely independent woman to a silly Sally. But she was happy and laughing and smiling, so it made for a comical sight. My grandchildren came in with my daughter, and although she recognized them, she was looking all over her bedroom for someone named, "Creoly." Seeing the children, she enlisted them in the search for Creoly. Unable to find her, she began to sing the alphabet song for them, except she could not get past A-B-C without confusing all the letters. She was so comical that the kids were laughing hysterically, and she was too. It was more than I could take.

She needed her prescription filled and some things from the store, and I needed to get out of there, so I asked her to give me her

# TENNYBOOTS!

ATM card from her Bank. When I returned from the store, I decided that in her present state I would keep the card. I then left to go home, leaving her with my nephew and my daughter for a while. I had not gotten home good before Russell called to tell me that Mama wanted her ATM card back. Knowing that there would be many people going and coming in her apartment, and in her present state, I told Mama that I would hold on to the card until I return. She threw a fit. She had Russell calling me all night, to bring her damn card and her money. She accused me of stealing her money and told everyone who called her that it was so.

Early the next morning I brought her ATM card. Even though she was still delirious, I didn't care what happened at that point. A sane Mama harassing me was bad enough, but a delirious Mama harassing me was just a horse of another color. Mama told everyone who visited her that weekend and everyone she spoke to on the telephone that I had stolen her money. Russell scolded her for saying it, but in her state of mind, she fully believed it to be true and she yelled at him too. Mama's friends and some of our family members began to call to tell me that Mama had accused me of stealing her money. They assured me that they knew it wasn't true and that I should not worry about it. I felt like two cents. I knew I had not stolen her money; Russell and my daughter knew, My cousin Myrna knew, and Mama's friends and church members all knew that there was no reason for me to steal Mama's money. But once that kind of accusation is leveled, even if they take it back, they cannot pull it from people's minds. That suspicion hangs over you always.

I stayed away from Mama's apartment for at least four days. Russell was faithful and stayed with her the whole time. And just like the doctor had promised, by the time the antibiotic took effect and the infection cleared, the old Mama began to return. I went to see Mama on the fourth day after she had come home. She looked so small and sweet. Something compelled me to give her a hug. She had gone through so much and now she was back. She had no memory of accusing me of stealing her money. I did not mention it to her either. I knew that she had leveled the accusation during the time she was delirious. She would feel terrible about what she had said. I tried hard to resume my regular relationship with Mama. I attempted to push the stinging pain of the accusation down far enough so it would not affect me caring for her. I only wound up masking it until the next time and the next time...

About one week later, Mama called me on the telephone one night and said, "Ju, I didn't know that I accused you of stealing my money. I'm so sorry, I know that you would not take my money—you give me money. But I'm hearing that I was out of my mind. I am so sorry, Ju, that hurt me to hear that. I'm sorry."

The apology was sincere and rare and I accepted it.

"I know you didn't mean it, Mama. I accept your apology. Thank you for apologizing. Who told you that?"

Mama never apologized. I was thankful but now disheartened that someone had told her that she had been out of her mind and that she had accused me of taking her money.

"I don't know. I just heard it. Um. Somebody told me something or other..."

Mama was a bad liar. It was clear she was protecting someone by not saying who had told her. I let it go. Mama was terribly frightened of getting Alzheimer's or, as she called it, "Oldtimers." She was constantly checking herself and defending herself anytime she thought someone had accused her of being forgetful

"I don't have no Oldtimers," she would say if someone would say that she didn't remember something.

The revelation that she had lost her mind for a few days, was devastating to her. I wanted to protect her from that knowledge. But having a large family with loose lips, keeping it from Mama was bound to be hard. Someone would tell her eventually. I knew that she would also be devastated to learn that she had accused me of stealing her money. I later learned that it was Russell, who was incensed that Mama had continued to accuse me of stealing her money after he felt she should have known better, that he had told her it wasn't right for her to say that about me. I understood his concern for my feelings, but my concern for Mama's mental state trumped my desire to get her told. I didn't want her ruminating on having lost her mind so much that she became depressed. I needed her to return to her old self to lessen the impact of caring for her on me.

A few years later, the time came when I took over Mama's finances. She was making trips to the bank often and her savings account at Carver was drained. Every time she used her card, she would *hide* it, and misplace it from herself. Because the only government ID card she had was her driver's license—which had expired when she was 83-years-old—we were at the mercy of the bank to supply her a new card based on the personal relationship they had with her.

Mama's retirement income comprised a small pension and social security. Each month after tithing 10% of her income to her church; and paying rent, insurance, cable, and buying food, Mama had little money left. The gap between what Mama had and what she needed to live with dignity was expanding. I took over her income, paid her bills and bought her food. I also provided cash to Mama based on an as-needed basis.

It wasn't Mama but family members who had previously derived some benefit from Mama being in charge of her own money, who now leveled the charges I was stealing Mama's money. The charges were hurtful, and too often I tried to prove to the family how Mama's income was spent on her. My daughter, Cricket, told me that I didn't owe anyone an explanation. Next time someone flung the accusation at me, I threw back an offer for the person to take over Mama's care and her money. And that ended that. Mama was a handful to deal with and the money she received monthly was just enough that she was over the limit by a few dollars for Medicaid. I begin to hear that family members were saying that caring for Mama wasn't worth her check, because Mama was a pistol.

Still, Mama and I had many fights over her money. She didn't accuse me of stealing it but at various times, she was going to "call the law" on me to make me give her her damn money. Or she would want me to give her back her ATM card so she could manage herself. Or she wanted money to give to a great-grandchild. Or she was paying her great-grand-child's cable bill. And on and on it went. Some months I gave in and gave her the cash while holding on to her card. Within a week all of her money would be gone. Rather than *die poor pig*, Mama would *root hog*, remain proud and stubborn and would not ask for more money. One time she had asked for money and I told her it sounded like a personal problem, handle it. And she never asked again. Although, I didn't make it obvious, despite her telling me she could handle her own affairs, those times when she ran out of money, I sent care packages to her by my daughter, instructing her to not let on that it was from me. The next time Mama would demand all of her money from me, I would hold fast and not give in. But the abuse I had to suffer when I held my ground was unbearable. Mama would call and call and call me until I blocked her calls. In the wee hours of the morning, late at night, all the calls would start the same.

"Judy, give me my money."

"You are gonna give me money or I'll call the law on you."

I would hang up the phone on her and call my cousin, Bea, or Cricket, Myrna, or anyone else who would still listen to my complaints. Then she would call my sister, Edie, who was not long suffering. Edie would try to reason with her and then hang up the phone when she could not be persuaded to back down. Then she would call my cousin, Myrna. She would tell Pinky and Ashley, and the folks on the bench. Russell would hear and admonish her. And when desperate, she would even tell my daughter, Cricket, whom she usually allowed to stay above the fray.

I initially tried cooking her food and bringing it over in plastic containers for her to eat. But that didn't work because each week, they left the containers in the refrigerator with wasted food, which she said she either forgot about or wasn't hungry enough to eat it.

# TENNYBOOTS!

Since the meals I prepared were nutritious and included beets and liver and onions that were blood builders and which Mama claimed to like, wasting the food by not eating it was costly. One day, I had cooked Mama's food and was bringing it to her. She was sitting on the bench when I pulled up in the car. When I got in earshot, I heard Mama say:

"Here she come with that old food. I already know what she got in there. I'm gonna leave that shit in the refrigerator like the others. I'm tired of that shit. Next week when she come she will have to take it out and throw it away. When she ask me why I didn't eat it, I'll tell her I forgot. And then she'll be bringing some more old food. Every week the same thing."

Mama's voice was louder than she could hear. And her whispers were inadvertent stage whispers. She didn't know that I heard her, but her friends on the bench did.

Someone laughed and said, "Ms. Florence, you are too much."

That emboldened Mama until she looked up and I was upon her.

She then looked up at me and said, "Oh, Judy. What you bring me today?

"Shrimps and grits and a bacon, lettuce and tomato sandwich," I lied.

That sounded fantastic to her, I imagine her mouth *starting to water;* I tried hard not to laugh.

"Ooooh give it here. I'm supposed to be allergic to shrimps you remember the last time I ate them I was sick as a dog. I shit all over myself and Ashley and Asia had to put me in the tub. They cleaned my ass up till I was shining. But I think I can eat em now. Just one at a time. As long as I don't eat too much."

"Okay, do you." I hooked the bag on her walker and turned around to walk back to the car. Mama's friends on the bench began to warn Mama that she should not eat the shrimp if she was allergic to them. I heard them lamenting that I should not have made her shrimps knowing that she could not eat them. As I pulled away Mama was digging into the bag to bring out the food. I always put plasticware and napkins in her bags so she could eat outside if she chose to. I imagine her glee in anticipation of eating the shrimps and BLT, and then her disappointment to discover that she only had liver with onions, beets, yams, and fresh spinach, with a big slice of cornbread to make cush when she got upstairs. I know she cussed me out, but I laughed about it all the way home.

That was the last bowl of cooked food I brought her. Unless she specifically asked for something. Sometimes she asked for hamburgers or the flanken ribs I make. But that was it. I started buying her food and staples to have in the apartment to microwave and eat as she saw fit. Plus, Ashley and Asia would bring her cooked food to eat; Pinky would bring her dinners from the restaurant; Russell would bring her fish sandwiches, and Cricket would also bring her food. Her friends would buy her food. She was never without food.

At some point, Dr. Yoe suggested that she eat more blood food like kidneys, spleen and blood sausage. Mama was used to eating boudin in Opelousas and agreed to eat blood sausages. She told me she loved them and it reminded her of home. But one evening when I had stopped by the El Cuchifrito Spanish Restaurant to get her a few sausages, and left her in the car, she complained about the sausages to my sister and cousin.

"There she go, buying me those old black ass sausages."

And that's how it continued. I could never please her. She tired of eating this or that or that or this. And unless she requested something specifically, I stopped bringing cooked food.

Mama recovered from the temporary delirium caused by the UTI, but after that was not quite the same. She is stubbornly independent still, but she began to acknowledge that the way she processes things now was somehow different. On a day-to-day basis, it's not noticeable because she mostly is fine. But she has bouts where she doesn't remember some things she did or said previously. She has no diagnosis of Alzheimer's, dementia or any significant cognitive loss. But something, some days, is different. Coupled with her wily ways, I don't really know if she is telling the truth or pulling my leg when she says she doesn't remember doing or saying something or acting a certain way. The good thing is that after fighting against *Oldtimers* for so long, Mama is finally okay with the fact that on some days she may not be "in her right mind" (her words, not mine.) Not only has she embraced this other mindedness, but she uses it as an excuse to get herself out of mischief that she has created, saying more than once, that she doesn't remember or she's not sure where her mind was on any given day.

Today the Shawnee yellow bracelet was her guide in finding her way back to this moment. Today, Mama is not lost or claiming to be.

****

## Chapter Twenty

### Jim Crow and Dr. Buzzard

Mama calls me at 7:00 on Sunday Morning for Sunday School that begins at 9:30.

"Ju, I am ready," she says, "pick me up at 9, I've been dressed since 6."

She knows I'm coming, why is she calling me so damn early on Sunday morning for a 9 o'clock pick up, but I tell her okay. Since I was up, I left early. She was waiting in the lobby. Her colors complement each other well, but her belt is twisting around her waist, and her stockings are sagging. All in all, she looks fine. She's sporting a burgundy derby, and for some reason, she is wearing the clip-on earrings my friend, Vy gave her for Christmas, alongside her pierced ones. I don't disparage her when she asks for my opinion. She's very sensitive and if I say something she believes to be negative, she yells at me and says it isn't so, therefore; I choose my critique carefully. I put her walker in the back seat and help her get into the car. She doesn't require much help this morning. She gets herself all settled in the back seat behind me and I drive off.

"How I look? Mama's feeling like shouting today," she shouts, which catches me off guard and scares the crap out of me

# TENNYBOOTS!

because she is sitting in the seat directly behind me and the unexpected, impromptu shouting is at the back of my head.

"Mama, warn somebody when you get to shouting in the car, please."

Ignoring me, she's revving up and *getting her church on*.

"Ain't got no pain, my eyes are seeing good, I'm in my right mind, and I am just thanking God."

"Do I look okay?" she asks again.

"You are wearing that royal blue Mama. Are your legs cold?"

"No, I'm warm!"

"You know you can wear that pantsuit again that I bought you. You can change the top or wear the same one. It's pretty cold out here for just those French Coffee pantyhose on your legs."

"I don't wear pants to church. And I'm warm."

I swear she says things just to annoy me. But I'm not taking the bait today.

"Okay, I guess you'll just have to *root hog or die poor pig*."

That Gullah-ism didn't apply to what I was saying, but it always made her laugh so I found ways of inserting it in our conversations. We're too early again, and the sexton hasn't gotten there yet to open the doors, so we have to wait in the car. This gives her the opportunity to orient herself in the present by remembering the past. But first she takes out her broken piece of a mirror to check her face and make sure her nose is clean. I see the mirror and sigh. I've asked her to get rid of it because it's an accident waiting to happen. I make a mental note to steal it out of her bag on the way home. If I ask for it, she will fight to keep it. But it's a losing cause: she always buys the same glass mirrors from the same guy at the Harlem Mart, they always break, and she always carries a

# TENNYBOOTS!

jagged piece of mirror in her bags to ensure that her face is clean. That no one has been cut by the damn thing yet is a miracle.

"I remember when my church was a movie theater, and on that corner over there was the Schrafft's restaurant. It had a soda fountain and we would go there on dates. The second time I came to New York City, me and Fan lived in that building, with a woman named, Ms. Poole. Down the block we'd go to the place that had the amateur hours shows, they was so much fun. I've come a long way from Opelousas, I don't ever want to go back. If only Momma could see me now."

The mention of her Momma stirs up memories that she must share. Whether because of grief or nostalgia I have no idea, she starts right in this morning:

*Poor Momma, she was always sick. Momma got sick after she had the first baby, my sister, Mildred. She was married at 19, well, IF she was married. I think they jumped a broom. She had Mildred when she was 20. She never got better after that. Momma used to have headaches. Somebody said Momma had been hoodooed. Nobody would lock they doors so people could come into your house and take whatever they wanted—your flour, corn-meal, and your rice when we wasn't there. Most people didn't bother your things, but one family, the Damps, they was different. Finally, we bought a lock and chain and put it on the door. Then they came through the window, so it was no use.*

*One day Momma found a strand of her hair and some pink powder tied up in a lil sachet sack, sewed into her pillow. They said that was the hoodoo that made Momma sick. Somebody told Momma to go see Dr. Buzzard, I never saw a Dr. Buzzard but everybody knew he was the hoodoo doctor. Momma told us that Dr. Buzzard said to take the sachet sack to the stream, then turn her back to the shore and throw the hoodoo thing over the left shoulder and let it flow into the stream and let it drain down into a big...we call it Callahan—into a big body of water. So, we did. We all went there with Momma. And we helped her to do what Dr. Buzzard told her. Fannie threw the hoodoo thing into the stream and we ran alongside it until we couldn't see it no more. But Momma still suffered with headaches. Later, some people told Momma that she was supposed to be the one to throw it in the Callahan, not us, and that's probably why it never worked. Anyway, she never stopped suffering with those headaches. And that's why I left school early and went to* work to buy her the medicine she needed for her headaches and stomachaches. Years later I learned that the medicine was just BC powder for headaches and neuralgia.

She roars with laughter here. I laugh too about Dr. Buzzard and his fixes that were rendered impotent by BC powder. It seems so foolish that this was the *medicine* that Grandma Lindy so badly needed. Mama keeps pace with the memories, she's on a roll now; one memory leads to another and I recline my seat, close my eyes and listen, filling in the gaps with my own memory of these stories.

*I remember my step-father used to take us to the fair when it was in town. You know like a carnival. We would be coming back on the road about three miles from our house in pitch-black dark. All of a sudden Papa Steve would say, 'Hey, did you see that man crossing the road?' We would say, where Papa Steve, where Papa Steve, and he would say 'Right there, that's a ghost, that's a ghost.' We would all jump on him. He would be carrying some of us on his back, some of us on his front. Then finally, he would tell us that the ghost had passed. By the time we would get almost to the house and go through the gate, he would say, 'Look, there's six white dogs jumping through the fields.' What he wanna say that for? We would break the door down getting in the house, we would get under those beds we had. It wasn't like beds now, there was nowhere to really get under it. But we would bury our heads we was so scared.*

*We had made those corn shuck mattresses. Me and Momma would take the wagon out to the woods. And we had long sticks, ricans we call them. And we would use those ricans to get the moss from the trees. Then we would go home and lay the moss out on the grass to dry. It had to be black to put it in the mattress. Momma would sew some yellow cotton into sacks and leave one hole where we would stuff it with black moss. We used corn shucks for the bottom part. And that was laid out on the floor. We ain't had no real mattress, that was our mattress, and we would get up under those beds running from the ghosts.*

Mama cuts off here, picturing the mayhem in her mind. She laughs at the memories, a big laugh that collects the merriment, mischief and fun, and sends it back out into the universe as though she is once again a child walking home from the fair, being scared by ghost stories her Papa Steve is telling.

# TENNYBOOTS!

"What a life!" Mama exclaims more to herself than to me. That memory leads to another about Papa Steve.

"Ju, you remember when we went to Papa Steve's funeral, I took you and Gay. Edie didn't go cause she had to go to school. We went on the Silver Meteor and then we changed trains in New Orleans to the Southern Pacific Railway, you remember don't you?"

"Yes, Boy, do I remember. Those Jim Crow white folks were no joke."

We traveled many miles and hours and across the longest lake I had ever seen, Lake Pontchartrain, with no rails on either side of us to keep the train from falling into the vast black lake. Or so it seemed to my five-year-old anxieties. Mama had ramped up the scary ride over Lake Pontchartrain before we came, so I was already afraid before we ever stepped foot on the train. Mama could really tell foreboding stories. Come to think about it, she was the first Princess of doom and gloom I've ever known. Maybe Mama's anxieties were passed down to me. Even now when I think of it, my breath quickens. The Silver Meteor brought us only as far as New Orleans where it dumped us onto a deserted platform in the middle of the night. As far as we could see, the night was black with dark blue patches where a far-off moon threatened to reach through the night and grab us in its dark shadows. The air was rent with scary southern night noises. More so because we were city kids and not used to such quiet darkness where the plaintive, nocturnal calls of insects and animals could be heard so distinctly. The Colored Waiting Room in New Orleans was a short platform and nothing more, no shelter, no seats, and no one else. It was just the five of us—Mama and her two sisters, Aunt Mildred and Aunt Fannie, and me and Gay—at the edge of a dark railroad station. My aunts had fancy, matched sets of creamy white and red colored Samsonite luggage, and those hatboxes Ophelia DeVore's models used that always looked so glamorous. My aunts had been very careful with their luggage in the overhead rack on the Silver Meteor from Pennsylvania Station in New York City. But now, the luggage looked out of place and pretentious piled haphazardly against our suitcases at the end of the deserted platform that doubled as the Colored Waiting Room.

# TENNYBOOTS!

Mama and her sisters spoke in hushed tones, way too quiet for an empty platform, seemingly afraid to be overheard by all of the people who weren't even there. This only added to my disquietude. Looking around trying to make sense of the dark, in my almost 5-year-old voice, I asked Mama, "Dould we be afwaid of boogermen?" A lingering lisp betrayed my precociousness until I was six, when it just evaporated one day. Mama always said it was to keep me humble.

Putting forth a brave face, Mama laughed and said, "Ain't no boogiemen here cept for the ones you bring inside you."

Her answer didn't make me feel much better, because then I was worried that I had brought some inside of me. I started doing a dance like an itch had got a hold of me, to shake those boogiemen loose when Mama asked what was wrong with me.

"Are you cold, Judy?"

"No Mama. I'm just dancing."

"Dancing, Girl! You hear music somewhere?"

My sister Gay, who, even as young as six-years-old had perfected the art of conning anyone to do anything, had gotten Mama to pick her up and had fallen asleep with her head on her shoulder and her long skinny legs wrapped around Mama's waist. Although cranky and tired too, and shivering more from fear than cold, I stopped dancing the boogiemen out of me and stood straight as the ushers in church on the First Sunday, stretching my four-year-old eyes wide to see through the blue-black night, first in front of me, and then behind me, still sensing danger in the unfamiliar, and the adults' hushed tones.

Now I know, but I didn't then: it was 1957 in the Jim Crow South, and we were standing at the "Colored" section of the platform which is why it was even darker and scarier than it should have been. The fear that is still so palpable to me six decades later, was for real boogiemen, even if I didn't know it then. I remember the sad, moaning sounds the Silver Meteor made when it left us on

# TENNYBOOTS!

that platform; and the welcoming noise the big black Southern Pacific Railway train made when it finally came rumbling into the station, indistinguishable from the night except for its loud noise and its one bright headlight parting a way out of the dark night. Although we were right near a door when the train came to a stop, they didn't open it until the conductor looked out at the platform, and then opened the doors first where the white people, who had been sheltered in a before unseen waiting room, were standing.

With derision in his voice, the conductor told my Aunt Mildred, who was carrying her beautiful cream and red Samsonite luggage with the hatbox to match, the proud matriarch of our family, whom we all revered, "Aunty, stand back, wait your turn."

The five of us were the last to board the train from New Orleans to Opelousas. Mama was fidgeting with the reams of tickets when the train started revving up to leave even before we had securely mounted the rickety old metal steps protruding from the colored section of the train. Even at our young age—I was four going on five, and Gay was already six—we were city kids from the projects of Harlem, and we had learned early how to stick up for what was right. We were already grumbling that it was not fair, that we were there first, and now, we're getting on last. I'm not sure if Gay really knew what was going on, Mama had wakened her from her sleep when the train came and stood her on the platform, but she was complaining right along with me.

I remember Mama and her sisters, Aunt Fannie and even our proud Aunt Mildred, quickly and quietly shushing us. Mama was cowardly and easygoing, Aunt Fannie was easier, but Aunt Mildred always held her ground and spoke her mind—except this time. Mama and Aunt Fannie seemed resigned to the unfair treatment. But Aunt Mildred was seething beneath her best wig and traveling hat. Mama told us to be quiet because we were in the South and Negroes had to act differently in the South. We were tired and sleepy so we didn't put up much of a fight. Mama piled our tan plaid suitcases—secured with brown leather straps to keep them from opening and spilling out the contents—near the back of the railroad car, between the bathroom and the door where the cars were coupled and made a pallet for us to sleep on. I remember little

# TENNYBOOTS!

after that until we finally got to Opelousas. I had made sure that I would be asleep during that long ride over Lake Pontchartrain that Mama had ominously described.

I didn't understand it then, but Mama, Aunt Fannie, and Aunt Mildred all transformed once the train rambled further south. They began to avert their eyes when someone spoke to them, say *yes ma'am, no sir*, and became very compliant. By the time we got off the train in Opelousas several hours later, Mama, Aunt Mildred, and Aunt Fannie were fully complicit with the dictates of the Jim Crow South. As Gay and I went skipping down the street near the Southern Pacific Railroad Station, Mama and our aunts each reminded us in their own way, that we should step aside if a white person was walking toward us. Aunt Mildred told us in a no-nonsense way that gave no room for questioning. Our very sweet and nice Aunt Fannie told us in a pleading, cautionary tone with a lot of baby this baby that's thrown in. And Mama told us matter-of-factly as though she was telling us not to cross the street without holding someone's hand. Neither I, nor Gay listened to either of them during the week we spent in Opelousas, and we were constantly having to be reminded to step in the gutter and let the white folks have the right of way. Now that made no sense to us. Mama never let us play in the streets in Harlem and now she was telling us to step in the gutter to allow grown folks to pass...

Mama interrupts my thoughts again asking, "Ju, you remember Papa Steve's funeral and wake don't you?"

I nod my head, slowly, still thinking about the train ride, and then respond, "Boy do I."

In 1957, when we finally arrived at my grandparents' house on Mill Street, at the end of Academy Street, in St. Landry's Parish in Opelousas, Papa Steve's body was being waked in the house. Gay took one look at the dead man laid out in the parlor and hauled ass. Gay had a head full of thick, longish hair and had unplaited one braid, like she was wont to do, on the train. Mama was always getting after her about playing in her hair. The image of Gay running down the road with her hair wild and Mama trying to catch her, made me double over in laughter. What a sight we Harlemites

# TENNYBOOTS!

were to the genteel southerners gathered for a respectable wake of Papa Steve. Mama had to run to catch up with her way down the road. Gay was like that. She would react to things with little forethought about consequences. She had never been in Opelousas before. She had no idea where she was going, but she took off running and hollering, anyway. Mama was athletic and finally caught up with her, but it took a lot of cajoling and pleading to get her back inside. One elder suggested that a rican switch off the pecan tree in the front yard would work just fine on her. Mama wasn't keen on hitting us, and we certainly had never been hit with a rican switch off of a pecan tree, whatever that was. Somehow, Mama finally got Gay to settle down and come back into the house. For the entire visit, Gay was particular about not going near the parlor where Papa Steve was hanging out until the burial, in the front room of Grandma Lindy's house. I remember a casket and a dead man in the living room. I had never seen him alive, so there was no emotional reaction to seeing him dead, but having a body in the same house where we would sleep was a little scary. Mama kept calling something a shroud, I surmised it was Papa Steve or something that he wore. I was tired, scared and confused but Gay's escapade had eclipsed any reaction other than laughter, I may have had.

After all of that, we finally got to meet our grandmother, Grandma Lindy. Her name was Malinda, they named her after her father's mother, Melinda, but people called her Lindy. I wasn't sure if we were to call her Grandma Malindy or Grandma Lindy so I just squished the words together real fast-like so no one could really tell how I split the Ma and Lindy. My older cousins called her Big Mama. But Mama kept referring to her as "Grandmalindy" so that's what I went with.

Most southern people had the habit of calling Gay Gail, which she hated. Only Aunt Mildred could get away with it. Grandma Lindy made that mistake right off the bat, saying, "This must be Gail." Gay immediately corrected her: "Gaynell or Gay," she said in the best New York City accent she could muster. People had no problem saying Judy when they heard both syllables, but I wasn't sure whether Grandma Lindy could hear that well and might butcher my name, by calling me "Julie" as people sometimes did. I knew that if she did that Gay would have a fit of laughing, and mock Grandma Lindy by calling me Julie for the rest of the trip. I planned to preempt it. After Gay corrected her, I immediately introduced myself, saying, "And I am Ju-dy," being very careful to enunciate the "D."

Grandma Lindy replied in a long, slow, southern drawl that matched the cadence of her chair rocking back and forth, "Baby, I would know you anywhere."

How she would know me, I wasn't sure, except everyone told me that I looked like Mama, so maybe she could recognize the Mama in my face or the Mama in my hands.

Gay's eyes scanned Grandma Lindy, looking for anything to make fun of, and when she found it, whispered loudly to me to look at the big ball of skin on the top of her foot. Foolishly, I looked down at Grandma Lindy's foot, then the ball of skin, and then at Gay, who was contorting herself into a fit of ill-hidden giggles while pointing at her own feet, like someone whose very scratchy crinoline had them in its grip.

Grandma Lindy had a skin growth about the size of a large brown egg that pushed her stockings to their limit and squished its way past the top of her slippers like a fat tube of pork sausage. It was so strange that Mama had never even mentioned it, given as to how it was so prominent. Gay, ever the mischief-maker, was doing a terrible job of stifling her laughter and surreptitiously pointing to her own foot every time no one was looking her way. It took all the control that a soon to be a five-year-old child could muster for me to not burst out laughing at Gay's foolishness. It was bad enough that we were city kids who didn't say yes ma'am, no ma'am when asked a question. We cavalierly said "yeah" or "no, "and sometimes we didn't even bother to speak -- we just shook or nodded our heads while breathing through open mouths, or hunched our shoulders like the dunces in the burgundy leather set of Fairy Tales books Mama had bought from the traveling salesman on credit. And now, here we were when we should have been on our best behavior, convulsed by a fit of jerking giggles that had to look like a terrible case of sibling tics.

# TENNYBOOTS!

Despite our bad manners, Grandma Lindy was sweet, welcoming and very southern. She was very glad to see us, and she excused our mischief. She wore a hairnet over her hair and some round wire-framed spectacles, perched a good distance from her eyes, on the bridge of a wide, flat nose. I could see Mama and Aunt Fannie in her face, but not Aunt Mildred so much. She moved slowly, and oddly referred to herself in the third person as in, "Old Lindy is sure glad to see y'all. Old Lindy have some sweet tea in there, get yaself something to eat and drink. Y'all can have whatever you want in Old Lindy's house."

We had come so far, and we were finally meeting Mama's Momma. You could tell that she had been very fond of her husband, Papa Steve. Her voice became animated when she spoke of "Old Steve" in such a loving way. It was also odd to see Mama and our aunts acting like daughters. Grandma Lindy told Mama to fix us some preserves from the safe that looked like a cupboard. There were jars and jars of preserves she had canned and put away. I kept looking for cans when everything was in small glass jars. At first, I was so confused. But by then I was realizing that things were very different down south so I shouldn't do my usual routine of peppering folks with questions when something wasn't was; I'd just wait and try to figure some things out.

There was also pecan pie, made with pecans from the big pecan tree in the front yard I had noticed when Mama was chasing Gay down the road; and a lot of fried chicken that I hoped hadn't been made from chickens like the ones that were strutting proudly around the yard. We ate like we were hungry because we were, and then Mama put us to bed in another room. The bed I went to sleep in was Papa Steve's bed. I must have slept for a long time because Mama came to wake me up.

The trip to bury Papa Steve over six decades ago was pushing vividly through Mama's memory now too. Mama had been just going with the flow, with her eyes closed, when she raises up, excited, as the memory quickens in her consciousness. It was eerie that we both arrived at the same place in our memories at the very same time.

## TENNYBOOTS!

"Yeah, you remember when I came to get you out of the bed? Papa Steve was holding on to you and wouldn't let go. I kept pulling you and you was stuck in the bed, and I said, Papa Steve, let my baby go! And finally, I got you off that bed."

Mama tosses her head back, and then as she hits her right thigh with her open palm, her head comes down in unison and she laughs wildly. I laugh too. It's a story I have heard so many times now, that even if I don't really think I remember it, I know that one of my arms was being pulled down between the bed and the wall, supposedly by the ghost of Papa Steve, while Mama was pulling hard to get me away from the bed. I remember an old, black metal Winchester rifle leaning against the wall by my head. It was my first time being that close to the cold black shaft of a real rifle. I was afraid that one wrong move could set it off, and I'd be as dead as Papa Steve. Even as a child, my mind raced to every possible scenario as I made plans to resolve them. The adults in the house were convinced that Papa Steve's ghost was pulling on me because I was in his bed, or that he was coming back for his old Winchester rifle, something he loved dearly, and I was in the way. He had been a much better hunter than he had been a farmer, and he and his Winchester were never far apart.

Because the Haints had come for me in Papa Steve's bed, they had to pass me over his casket at the burial in the churchyard of Little Zion Baptist Church, (where Mama was baptized at seven-years-old), to ward off the spirits. They wanted to pass Gay over too, just in case, but Gay would have no part of it. Her long legs stiffly dug into the soft mound of earth they had removed from the hole. They let her be before she had kicked it all back into the hole even before they let the casket down. In Opelousas they didn't really bury the bodies deep in the ground. The hole was dug to secure the crypt that Papa Steve would go in.

Mama is playing back the memories of the story in her mind now.

"Yeah Momma said Papa Steve was coming for you, cause you were born with the veil on your face."

# TENNYBOOTS!

"The caul," I say.

"Yeah, the veil," Mama says, unwilling to leave me with a caul or the last word on the subject. I chuckle to myself.

That's another story I have heard over and over again. I was born with a veil over my face and I am supposed to have a special talent to see ghosts. I'm uncertain if I've ever cashed in on it.

"Ma, other than the ghost stories Papa Steve told you, did you ever really see ghosts?"

I ask because when we were kids Mama and DadDee always told us a lot of ghost stories about walking down the road and seeing white balls of fire, or white dogs, or ghosts dressed all in white crossing the road or haunting the night or hearing noises when no one was around. I suspected after a while that those ghost stories were tall tales or family lore. It wasn't lost on me that everything bad was white. Mama admits that the closest she came to a real ghost was when she and her Momma were lying on the porch and heard chains rattling.

With her eyes closed, Mama tells that story: *That night, as usual, Momma was sick, and when she was sick, lying flat on the hard floor of the porch made her feel better. Since I was her stickin' plaster and went everywhere Momma went, I was laying down on the porch with her. It was about three in the morning and it was pitch black outside cause we had no lights and all of a sudden we heard chains rattling. I said to Momma; you hear those chains rattling? Momma said it's probably a ghost, baby; they don't bother you if you don't bother them. So, I laid back down. Then the chains got closer. I was getting up off that porch and told Momma if that's a ghost, he's coming to visit let's go in the house. By that time, the ghost was at the porch. Me and Momma both started hollering. It was so black we couldn't see the whites of our eyeballs, so we couldn't see the ghost. But just then the ghost spoke and said, 'Wait don't run, I ain't gon harm ya.' By that time, I was hollering Pa-pa Steve, Pa-pa Steve. I didn't want to run in the house and leave Momma who was slow bout getting up, but I was too scared to stay on the porch, so I kept hollering and jumping in place. Papa Steve came running out with the kerosene lamp. By the light of the lamp, we could see that the ghost was a man who had escaped from the chain gang. And then I started hollering again. He was wearing the clothes*

# TENNYBOOTS!

*and still had the irons on his legs and hands. He told Papa Steve, 'I ain't gon harm ya. I been in those woods for days, and I just need something to eat and a place to rest, I ain't been sleep in days.' Papa Steve told him 'Okay, we can put you in the barn and give you a bit to eat.' We ain't had much to eat ourselves, but Papa Steve scraped up some cush for him to eat, and we had some cream from the cow, he gave him that and took him to the barn and made him a pallet in the wagon. The next morning Papa Steve called the 'Sheriff.*

"Y'all turned him in," I ask—a wail—more than a question.

"Yeah, we didn't know what he would do, he had escaped from the chain gang, he still had those chains on him. When the Sheriff came they was nice, they said: 'Uncle, hey there, Uncle, we ain't gon hurt you none, just gon get you cleaned up.' Then they took him away.

I ask Mama if they even knew what became of him. She shook her head no. Now, I am pissed that the story doesn't end with them bucking the system, sparing the guy, and helping to free him of his shackles. Uncle Toms, I judge them. I had enough of the stories for today; I return my seat to driving position, and just then, thankfully the sexton comes and opens the doors to the church.

I return a few hours later to pick Mama up from church and she has had such a good time she is not ready to go home; she is going to another church until around 5:00 P.M. she decides. She tells Sara, of the fourth generation, the latest child that Mama raised, to ask me if I will take her to the other church.

Because I had gotten out and walked into the Church's vestibule, I overhear Mama asking Sara in a very loud voice in front of the church people, "What she say? I bet she ain't gonna do it!"

To which I say, "Sure baby, whatever your sweet heart desires."

Caught, she put her hand up to her mouth as if to stuff the words back in. Yeah Mama, eat your words I think. Never had I refused to take her to another church program and pick her up. She was just being messy and showing off in front of her church crowd.

# TENNYBOOTS!

    Sara gets Mama, her walker, and herself into the car and I bring them to Amsterdam Avenue and 130th Street. I go back home to finish my Sunday Morning Mama story and to wait until 5:00 P.M. to pick her up. Sara calls at 4:30 to let me know they are ready. I'm not finished my story yet, so I sit at my dining room table finishing the story and pick them up close to 5:00.

****

# TENNYBOOTS!

## Chapter Twenty-One

### V.I.P. Hits Turbulence

The winter of 2015, when Mama was turning 96 years old, Nelson Vails, one of the kids who grew up in the projects with us, contacted Mama through her Facebook page—yes Mama has a FB page—and told her that a producer was making a documentary on his life and he wanted her to be in it. Nelson was the youngest child of the Vails' family, a family whose parents, Bob and Louise Vails, had a knack for raising their children with the confidence that lead them to pursue and excel in untraditional pursuits. One had become a Black cowboy in Oregon, one had traveled to San Francisco, California to live and go to college before it was popular in our community, one had won a "Fancy Pants" contest that came with a 67 Mustang, one was a famous dancer with La Roque Bey African Dance Troupe, one had been part of a group of all Black Rangers in Korea, and one had designed leather outer garments and had a notable collection of war memorabilia. The tradition extended to the next generation amongst them, a realtor, a pediatrician, a restaurateur, and a highly sought-after film industry wardrobe stylist. Nelson, the baby of a family of ten, had morphed from a spoiled brat, climbing trees or falling out on the ground when he didn't get his way into a champion who won the silver medal in the 1986 Olympics in cycling. An improbable journey took Nelson from the projects as a teen father, via a bicycle messenger job, to the world, riding his bicycle. As a kid, he entertained us riding not down, but UP the stoop on his bicycle. Both his parents, Ms.

# TENNYBOOTS!

Louise and Mr. Bob are departed and dearly missed, and Mama and only a few other parents from our childhood are left in the building.

As promised, one evening Nelson and his producers and cameramen called to say they were on their way to interview Mama about Nelson's early life. Mama got all gussied up in her robin's egg blue suit, tied a pink bow at her neck, and waited for Nelson to come. The time they had promised to come had passed and Mama became impatient and convinced herself that they weren't coming when Nelson texted me to say that they were five minutes away. Mama was giddy with expectation and babbling away:

"What he want with me, what am I supposed to say?" she asked, trying to stifle her excitement. "I remember when he was born, his mother said she was going to name him after Nelson Rockefeller so he would be rich. Did he get rich?"

I hunched my shoulders up to signal to her that I didn't know the answer to that question. I certainly did not want to give a snide answer that she would repeat with a tag that Judy said it in a documentary.

Nelson and the cameraman, Scott, and another guy knocked on the door. With a broom in my hand, I opened the door and welcomed them in. I had Mama all ready and sitting in the new rocking chair that I had just bought for her hoping that the rocking chair would temper her proclivity to say something inappropriate. My thinking was that if she looked like the perfect little old lady maybe she would act like one. I hadn't seen Nelson in years. He hadn't changed much, the Vails all have a distinctive look, both males and females and you can tell them anywhere. Mama was in rare form and her memory of Nelson and his family was sharp. She didn't need much prodding to begin talking.

"I remember when Nelson was born, he was the last baby and Louise was well into her forties when she had him... Nelson had built those things, what they call them? She looked around for help with the name of the 'thing." Yeah, skateboards. He built long ones with a long piece of wood and roller skate wheels. Once he built them then everybody had one, but he was the first. His mother

# TENNYBOOTS!

named him after Nelson Rockefeller so he would be rich, I don't know if he ever got rich!"

My great-niece, Ashley, who was standing with me in the background crossing our fingers, gasped, and said, "Oh no she didn't just say that!"

Rolling my eyes to the heavens for help, I replied to my niece, "Let's just hope that is the most egregious thing she says."

The cameraman, like everyone Mama meets, loved her storytelling and sassiness, and the camera kept rolling. As the object of everyone's attention in the room, Mama flourished. She has definitely become more confident with age. Her ninth decade is more than she could have ever imagined as a sharecropping child. I, meanwhile, was sitting on proverbial pins and needles, hoping that she didn't say anything too untoward, as she can and will do whenever all eyes are on her. Finally, the interview ended and I breathed a huge sigh of relief because the worst thing she had said was to ask if Nelson were rich yet—I could live with that. It was funny. Scott, the cameraman, liked my painting of a typical day in the projects and filmed that, then we said goodbye as Nelson had to meet with childhood friends downstairs and attend a family reunion dinner at Amy Ruth's.

Mama was euphoric after they left.

"How was I? Was I good? Did I say the right thing? I remember when he was born. Does he have a lot of money yet? What is this for, a movie? I am going to be in a movie? When, why me...?" And on and on she went.

My nephew, Russell, who was pining to be in the movie, had just come in and asked, "Ma, you didn't say anything crazy, did she Ju? Ju, you monitored her right? Where'd they go? I have a lot to say about Nelson. Nobody had legs as big as that dude's, those muscles were like this!" (demonstrating with his hands how big Nelson's muscles were.)

# TENNYBOOTS!

Mama finally settled down, but not before she had gotten on the phone and told everyone she knew that she was going to be in Nelson's movie. I left her that night, leaning on the counter, talking on the kitchen phone, still attached to the wall after 50 years, twirling the old yellow cord and feeling happy, useful and important.

The next time we saw the Vails' family was at their brother Preston's funeral a few months later. Mama had taken to eulogizing people at funerals. She always had a lot to say, but I could never be sure what she would say. My nephew and I had taken to going to the front with her, pretending we were there to support her walking. But the real reason we were there was to yank her away—like Sandman at Amateur Hour at the Apollo—if Mama were saying something out of place, or if she was going on for way too long. And these funerals were not her contemporaries, who were already all dead. But she had friends in all age groups, from one to ninety-four. She is the oldest living person in her building.

Nelson told me at the funeral that Mama's part in the movie had gone well, and that they would have a premiere in February 2016. I told Mama. And she was trying not to show her excitement, but feeling absolute delight, she began musing over the upcoming premiere.

"Oh hell, I have to live at least until then. I have to see myself in the movie. When is it? Did I do okay? I wonder how will I look?" She continued to bask in the news of the upcoming premiere. Willing God to live for this or that had been something she was doing since at least 2004 when my twin grandchildren were born. So far, God had been willing and Mama had lived to experience the thing she wanted to.

I reassured her it wasn't too far off and I was sure that she would live to see herself on the big screen and that I was sure that she looked just fine with the robin's egg blue suit setting off her silver hair. She was pleased. Not too much later Nelson's niece contacted me and told me we would get VIP tickets for the premiere and the film. I told Mama and then set out to make it a

# TENNYBOOTS!

fabulous night for her. Mama was beside herself with anticipation and excitement. It looked like she would live to make the premiere.

I love dressing Mama up, and she enjoys to be dressed up. I also love vintage style clothing from the 50s and that was the look I had in mind for the premier. Shopping online, I found the perfect outfit, a 50s style dress in a shiny bone or off-white colored fabric. I then searched and found a crinoline from a vintage store in Greenwich Village, where I also got her a vintage choker. I got her new underwear and silk stockings with seams from the old lingerie store on 125th Street, that still pulled stockings out of boxes stacked in order that only the saleswoman could decipher. I got her sheer stockings with a seam down the back. Each time I got another article of clothing, I told her about it, increasing her excitement until she couldn't take anymore.

She'd say, "all right Ju, whatever you want; I know you will get it all together."

I don't think she ever really grasped the concept of how big this was. A movie premiere and she was in the movie and was a VIP, just was not in the lexicon of a "black gal" called, "tenny boots," from sharecropping beginnings, who had lived a simple life until she turned 95. But she was a good sport. And I enjoyed watching her excitement.

On the day of the event, my grandnieces overheard her on the phone talking to her church family, wiggling her rump and bragging about the event.

"I don't know if I'll be at church tomorrow, you know I'm in a movie, yeah, chile, I am going tonight. Judy said it's a big deal, she's getting me all dressed up, and we are going to see the movie, so I don't know if I will get to church tomorrow, I may be too worn out from the big night." Oh, how she loved to brag anyway, and this gave her something big to brag about.

I asked Ashley, who's a talented but yet unrealized designer and fashionista, to give Mama a 50s style hairdo. I also wanted to get her approval on the outfit.

## TENNYBOOTS!

I knew I had the perfect combination and wanted to surprise her. On the night of the premiere, she called me and asked me to bring hair spray because the style she had given Mama had dropped. When I got there Mama had taken her bath and was getting her hair done again. We stopped to try the dress on. Luckily, everything fit perfectly. I had not tried it on earlier and did not have a backup. I took it off of her, ironed it, and we got her dressed again. I had bought some underwear that would push up her 97 years old *titties* as she called them, to show some cleavage. We shined her up with Vaseline (the only thing she's ever used on her skin, except for Artra—a skin lightener and Noxzema in the 60s) and some scented cream with glitter; Vaseline so that the shine would last all night, and the other stuff for light fragrance and effect. I polished her nails, and we put the crinoline on her. The waistline was narrow, so it went over her head instead of pulling it over her rump.

"I feel like a big child, I used to put these 'crindalyns' on y'all when y'all was children. Now I feel like a big child."

"Turnabout is fair play," I teased her. "It's your time to wear crinolines now."

I tried to put some lip-gloss on her lips, but that's where she drew the line.

"No, I don't wear no makeup, it makes me look like a monkey," she said, placing her hand in front of her face, refusing the lip gloss.

"And don't let them put no lipstick on me when I die."

Funeral instructions were always sprinkled into regular conversations now. It wasn't morbid, just prudent planning. She looked fine, so I didn't insist, and true, she had never worn makeup. A red sponge powder puff she would use to keep the shine off of her face, but that was it. After she was all dressed, Ashley put more curls in her hair and then finger pulled it out in a soft and sassy 50s style. The look was complete and Ashley, the would-be designer-fashionista absolutely loved it! I'd bought a shrug for her arms in

## TENNYBOOTS!

case she complained that too much of her arms was out—she didn't like the excess fat hanging off her arms to show. She was riding on such a high; she didn't complain one bit. I used the shrug as her sweater, put on her coat, a tan camel hair with a wide collar that could double as a hood, and we set out on a snowy night in March to go to Mama's premiere.

She had been refusing to go out in *"all that snow, I might slip and fall,"* for weeks of snow; but had no problem leaving the house with new snow falling yet again, to go to the premier. The new My Image Studio Theatre, (MIST), is in the lobby of the Kalahari building here in Harlem. The MIST's mission is to show movies and documentaries in the images of Black and other peoples of color, so it was the perfect place to have the premiere. I had suggested this theater to Nelson and his crew when they were filming in December, and Nelson's niece lives in the building, so it had all come together. The venue was excellent, and only one block away. That Mama who had lived half a block away for 67 years would be in one of the theater's first documentaries in her 97th year was almost too much to wrap our heads around.

The snow was falling like confetti around us when we left the building adding to the magical quality of the night. We crossed the street in front of Mama's building where the snow was just barely dusting the curb. Mama was pushing her walker like Cinderella's coach, as Ashley's boyfriend, James, and I walked on either side, like footmen. We cut through the African Market, across the street from Mama's building, which leads out to 116th Street and walked a few yards to the theater. At the entrance, we walked in on a red carpet. A table to the right was for registering; we gave our names, they listed us as Florence Edwards and her guest for VIP treatment. They put red bands on our wrists and gave us our swag bags. We went to the coat check and then into the reception area, the restaurant part where they had set up hors d'oeuvres and drinks. People were dressed beautifully for the occasion. Nelson greeted Mama, dressed in a black tux with a red cummerbund and bow tie.

Mama's eyes flitted from one incredible sight to another, unable to take it all in at once. I was pretty impressed myself.

# TENNYBOOTS!

"Ju, I didn't know it was all this. I didn't know it would be like this," she exclaimed like an excited child.

"I didn't know it either, but I didn't say that instead, I said, You hit the big time Mama Flo," beaming and adding to her excitement.

It really was beyond her comprehension. Even before she took off her coat, the paparazzi were snapping her picture. She easily was the oldest and most diva beautiful belle of the ball. The dress and her hair morphed into a very glamorous look. People recognized the period, and we heard them call out, Marilyn Monroe, Billie Holiday, Lena Horne, and other fabulous ladies of yore. Mama beamed with pride when person after person came up to her and asked to take her picture. She really was the belle of the ball. I was so happy for her. It was everything I had hoped it to be.

Many of my childhood friends were there. We grew up in a very close-knit building, and 60 years later we still turn out en masse to represent 20 West 115th Street. It was really good to see the various members of the Vails family, Percy Robinson, Lucille and Herl Finney, Michael Ferguson, Andre, (Shirley's boy) and others. My nephew, Russell also came later and helped with Mama. There is an abounding love for the people you've grown up with, at least in the projects, where we were really one big family, that is very different from anything I've ever experienced. That love was palpable as we relived the celebration of Nelson's victory at the 1986 Olympics—a project boy made good. He had made us all proud.

I got us both something to eat and drink, being very careful so that Mama wouldn't spill anything on her dress. I placed a napkin on her chest to catch the accidental drops of food. Mama has this habit of eating chicken and meat by grabbing it with her whole hand, and even the backs of her hands are usually a greasy, sticky mess when she's done. I carefully wiped her hands, back and front, making sure they were clean before she touched her dress again. While taking my time to wipe each finger individually, I noticed how old and wrinkly her hands were. A few of her fingers were bent in rebellious ways. Funny, I hadn't noticed this before.

# TENNYBOOTS!

Her hands, that had worked so hard, hoeing fields and picking cotton for her sick mother, cleaning other people's homes, taking care of other people's kids, and cleaning offices had really aged over the years, so much more than her face, or even her pushed up "titties." Her hands, more than any other part of her body, had logged the miles of her life—bent, battered and wrinkled, but still functioning as intended. The dazzling ring she is wearing, a favorite piece of costume jewelry, was in perfect juxtaposition to the weathered hands—fake and flashy where her hands had been authentic and unwavering. I am bursting with pride for Mama that this moment is flawless for her and so much more than she could have ever imagined it to be. I consider it a privilege to have been able to make it all come together for her.

I steal a glance at my own hands that are small and shaped exactly like hers, searching for any hints that they will age in thirty-three years to look like hers now. She catches me studying her hands.

"What, do my hands look old?" she asks alarmed and about to be embarassed, reading my thoughts.

"No, they are perfect," I lie and say. "I'm checking out your bling."

"Oh," she answers, sounding relieved.

People are still having her stand up and take pictures with them, telling her how beautiful she looks. An announcer interrupts the revelry for a scripted program of prayer, speakers and the Memorial Baptist Church Gospel Choir. Mama asks me if she should get up and say something. Oh boy, I chuckle to myself. This desire to speak at every occasion is recent, it has come with old age, the older she gets, the more she believes she needs to address every occasion. I tell her no; they have a script and the people who they want to speak are already chosen. No off the cuff, impromptu rambling tonight, Flo.

After the reception, we went into the VIP theater and had front row seats. Mama and Ms. Helen, the other nonagenarian from the building, who represents our parents in the movie, both have walkers, so we sat the ladies in front and banished the walkers to the back of the theater to wait for the movie to begin. I sneak a wink at Deborah, Ms. Helen's daughter. We have often commiserated on the trials and tribulations of caring for an aging independent and often stubborn mother. So far, tonight is easy for both of us.

The movie begins. Although this audience is racially mixed, we, who are from the *hood* and are versed in the Black tradition of call and response, applaud and talk back at the screen when the footage of Nelson winning the silver medal is shown. On that actual day 28 years ago, news reporters and neighbors had gathered in the Vails' apartment on the first floor, to cheer Nelson on. We all believed that he could have easily won the gold. Tonight, we are transported back to that moment, and once again cheer him on as the memory of that day was replayed on the silver screen. We ooh and ahh as old snapshots of his parents,

Ms. Louise and Mr. Bob are shown. As the movie continues, our childhood friends, and their children who are featured in the movie show up on the screen. My nephew, Russell, gets a lot of play as he talks about growing up in Nelson's tracks. Mama is sitting and watching wide-eyed. She has not dozed off the whole time.

"When am I going on, you think I'm in it," she asks, barely able to contain her excitement.

"Yes, Nelson said you are in it and your part came out good," I tell her while holding my breath hoping that her part has not been cut.

Finally, towards the end, I see myself, on the screen, opening the door with a broom in my hand, (Damn it why in the hell is that there? And why did I have that broom?), as the camera crew comes in filming? The crowd yells my name. But thankfully me and the broom flash quickly. The camera pans to Mama sitting in her rocking chair reminiscing, and sure enough, on the huge silver screen she is telling the story about how Nelson got his name, and at the part where she asks if he's rich, the audience howls with laughter. Mama is mesmerized, sitting with her mouth open, gazing at herself on a big screen in a movie theater. When her part is over, I hear people saying, "Ms. Florence, there she is, there she is!" Mama sits there awed and dumbfounded, not able to fathom the arc her journey has taken from sharecropper in the red dust of Louisiana to a movie screen in New York City—Improbable, to be sure, but realized, in the most un-matter-of-fact way, in her 97th year. Hot dammit Mama, you did it.

The movie ends, we applaud loudly, and the Q & A is ready to begin. Nelson's oldest brother, Robert Vails, is being recognized for being one of the few Black Rangers in Korea during the war. We leave because it's getting late, and I really want to get Mama in before 10 P.M. Many people exit the theater to leave at that time and are all gathered around Mama in the foyer of the restaurant area.

Once again Mama is over the moon in being the star of the hour. She's doing everything but signing autographs. My face and heart are all smiles thinking of her happiness.

People from our block are telling her how good she looks when I hear her say, "Yeah I'm 96, but I'm doing good, they wanted to put me in a nursing home, but I wouldn't let them, I am still here. I refused to go to that nursing home."

I can't believe my ears, I stop mouth wide open—the smiles drop off my heart and face and confusion takes over—hoping to extinguish this nonsense I quickly say, "Mama, that is not true, why would you say that? No one ever said they were going to put you in a nursing home."

I thought we had that nursing home mess all cleared up the last time she had gone to her church with that lie. But Mama is too invested in the story of how we did her wrong and how she overcame, to stop now and too caught up in the crowd's adulation.

She raises her voice and says, "Oh yeah, y'all was, I heard y'all talking about it."

# TENNYBOOTS!

Well, gotdamn. Billie Holiday had gone all Joe Louis in a matter of minutes. I feel like I just got sucker-punched.

"Ma, you really need to stop it, no one has ever even considered sending you to a nursing home. I wish you would stop saying that crap."

Her audience, old friends, my best friend Lucille Finney, and people who know her well, were laughing with her, and that just added fuel to her fire. Furious with her, I had to get the hell away from her. Every time. Every single time!

I left her with her adoring crowd and my nephew, Russell, and went to the ladies' room. In the time that it took me to use the bathroom and wash my hands, Mama had managed to offend another unsuspecting soul. As I got close to where Mama was holding court—and make no bones about it holding court is precisely what she was doing. She had the attention of a crowd, she could have just basked in it, but no. When I got close to where she had a crowd around her someone said, "Oh boy, you'd better get Flo before she says something else."

Stick a fork in me. I was done. I didn't even want to know, but I had brought her here and that made me at least responsible in part for anything she said.

A beautiful young woman said, "Oh, I just found out I was the ugliest little thing as a baby, but now I am beautiful!"

My mouth flew open. I apologized to the young woman and told her, "That's not true, you've always been beautiful, inside and out," which she has. I had to loud talk over Mama, who was loudly defending her ugly remarks saying "Yes she was. Uh-huh. But she's beautiful now." The crowd had abandoned her to go their separate ways. And I was left with her. I could see if she drank and had gotten a little tipsy on the wine. But she didn't. She just had this knack for showing off when she had an audience. I wanted to yank her butt out of there. But the woman was as gracious as she is beautiful and said she didn't mind; she was glad that it had a happy ending and that she was beautiful now when it counts.

# TENNYBOOTS!

Russell returned with our coats, and I told him, "Quick, dress her and let's get her out of here before I kill her!"

A few stragglers defended Mama by saying that at 96, she can say anything she wants. That is not the way I see it and is definitely where Mama and I butt heads. If she were demented and didn't know what she was saying I could understand. But to say hurtful and cruel things and lie on people just because she has reached advanced years, nope. I don't subscribe to that.

I tell her again, "Ma, you cannot say things like that. You owe her an apology."

She doesn't see it that way and starts to try to defend the indefensible. And then I just let it go, remembering that this Mama is never wrong and will never apologize. I remember that Mama's criticism of us is always done publicly, something I've always hated and never understood. She would wait clear until she was outside sitting on the bench to criticize us when she could have said it privately in our home. None of the other parents did that. Except for maybe Ms. Lucy, who was the unofficial mayor of our building. But at least she made up for it by bragging on her kids with outrageous lies.

I just don't get it. We walk back home in silence. Slowing down as she catches her breath, I am thankful for the mantel of fallen snow on the ground. Mama, in her boots, has to give all her attention to sure-footing the snow. Either she is too winded or senses my mood, and thankfully doesn't utter a peep.

I finally get her home, and she says, "Ju thanks I had such a good time."

"Well bowl me over with a feather, that's how you repay me."

I think this but do not say it. I'm over Mama tonight and don't want to interact with her at all, even to argue. She begins to tell Ashley all about the evening. I help her to take off her dress, and crinoline, her push-up bra underwear, her silk stockings with the seam down the back and snow boots. I put everything away and say goodnight. The evening had been perfect until...

I walk home pruning my recollections for reasons for Mama's behavior. I found none. The snow falling quietly, landing in pillow-top-fluffy piles, is the perfect accompaniment for my state of mind. The next morning, I am still angry with Mama when she calls me to bring her to church. She wears her pantsuit again, the one I had bought her, thankful for its warmth. I do not bring up the nonsense of last night, and neither does she. Riding to church she is orienting herself in the present.

"This is where we were last night, right?"

"Nope, we were on 116th Street, this is 115th Street."

"Oh, right, right," she says, trying to recover without being wrong because being wrong might mean she is losing it.

"I see, this is 115th, we was on the other block."

I don't feel like the small talk so I don't respond. We get to church and they have not cleared a path to the door yet so I have to hoist her up over the slushy snow. A church deacon finally comes out to help. I push her into the church with the deacon and ushers, using her walker as a wheelchair, and tell her I'll pick her up later. I don't even bother to take her picture this morning.

****

# TENNYBOOTS!

## Chapter Twenty-Two

## Saturday Night Revelry

Five generations of Mama's family filled her apartment on a rainy Saturday night. The ages range from a year old to Mama at 96. It was rowdy and impromptu and Mama loved it. Mama in the midst was holding court as well as anyone, and certainly better than me a closet introvert. She was telling stories, dishing the dirt, and stirring the pot with gossip as usual. Unfazed by the two-year-old who had jumped on her back as she sat in her rocking chair, Mama held the room and conversation together so well I marveled at her perseverance and willful refusal to succumb to old age.

At one point she began to tell us again the story of her sister Nettie's birth. She had only gotten as far as Papa Steve asking if he should go fetch Ouzine or Madame Tout Tout, the Creole midwives, when I interrupted saying, "Oh yes, we remember that story." Mama's recounting of her stories is each time brand new to her. She tells them in meticulous detail and leaves nothing out—not one word.

But tonight, she was competing with a one-year-old, a two-year-old, a five-year-old, and two nine-year-olds. All of them, including Mama, were speaking at the same time vying for undivided attention. Something had to give. Even my nine-year-old granddaughter, Chloe, had heard the story so many times that she could finish it herself and had put out her hand to let Mama know that we had heard that story enough today. There's no rhyme or reason which stories get told when and for how long. I often look for the message: is the story a visitation or is it a longing. Is it revealing something or just keeping company? Is there a message we should be discerning? I could not answer these questions and tonight is no different, but Mama's baby sister, Aunt Nettie, had hung around all day in the telling.

The house phone rang at just the right time and it was for Mama. The telephone is still tethered to the kitchen wall, once

# TENNYBOOTS!

canary yellow with a clear plastic dial, now clouded by the years, still broken on number eight where my sister, Gay, ripped off the old metal telephone lock almost 50 years ago. I've tried to replace that dinosaur with cordless phones many times. But they get lost, or the batteries die, or the buttons are too small, or Mama sits on the phone and can't hear it ring. No matter which phone I buy, when Mama's fingers fail to dial the right number, she insists, "*That operator won't allow me to call your number. She keeps saying try the number again, hell I dialed the right number, so I said shit and hung up on her!*"

No amount of explaining can convince Mama that she's mis-dialed, and the recording is not an operator. We keep the stationary landline phone on the wall in the kitchen, just in case. She gets her exercise walking to and from the phone. You can hear her hollering, "I'm coming, hold on, just hold on. Moving slow, but I'm coming," when she is called to the phone, talking all the while until she gets there.

So, it is now. With one forward motion she shakes the two-year-old off her back like a much younger woman, rocks herself to a standing position and leaves the room to take the call. Her colorful pants are not all the way pulled up and her underpants are showing. One of the kids hollers out, "You're sagging Mama." Her response——she stops, laughs, does a booty-shaking dance, then continues on her way to answer the phone.

When the call is over she returns to the living room and gives up the gossip, once again adding her voice to the mix of stories being told around the room.

The two-year-old eyes a box of croissants on the kitchen table that I had bought from Costco and brings it into the living room. Mama takes it from her and doles out one half of a croissant to everyone. She shares her two liter-sized Pepsi Cola with the children, against their parents' wishes in plastic red cups. For a few precious moments, silence hushes the room, as stolen sips of soda washed down mouthfuls of croissants. The croissants now a buttery memory and thirsts quenched, the gaiety returns to the room with Mama in the middle, alive and vibrant and couldn't be happier.

# TENNYBOOTS!

Saturday night's rain gave birth to a dreary Sunday morning; the rain had stopped before dawn, but gray clouds hung like floppy hats over the morning. I call Mama on my way to pick her up for church expecting an easy Sunday morning. As lively as she was last night, Mama appears in the doorway in stark contrast, with her head down and looking weary this morning. Wielding her walker down the ramp towards the parking lot more like a wagon than a chariot——strictly for utilitarian purposes, her complaints, leaden on the damp morning air, heavy with rare self-pity, reached me before she did.

"Nobody was wake to zip up my dress I didn't want to wake them up. My fingers are stiff and these old shoes done got too big again. "

Sara had not come to stay the night so I had to get out of the car to situate Mama. No two-step and we're in routine this morning. Getting Mama into the car was clumsy and labored. I had to give her an extra push to get her rump on the back seat of the car. Even her walker felt heavier when I put it in the trunk, remembering to remove her Sunday black patent leather pocketbook off of the handle and place it beside her on the seat.

"This is when I feel like crying," she said, closing her eyes and screwing her face up to cry. Mama wasn't a crier, so when she did you knew her spirits were low.

From the rearview mirror, I could see that her face was dry and ashy and tears pricking her eyes had already spilled. When I stopped in front of the church, I turned and faced her locking eyes and told her she looked peachy keen. I took the oil I keep just for her out of the glove compartment, oiled her face and hands, zipped up her dress and told her she was the cutest 96-year-old ever. Stuffing Shake Shack napkins into the toes of the shoes that were too big this week and swung her legs out of the car. I got her walker from the trunk and placed it in front of her. She eased herself down, steadying herself with the walker, and out of the car. Her mood lightened as the sun's lazy rays pierced the clouds. Mama and her walker with the patent-leather pocketbook hanging on its

## TENNYBOOTS!

handle ambled towards the church doors flung open by the deacon who saw us pull up. Pity party averted. Phew.

Mama's 96th year tumbled into her 97th and slid into her 98th like a runner at second base. She is beat-up and dusty but still in the game. She is showing no signs of slowing down. Her promise to live to be 103 is marching towards reality. It freaks me out and blesses me at the same time. If she lives to be 103, I will be 70. Caring for her will surely kill me by then and she will step over me and find a new caregiver as she has promised to do. Those revelations I had at the end of her 94th year about how it was me who had to adjust and the blessings that were forthcoming when I allowed her to do her thing—malarkey! That was nothing more than nostalgic reflections at the end of a year. Mama continued to do to suit herself whether it was prudent or safe or rude. Between the highs and the lows, Mama's outright abuse at times and my reactions to her have taken a hell of a toll on a daughter who only wished to shepherd a mother to the end with dignity. I wish everyone could experience the joys of a parent living such a long full life on her terms—but without the physiological damage it does to the person toiling to facilitate the living. Caring for Mama taxes all of me. It is as though I have two selves each demanding my attention. But one must take a backseat to the urgency of the other.

My control of Mama's money continued to be an issue that created much anxiety for her and headaches for me. I paid her rent and other bills, bought her food and supplies and clothing and gave her $100 per week for pocket money. Although I had to supplement what she received from social security and her small office-cleaning pension check, sometimes that was not enough for her. During those times she demanded more. As check day neared instead of discussing the need for some more spending that month, Mama's plotting would rev up. We could never have a civil unemotional conversation about her wanting more money. She would work herself up to where she considered any response by me a rejection. At those times she would threaten to, "Call the law," on me and watch them, "Haul your ass to court." Other times her threats were to, "Go the bank and tell them you won't give me my card." Ignoring Mama's money demands were out of the question. I couldn't ignore her even if I wanted to. At these times, her phone-calling prowess was on point. No operators refused to connect her with me, and she would call me all night and throughout the day pleading and then demanding me to give her the $500, or whatever amount of money she wanted. She would lobby my sister, or my cousin, Myrna, her grandchildren and even some of the people on the bench, to tell me to give her *her damn money*. No amount of rational discussion would do. In the past when I would give in to her demands to give her the cash or her cards, both would disappear. Sometimes she attempted to hide the money or the cards and hid it from herself, or gave it away. At those times, she would boast that she didn't need me to take care of her because she could care for herself. A few times, at the point of losing it, I would give in and give her the cash and tell her not to call me when she ran out of food or needed something. As always, before the week was over, the money was gone and she had run out of food. Proud and not willing to admit that I had been right, she would prove to me she did not need me. She would rather do without than to call and admit defeat. The great-grandchildren would let me know that Mama had no money, and I would buy food and send it to her by my daughter, or Ashley, who lived with her. With the caveat that they not tell her it came from me.

Obama caused one of our biggest fights over money in her 97th year. Well not actually Obama but an Obama ring Mama saw at the Harlem Mart and wanted at the very moment I was away, and would not wait to own it. I was over 800 miles away when I got the call.

"Ju, I'm gone borrow $50 from Ashley and $50 from Linda to buy me a ring."

"Ma, what kind of ring? Is it *hot*? Do you know the person selling it?

"No, it ain't hot, the man at the Mart got it. You know him, *so and so's* wife, he goes to my church."

"Ma, I do not understand who you are talking about, but if the ring ain't hot then it can wait until I get back in two days."

"No. Judy. The man got the ring now. I want to get it now."

"Ma, is the ring a one of a kind? Does anyone know this guy? Is the ring real?"

"Yeah, Judy. It's a real gold Obama ring. I can't describe it dammit. I want my money to buy the ring now."

"Ma, let me call someone and ask about it? Does anyone know this guy?"

"Shit Judy, you gone give me my money. I'm gone borrow it till you get back."

"No Ma, don't go borrowing no money. You don't..."

I heard the phone click. Five minutes later my grandniece calls.

"Ju, did you say that I should lend Mama $50 for a ring?"

"Ashley, I am so confused. Mama called me and told me that she was going to buy a ring. I asked her if it's *hot* that she can't wait until I return. What, pray tell is all the rigamarole about this ring?"

Ashley didn't understand either and told Mama that she would not lend her the $50 until someone checked out the man selling the "pure gold Obama ring" for $100 cash, and that I would be back in two days she could wait until then.

I had called Mama's friend Linda and asked if she knew anything about the ring. She knew the guy but he was not at the shop that day, she said she would check it out the next day. Next thing I knew I got a call from my niece, Pinky, Mama's oldest grandchild and fierce protector of Mama against me. Mama was always carrying bones and bringing bones between Pinky and me or reporting some allegedly egregious thing that I had done to her. With Mama's passion for dividing and conquering us, the thing I had said or done grew in the telling to the extent that when *my words or actions* returned to me, as they always did, in the heat of an argument, my part was unrecognizable.

# TENNYBOOTS!

As it was with Pinky's text: "Ju, why you got Mama out here taking up a collection like she's in church begging for a love offering to buy the Obama ring? Where's her money? This is no way to treat her, you need to be ashamed of yourself."

For years, I grieved each false attack and allegation against me about how I failed to do right by Mama. I felt obligated to prove that I had not done the thing that Mama or family members had accused me of doing to Mama. My daughter, who has a very healthy way of staying above the fray in a family known for drama, finally convinced me that I did not have to acknowledge the attacks. I was learning to let them roll off my back, but although I did not respond to Pinky's text, the thought that Mama was taking a collection on the bench distressed me.

By the time I got home two days later, Mama had bought the Obama ring, and it had immediately gotten stuck on her finger. Not wanting to tell anyone that the damn thing was stuck, she had soaped it, and twisted it, and rubbed alcohol on it, until the brass of the *gold* Obama ring had turned green in places. Right before I was about to take her to the emergency room to get the damn ring cut off of her, it slid off her finger. When I left her apartment to pay off the collection money for the ring, I suggested that she not put the ring back on until it was sized for her finger. Chagrined, she bristled at my suggestion and formed a retort, but either shame or exhaustion trapped the words in her mouth; I got out of the door without hearing a peep from Mama.

Her debts paid; I went to see the man at the Harlem Mart who sold her the ring. The guy sold belts and other brass items. He claimed that he never told Mama the ring was gold and recounted how Mama would come by sometimes and look at the jewelry in his case. She had been wanting the Obama ring for some time. He promised to resize it for her. Like so many things Mama did now, it baffled me why her pining for the Obama ring reached its climax on that day and she would not be put off. The Obama ring soon became a favorite piece of her jewelry. For her 98th birthday, I got her a birthday card signed by Obama. She was beside herself with excitement when she received it and treasured it. I hung it in her room where she could look at it often.

# TENNYBOOTS!

"How did Obama know it was my birthday, Ju. Who told him?"

"It must have been the ring Mama. It must have been the ring."

When I left her that day, she was looking from the ring to the card from the card to the ring, as though each held a clue.

Mama's yearly birthday celebrations are a big deal. The community comes together to celebrate in the backyard of the projects. We have cake and ice cream and people bring cooked food. Mama gets gifts and dollar bills pinned on her with stick pins. Mama loves the money and attention. All of Mama's young men would come to show Mama some love. She loved their fawning over her. I would dress her up for the occasion, wrap a cape around her if the October weather was chilly and place a birthday crown on her head. Mama would turn another year closer to 100, the oldest person on her side of the projects. We would stay out until dark and sing all three versions of Happy Birthday to her by the light of the candles.

As the countdown to her 100th year began, Russell planned a big 99th birthday for Mama at Harlem Shake Shack where her title of Ms. Harlem Classic reigned in perpetuity. She had asked me to buy her some boots, "With a heel, not those old lady boots you usually get me—something dressy." I obliged. She planned on wearing her roaring 20s dress and a black jacket threaded with gold lame. She would sport a black and purple Fascinator on her head. Googling "Jazzy Boots with heel," I bought the boots online because her favorite shoe store in the neighborhood had made way for development in the ongoing gentrification of Harlem. A post-it on my laptop reminded me to order them a half size larger for the swelling of her feet that had shoes fitting one week and not the next. The Black leather boots with a two and a half-inch heel—way too high for me—were just right for Mama, who still attempted to wear heels to church every Sunday when she could. They were the pull on-push down type. Mama pulled them on easily the night of the party. And pushed them down to a stylish position near her calves. Dressed up and her walker decorated with gold ribbons tied

# TENNYBOOTS!

to huge gold mylar balloons broadcasting her 99 years of living, she sauntered into Harlem Shake to a crowded room, once again the belle of the ball.

The party was loud and lively and Mama entertained and enjoyed every minute. Russell had brought large poster boards with her picture on it and the guests signed their names and wishes for her in felt pens. A 99th birthday was no runner-up affair to Mama, she embraced it fully on its own terms and enjoyed her guests, the attention and gifts. My sister, nephew, and nieces came up from North Carolina for the occasion. Mama received a lot of cash and was thrilled, because money makes her smile. I took the money that her guests had pinned on her along with the gifts in cards and secured it for her. She had counted it several times and knew the exact amount I was holding for her. She also had stashed some away without my knowledge.

Sunday morning after the big party Mama would not miss church. When I met her on the ramp coming down to the parking lot that morning, she was wearing a pair of fake uggs and wielding her walker with a pair of shoes and her dress boots atop the plastic seat.

"Ju, can you put these boots on me? I been trying for half a hour."

"Where my birthday money? I want to buy me a shade for my living room, a curtain, and some other things. But I want to buy it myself. Maybe you can take me up to that place on 125th Street. They say I can get the shade there if I bring the old roller with me. "

I took the boots from Mama, helped her onto the seat with her legs dangling from the car and removed the furry fake uggs boots that she had worn downstairs. I pulled, I jiggled, I twisted and turned them, but those jazzy high-heeled boots were not getting on Mama that day. A muscle cramp seized my back and made me jump to straighten it out.

"Ma, I'm sorry, you will need to wear those shoes you brought down. I cannot get these boots on you today. "

# TENNYBOOTS!

I said this as I was putting the walker in the car and walking back around to close Mama's door.

"Judy you *can* get them on me. You didn't try hard enough. Give them to me." She was yelling.

I started to put the jazzy boots in the trunk with the walker, but she demanded I give them to her at her seat. All the way to church, I heard Mama in the back seat, *cussing* me out while trying to get those boots on. When we stopped in front of the church it was early, and Mama demanded again that I put the boots on her. Squatting down in a way that would not cramp my back this time, I tried again, knowing how much she wanted to show off in church, but could not get those boots on her. I cursed myself for not getting a side zipper that would have been easier to get on her. But the side zipper boots were flat or too high. I got her out of the car and placed the walker in front of her.

"Where my boots give em to me. "

By this time, she was crying, and I felt like shit. When I was in seventh grade, I had bought myself a pair of black, rubber, Russian Boots, and I wore them for a month with no rain in sight. I knew the feeling. She slung her four boots atop of her walker and took herself into the church using her walker like a department store shopping cart.

Her deacon called to say that they would bring her home after a meeting. When she got home, she called to ask me if I could take her to get her shade and roller on Tuesday. I said yes.
On that Tuesday after work, I called her and told her to come down. She still had an attitude with me.

"Hey Ma."

"Hi Judy, you got my money?"

"Yep." The "Judy" was a dead giveaway that she was salty with me.

"Give it to me then."

"Can you wait until we get into the car?"

"How much is it?"

"The same amount it was at your party, Ma. It hasn't grown or shrunk."

"Humph, I don't know that. Money seems to walk round here."

I ignore her dig at me. She's a sight today. From her head to her toe, she is sporting a gay assortment of colors and textures and patterns, which conjures up images of the old rag man whose horse-drawn wagon was a staple in our 1950s Harlem neighborhood. He had stacks and stacks of all color rags in his wagon and would begin hollering his pitch half way up the block, "Rag Man, Rag Man." Now, for the life of me, I can't remember what the rag man did with the rags. Was he collecting rags or selling them? The horse had wanted to part of the spectacle and stood with blinders and sometimes a feed bag looking straight ahead. I was going to ask Mama, but she has taken herself to the back door of the car and is fumbling at the open door trying to get herself in without waiting for help—a signal that she's ornery today. At 99, her upper body strength is that of a woman half her age and she has pulled herself onto the seat by the overhead strap, using her walker as a footstool in place of my bracing her. The walker rolls away at the moment she needs it most, and it's a good thing I expected all of it and am standing close by to heave her the rest of the way into the car.

"Hey, hey, hold it, you 'bout to throw my ass out the car."
"No Ma, I'm throwing your ass in the car."
"Who ask you to help. I didn't need the help. "
"I'll remember that next time Mama."
"That's okay, you gotta get old one day too, Judy. God don't like ugly and he ain't too fond of pretty. You'll see."

# TENNYBOOTS!

By this time, I'm in the front seat and am getting ready to drive off after collapsing her walker and placing it in the back

"Where my money Ju?"

I take the money out of my pocket and hand it to her in the back seat, all $335 of it. I found out at the party that she had already given some of her birthday money to Sara, and I imagine some of it she stashed away before I gathered the rest. She grabs the money from my hand that is twisted awkwardly reaching behind me to the back seat, and I hear her arranging her bills and counting it. From the rearview mirror I can see her stuffing bills in various coat pockets.

"Ma, do you need me to help put your money away?"

"No. I got it in my pockets."

We pull up to the store now and there's no parking right in front. There's a hydrant a few yards away, enough room for me to park at the hydrant while getting Mama out and into the store.

"Ma, you are going in by yourself, right?"

"I don't know. I guess. You ain't coming in with me?"

The bravado she's had for days gives way to some uneasiness that I can't define.

"Let's see. I don't have a parking spot. Let me bring you into the store and we'll see if someone can help you."

Mama gets out of the car; I bring her walker around along with the roller shade. I stuff the roller shade into the canvas bag hanging on the walker and secure it between the straps. Mama walks in the wrong direction, I turn her and point toward the store. Side by side, Mama in her rag-man colored clothing and the pole of the roller shade protruding from the bag, resemble a Maypole about to be dressed. I turn on the hazard lights, lock the car doors and catch up with Mama just as she gets to the door of the store. She looks uncertain as we get into the store. A nice woman comes over and offers her help. I told her that my mother wanted some things and that I am parked near a hydrant and would return to check on her. She asked Mama what was she looking for.

As I was about to leave, I heard Mama's reply.

"Oh… I don't know. I want some curtains…and a shade for my roller," Mama said, not seeming so sure of herself anymore, while fumbling with her canvas bag to take the roller out.

The woman said, "Oh no dear, we haven't made those here in over 25 years."

Embarrassed that she had been wrong, Mama looked around to see if I was still in the store. I was. But I acted as though the problem was the store's and not Mama's insistence that they made roller shades.

"Miss, do you know of any stores around here that still cut shades to fit the roller?"

While waiting for the answer, I took the roller from the bag relieving Mama of her embarrassment and the Maypole at the same time. The sales woman didn't know of any stores in the neighborhood that still made shades from old rollers. She steered Mama toward the back to look for some curtains.

I returned about 20 minutes later and Mama and the saleswoman were at the cashier. Mama looked relieved and accomplished. And maybe a tad bit overwhelmed. I felt sorry for her. Maybe I should have tried harder to find a parking spot.

"Hey Mama, did you get what you wanted?"

She exhaled and smiled with me for the first time that day. I reached out and gave her a hug and said, "Go Mama, you did it!"

Another smile! The saleswoman realizing her part in Mama's success looked satisfied. Spending less than $100, Mama bought several lime green washcloths, a bedspread, a set of sheets, and a package of curtains hanging in a big white bag on the handle of her walker. Triumphant over shopping alone, for the first time since I had picked her up, her mood was light and gay like her ragman colored clothing. Contented with herself, she gathered her change, stuffed it into her pockets, and we walked to the car together as dusk was descending on 125th Street in Harlem. I put her packages into the car, along with her walker, and then came around to help her in. This time she was waiting for me.

****

# TENNYBOOTS!

## THE FINAL CHAPTER

Tuesday, April 16, 2019, was two hours old, when six months shy of her 100th birthday, Mama died as she had fought to live—like a big girl, seeking no one's help or accommodation. But she was never alone—ever. We had already released her from holding fast to this realm for her sake. During her last 16 days we let her know if she were ready, then so were we. Our aim was to liberate her. But the Ancestors were with her and did not leave. They kept watch over her, from the pink-light-comfort of her Momma and her sister, Fan, and the spirited mischief of my sister, Gay, to the matriarchal presence of her oldest sister, Aunt Mildred. Two days prior to her death, annoyed they had taken her shoes and would not return them, she cried out: "Mildred, Gay, give me my shoes," while trying to snatch them from the air, in a game of *Saluchi* she had not sanctioned. I knew that because in the unkind voice Mama reserved for me—or Ashley, she had stopped pleading and demanded that Gay and Aunt Mildred give her back her things *now*. Clue number one that the end was near: where her mother and sister, Fannie, were comforting Spirits, Gay and Aunt Mildred were becoming impatient—either she was going with them or she wasn't. Gay had a way with Mama, as her favorite child, she could get her to act and do things no one else could. Aunt Mildred, the family Matriarch did not dabble in the province of uncertainties, she spoke and things happened. I had missed the signs. Gay would bring Mama in. How perfect.

"Judy Edwards?" I recognized the number from St. Luke's on my caller ID.

"Yes?"

"This is Dr... calling from St Luke's Hospital."

"Yes, I see. Is Mama being difficult?"

"Er...no. I am sorry to say that she—"

"She died? Oh no… I will be right up."

    Not five minutes before the phone rang, the black and white poster board photo of Mama beaming, that was sitting on my windowsill, fell over. Was it at precisely the time of her death? Had the specter of her spirit exiting her body come by to say she was leaving? I would love to say this. But without being certain or having proof, I resist scripting her dying as she resisted me scripting her living. Whether she did or didn't I can't be certain. But I believe it to be true.

    Mama *dead*? *Gone*? Wow. Even though a Seer had told me on Saturday that she wouldn't make it to Easter Sunday, a week away, I couldn't believe that Mama would really leave, and now harder to believe that she was dead. What brought her into the hospital had not been acute. The doctors expected her to recover. They wanted to discharge her to a nursing home in the Bronx, the night before. They needed me to sign the release, and I had stayed away on Monday, holding out for a better choice. But now Mama was dead, who was I without her? Ten years we had done this. For ten long years. And now she was gone… I couldn't cry. I felt good about it in ways. For her sake and mine—because the next chapter would make her miserable.

    I called Cricket and Pinky. Pinky called Ashley and Asia and Russell. Russell brought Emi. Cricket called Edie. Ashley called Nikki and Raven and Sara; ten of us stood around the hospital bed where Mama's body lay waiting for us to say our last goodbyes before her body got cold. Beneath the body bag, covered by a sheet, you could see the outlines of her hands crossed over her chest in the classic death repose, her face and head exposed, looking serene

# TENNYBOOTS!

and unbothered. Her ebony skin held no traces of the lines on her forehead that were only just beginning to embed themselves into permanent markers of old age. The soft plastic body bag was the whitest white I'd ever seen. It was glowing—as though an infinite number of the brightest stars had replaced each plastic molecule to illuminate the darkness for her journey. The face was vintage Mama. Unchanged, it was the face I had run the back of my hand over so many times, comforting her, caressing her, and sometimes trying to tell if she was breathing. This time it was clear. No breath, faint or otherwise, would ever again cause her chest to rise, in the ritual practiced by those who care for the aged and the ill. It was finally over. Mama was dead. The woman I knew before I knew myself—was dead.

It had all began four months ago, on the third day of December before 2018 had said its goodbyes. Ashley found her. When her children were getting ready for school that morning Mama had not interacted with them and that bothered her. Ashley has the events of that morning etched in her mind, she would describe it over and over that day: "We had a morning routine. Every morning the girls went in Mama's room to show her their hair and uniforms and she would say to both, love you, and to Ryder—whose spirited nature didn't always jibe with the school's rules—be good, and give them a kiss! Riley could give or take the kiss; she waves bye but Ryder faithfully kisses her! This day she didn't wake up when Ryder said goodbye. It seemed strange. I hadn't brought her soda she had asked me to bring the night before, so I came in from taking them to school with the soda and went to wake her up, and to tell her I got her ginger-ale. But she didn't wake up after countless times of me screaming Ma Ma Ma MAAAA! So, I went to where Asia was sleeping, to get her to help me. I said, 'Bro, Mama isn't waking up, but she's breathing.' Asia said, 'Call Judy.' So, I went back to check again and Mama was having a seizure so I screamed, 'Asia get up now!' Asia came running and we grabbed her and tried to hold on to her but she began to slip off the bed so I wrapped my legs around her body and pulled her up, and then we called you. In the time that it took you to come, she had about seven seizures. I was never so scared in my life."

# TENNYBOOTS!

Rushing from my apartment four blocks away, I called for an ambulance. Leaving my car double parked outside, I ran into the building. By the time I got upstairs the ambulance still hadn't arrived, even though we can see the Fire Department on 5th Avenue from Mama's window. We called again, and finally EMTs, police officers, and Fire Department paramedics all arrived at the same time. They worked on Mama for a while, determining that it didn't appear to be a stroke, but seizures, as Ashley had thought. They took her to St. Luke's hospital with Ashley and Asia riding in the ambulance; I followed behind in my car. On the way to the hospital, I called my daughter, Cricket, who worked nearby, and she met us at the hospital. Mama wasn't responding well. I called Dr. Yoe to come to the hospital. The doctors asked what did Mama want, was she a DNR, did she have a MOLST? I hadn't heard of a MOLST before. It was a health care declaration that went into the what ifs.

We were at that point and they wanted to know Mama's wishes. She always said that when it's her time to go, let her go because she's been ready. I shared that with the doctors. Then the doctor asked about intubation. Would she want a tube shoved in her mouth and down her throat? That threw me, because I had just answered that she wanted no extraordinary measures. They wanted to intubate her because in her condition they didn't trust that she would breathe on her own. Whoa! Intubation sounded very serious. I didn't want to do it. Mama didn't want to, "Be on no machines." I had to honor her wishes. When I pressed the emergency room doctor for the trajectory of what would happen if they didn't intubate her, he said that she would likely die. All four of us were at Mama's bedside. Asia and Ashley screamed out, "Nooooo! That's our grandmother." Their response only made my decision harder. I looked over at my daughter, Cricket, the steady one, and she too was already crying and shaking her head, No. Nothing in my life had prepared me for this. Held captive in the gaze of my daughter and great-nieces, I questioned my capacity to make life and death decisions. They were watching my every move. I believe that had I sneezed they would have set upon me. We moved to the hallway off the emergency room. It was frigid. Now my teeth were chattering from the cold. It was too much. Who the hell was I to determine today that Mama should die? But it was according to her wishes. It sounded easy enough when we talked about in the abstract. As simple as a Venn diagram, if... then... but now a murky indecision sat beside the girls, daring me to follow Mama's wishes. It was too much. I needed air, but the doctors were waiting on me, and every minute counted they had said.

Thank God for Dr. Yoe, her hematologist. Dr. Yoe's treatment for Mama was always more aggressive than the staff doctors at the hospital. He knew her well and had witnessed to her grit and mettle many times over. Dr. Yoe came in asking for me: "Judy, they want to intubate her. I say yes. Give her everything and we withdraw what doesn't work. But at least we give her a fighting chance. She's a fighter. Let's let her decide by her fight. She's a fighter. And she's strong."

"Whatever you say, Dr. Yoe." The girls let out a collective sigh.

I was grateful for Dr. Yoe. Cricket and Ashley and Asia were all watching me like a hawk (as Mama would say) and didn't appear to trust that I'd decide what they wanted. I hoped to honor Mama's wishes, but I could see in their faces that neither one of them was ready for Mama to go without a fight for her life.

That's how Mama wound up on a ventilator. Word got out, and the family made their way to the hospital. By nighttime, me and 24 of Mama's grandchildren and great grandchildren were sitting around the hospital expecting Mama to die, but praying that she lived. The diagnosis was that Mama had a UTI that made her septic. The sepsis had caused the seizures. It didn't appear that she had epilepsy. For three days, lying in the ICU, intubated and hooked up to myriad machines, Mama was out of it. While we believed that she was giving us signs that she knew we were there, it was just what we were hoping. The doctors ordered a modified brain scan and pronounced that there was very little brain activity. Word got out that Mama was brain dead, which she wasn't. Dr. Yoe requested a full 24-hour scan, which showed activity. She remained intubated. On the third day, Mama squeezed open one eye and then the other but only for a moment—until Ryder came. Ryder is our theatrical child. She's also Mama's best buddy. Since birth. She was standing at the foot of her bed and was fake crying and saying, "Oh Mama, I miss you so much, please Mama wake up and let us know that you're okay." On cue, and recognizing her pal, Ryder's voice, Mama's eyes stretched open, walling around unfocused with the whites of her eyes exposed. Ryder jumped back hollering, "Oh my god, what's she doing, what's she doing." Mama scared the crap out of Ryder that day, but she opened her eyes and kept them open after that. With Mama's increasing consciousness came her resistance. She gnawed on the tube in her mouth that attached to the ventilator, pulled at it, and aggravated it until they had to restrain her hands. This was a good sign, they said. They needed her to be aware enough to take her off of the ventilator. Fighting back showed that she knew the tube was in her mouth and wanted it out. I lived at the hospital. Cricket came every day. Russell came often. Pinky, Ashley and Asia alternated days. Russell and his fiancé, Emi, and Pinky came two nights and allowed me to go home and sleep in a bed instead of the chairs in Mama's hospital room. Mama's other grandchildren came too. Thirteen-year-old Sydney, whose school was close by came every day after school and sat with Mama until six or seven o'clock.

Removing a tube, (Extubation) is as serious a decision as putting one in. A machine counted her breaths. There was a magic number she needed to take on her own, and when she reached it, they would remove the tube. On December 7th, the fourth day, after morning rounds the doctors on the floor in ICU decided that they would remove the tube. They warned us that if she couldn't sustain a certain amount of breaths per minute, they would consider putting the tube back in. I had taken to sending out text blasts to keep the large number of people concerned about Mama informed. Here are the blasts from day four.

*Friday morning 10:19 update: Good morning all. After yesterday's post we had a positively harrowing day. With blood pressure spikes, different medications, and disorientation from so much going on, Mama became physically combative with superhuman strength. So much so, I hauled ass out of there at 8:00 p.m. not to return yet. The full night of sleep in my bed was necessary and has restored me. Thank God and Ancestors for Cricket, who calmed her by singing "a Tisket a Tasket" and then she could leave at last; and for Pinky, who stayed the night and weathered the storm. Her nurse, Adaly,*

# TENNYBOOTS!

called just now. The issue today is to get her off the ventilator. Every time they administer the CPAP to get her breathing on her own, her pressure spikes and they have to put it back on. Ashley is there now. I will replace her. We are still limiting visitors to keep her calm. She needs to be able to *breathe fully on her own*. Sooner the better. Thank you all for prayers, vibes, healing wishes and support. This has been a week of lows, highs and uncertainties for sure; But friends, family, church family and other have sustained us. The ICU has been excellent in their care. Much love.

*Friday Evening Update 5:50 p.m.:* Good evening, the targeted prayers and thoughts and vibes are working very well. Ashley took the morning shift and found Mama calm and exhausted and resting. She reported that they were going to extubate Mama. They did. But Mama's breathing was very labored with wheezing. So, they re-intubated her. Cricket and Ashley attended the extubation and reported that Mama wasn't ready, she was gulping air. The Drs believe that her throat was swollen from all the moving around (remember Mama was a kung fu fighter yesterday.) She has been resting today. I didn't have to bail on her. Sara is with her now. Ashley is coordinating times to be with her. Asia and Raven are to follow. I'll go back tonight for the overnight shift. They are monitoring her mental state now. She is not knowingly engaging, but will follow commands when the nurse asks to open her mouth, etc. The hope now is that her mental state stays on par and they will give steroids to shrink airway swelling and then try to extubate again. Five days in, afraid of what comes next and traumatized by what has already happened, yours truly has fled several times—but remains hopeful that Mama will do to suit herself— whatever that is. For once, the family is working together and we think we are ready for whatever next is. My strong suit is not watching the numbers on the monitors go up and down like the Dow Jones. I will leave that for the professionals and am sitting tonight with blinders and headphones. As I've often told Mama-she ain't going to kill me. I got 33 years to get where she is. Lol. Until the next update. Ase.

*Saturday, December 8th 1:45 pm update comes from the Church of the Grotto where I ducked into on 114th street;* not for its brand of Catholicism, but for refuge from the cold and the pervasive sickness of the hospital. There's a huge Grotto at the front of the church, and a group is doing a homily? All I can understand is the response that sounds like, "Pray for us," punctuating the end of every sentence. There is not much new today. Mama rested until the maintenance people, speaking as though they were playing dominoes at a card table in the streets, woke her at 3 a.m. From that point on

# TENNYBOOTS!

*she was restless. She would throw up her hands demanding without words that I get her out of there. And I guess that is the story-the tediousness of it all. She has to be able to cough up secretions to breathe on her own. My friend, CEO of a "Best Nursing Home in the City" says it's hard work. She's not there today. Maybe tomorrow. She's still responding to commands. Putting up two fingers when asked. Seeing her raising those two crooked fingers let me know she still has fight left. I'm just sad that this is so hard for her. Last night, Asia had rolled her hair in yellow sponge curlers. She almost seemed at home preparing for church the next morning. I read from the Psalms for her. I also sang off beat some hymns we like: I Come To The Garden Alone and Jesus Keeps Me Near The Cross. She calmed and her heart rate and blood pressure lowered. The loudmouth nurses are back on the floor. No rest for the weary or the hospital patient. Peace.*

*Monday: it will happen today. Stay tuned.*

*Monday: She's doing fine. She only has a mask now. Oxygen through the nose next. Keep it going. All the doctors and staff here are ecstatic. Thanks to everyone. While she was smiling with the nurses and doctors initially, after they cleaned out her throat through her nose and did some other thing to release secretions, she became combative. When they left, she whispered in a very hoarse voice, "They are trying to kill me." It took a while for me to calm her down. They are doing it again but I warned her of what was coming and asked her to behave. She rolled her eyes. She's come a long way this week. We don't know what's next, but in attitude she's vintage Flo. When the doctor asked her what she wanted she replied, "I want to get out of here!" Thank you for those prayers. We hope for sustained breathing in the low 20s with no buildup of $CO2$. And most importantly Mama's patience with the process. She has no idea.*

*10th day update: 2 steps forward, 1 step back. On the 2nd day off the respirator, Mama's breathing became labored. She had several nebulizer treatments all day. By 9:00pm she became combative, and paranoid—refusing to eat and refusing her treatments. Then she planned her escape. She tried mightily to get out of bed and to leave the hospital. I finally left around midnight. I heard she got some sleep but is fighting everyone again today. She believes they are trying to kill her. And if you (family and friends) don't help her get out, you are aiding and abetting them. I've put a call into the doctors. Before the breathing issues had started, the plan was to get her walking on her walker. This has been overwhelming to us, and I am sure for you too, so I will stop the daily updates. But will respond if asked via text. I am taking a break*

# TENNYBOOTS!

*from the hospital today. Thank you for your continued prayers, thoughts, chants, etc. Love, Judy*

On the 13th day we moved by transport from the hospital to a nursing home at 7 P.M. Mama required temporary rehabilitation because the long days in the hospital had weakened her, and she needed to learn to walk with assistance of her walker again. Relieved that Mama would not be going directly home from the hospital, but wary of how she would react to being in a nursing home, I set about choosing one that would resemble her community, and also meet her needs. It also had to be near her home, where family members, Mama's friends and church family could get to her easily. But the best Nursing Homes, save St. Mary's a facility for People With Aids, were not in Harlem. One of my best friends, Diane, resides at Amsterdam House, on 112th Street and Amsterdam Avenue, where they take good care of the residents. It was number one on my list of five that the social worker had me choose, but there was no room. I settled on a nursing home in Harlem, with the caveat that Mama ain't no Cadillac, she's a Chevrolet. They don't have the newest furnishings or the best reputation, but they had a lot of Black workers and residents—so that Mama would feel comfortable—and they sponsored a Sunday morning church program. Mama was so ready to leave the hospital, although I later realized that she believed that she was going home.

Mama was still confused, but when she realized that the double room they assigned her was in a nursing home, her joy of being released from the hospital turned to despair. She took to her bed, slept and refused to do anything for four days. The admission director's promise to find a lively roommate for Mama influenced my decision to choose this particular facility. She had made good on that promise, and Mama's roommate, a heavyset woman, 15 years her junior, using a wheelchair but never confined, was *in every peas pickin'* and made Mama one of her *projects*. We called her our bonus. She loved to eat, and we showered her with care packages to show our gratitude. Although she had children, she hardly received visitors herself.

# TENNYBOOTS!

On the fifth day, the therapists from the *rehab* department, a phenomenal group of professionals, insisted that Mama get up and try. Try, she did. In time, Mama had regained what she had lost, plus more and won the hearts of the therapists and the staff.

Church had always been a big part of Mama's life. Reverend L.C. Simon baptized her at seven-years-old, at the Little Mount Zion Baptist Church in Opelousas, Louisiana. Mama was so happy to be baptized that she wanted to look her absolute best. Her best was a smallish, fancy blue dress—woman's clothes—that her Aunt Annie had handed down from the white folks she worked for to Mama's oldest sister, Mildred. The dress had hung off of Mama like a kindergarten kid in the dress-up corner; but she was proud to wear it after she emerged from the baptismal pool, even though its extra yardage dragged behind her like a train of a wedding dress. Like many a Black, migrating Baptist, once Mama would get to a new place, she would accept a local church's invitation to join a new church home. In Harlem, that Church was the LaGree Baptist Church, a South Carolina congregation that Ann Salley, her neighbor, attended. Mama's membership equaled my age, I had never known her to not be a member of LaGree. Every Sunday, I would dress Mama up in her Sunday best to attend the services. The residents wore their church hats and church clothes. Mama refused to go without me, so each Sunday I sat with her. Some days I enjoyed the service. Pinky joined us for a few Sundays. And one Sunday, her boys from the neighborhood, Egbert and Shickhouse, came through. The incentive I used to keep Mama steady in the hard work of rehabilitation was a promise to take her to LaGree on the first Sunday of the new year. Mama kept working hard. And I kept my promise.

On the first Sunday of 2019, Mama's 100th year on earth, I dressed her in winter white and wheeled her the six blocks from the facility to her church on Lenox Avenue. Mama looked nothing like what she had been through, and those members of the congregation, who had not visited her at the nursing home, couldn't stop exclaiming how good she looked. Basking in the love of her church home, Mama was the happiest I had seen her in a long time. Her church family fawned over her: they spoke their gratitude for God's Grace on her life from the pulpit and the Minister of Music played a medley of songs just for her. It filled my heart with joy for

# TENNYBOOTS!

Mama as I sat by her side. Her fighting spirit had shaken off death's certain grip and lived to tell the story. Mama's testimony filled in the details. She said she had been present with God and her recent Ancestors, but she they only allowed her to see His feet and layers of clothing, she could not see His face. Her Momma and sisters and Gay were all there, and she could sense they were happy to see her, but she could only see their backs. God had sent her home to finish her business, there was something she needed to do. So, she returned to us but soon she would leave again. Her church family didn't want to hear no death talk, everyone was planning for her 100th birthday in October. Mama laughed with them and said, "We'll see."

The countdown to Mama's last days began on April Fool's Day, the 21st day of Lent of 2019; two weeks to the day that Mama came home from the nursing home. It was the second anniversary of my dear friend Randy's death, and I deemed it a sign. Mama had tolerated the 100 days that Medicare would pay for a skilled nursing facility rather well. Although she mostly preferred to stay in her room, the staff could coax her into the recreation area, where she sat, read the paper, and watched television. A wonderful social worker named, Olefia, was fond of Mama and would braid her hair for her and cheer her up. Then, one night, an Aide discovered Mama on the floor near her bed. No one knew if she had fallen or slid off the edge while sitting on her bed. The Rehab had been okay, but there had been issues. Mama had gotten another UTI and was having a bout of delirium. The nurses called it *Sundowners*, but I insisted that they test for a UTI, and sure enough, she had one. Mama wanted to leave that day and got as far as the elevator trying to escape. She was hell bent on leaving and was fighting anyone that tried to stop her. Even Cricket could not calm Mama down. She pushed her wheelchair to the elevator, yelling at me to either help her leave, or leave her alone. She was fighting everyone who tried to reason with her. She was so strong and has much stamina in these bouts. By nine that evening, I couldn't take any more. My despair at Mama in a fit of delirium was not as dire as it was the first time it happened, but the threat of it becoming permanent always scared me to death. There was no way that I would care for a combative, demented Mama at her apartment. If we ever got to that point, I would have to place her in a Nursing Home permanently, against her wishes. Mama was also too vain to *live* that way. Being seen in the wheelchair embarrassed her. And she would always blame it on me, telling people that I had her in that old thing, never that she needed to be there until she had regained her strength. I had all of this weighing on me when I accepted the head nurse's assurance that they could handle Mama, that she would be okay.

The next morning, I returned very early to check on Mama. When I got off the elevator, I saw her. She was one of two residents sitting in the recreation room. They had pushed her into the corner with the table pushed up against her chair to restrain her. She had not slept all night and looked as though she had been in the fight of her life. I could tell she had flung her Ensure back at them, because her hair, face and clothing were full of specks of dried white liquid. When Mama realized that the person approaching her was me, she reached out and began to cry:

"Judy, look what they done to me. I can't get out of here, they won't let me leave."

I lost it seeing Mama like that. I flung the table away from her and kicked the chair that was barricading her way out. I wet a napkin at the sink near the microwave and wiped Mama's face clean, and told her not to worry, I would take care of it. Once Mama had regained a sense of empowerment by my being there, and with no regard for protocol or convention, I cursed everyone out! I had learned how to *cuss* well in law school, forever shredding the stigma that Black folks attached to cursing and sounding *ignorant*. When I look back on that day, that I had those four-letter words flying like a rich white man with privilege still brings me untold satisfaction. I had zero desire that those folks would respect Mama because of her daughter's quiet eloquence or profession, but that they would treat her as any one of them would want their own mother cared for under similar circumstances. Mama was their patient, and she deserved treatment at a professional level. If it took me cussing them all out, so be it. The added indignity was that these were Black people and folks of color mistreating an elder. Those who weren't doing the actual mistreating were complicit and allowed it to happen. Unconscionable in my estimation. I later heard that when word got out, which brought the administrative staff running to the third floor, my carrying on was distinguished from Mama's by, "Not the mother, the daughter!" I interacted only with the administrator and no one else. To her credit, the administrator, who was caring for her aged mother, understood my anger and my frustration. She did her best to set things right.

Mama loved the way I handled them.

"You told their asses off," she said with chest pumping approval when I got her situated back in her room.

"I know who I can get. I need Black or Linda to take care of them for me," Mama said, plotting revenge.

Too much sitting on the bench with gangsters I thought.

The ordeal had worn her out, and she was ready to go to bed. The nurse's aide got her washed up and put clean pajamas on her and she went to sleep. I stayed all night at the nursing home for several days, not trusting them with Mama's care. In a few days, Mama was her old self with no memory of the incident. For that I was thankful and once I realized she didn't remember I made certain no one brought it up to her.

I made plans to remove her from the nursing home after that. Her time was dwindling down, she was walking again and they had done as best they could for Mama. Mama was getting antsy and wanted to go home. All along she had been saying that no one ever left the nursing home and was never sure that she would.

At the end of March, I worked for two weeks in her apartment throwing out old things and making her room brand new. The second week of March, I brought Mama home from the nursing home. She seemed a little confused, but I attributed it to the fact that her discharge date had changed from last Friday to Monday, and convinced that she would never get out, Mama had worked herself up to a mood. Ecstatic to be going home, she thanked everyone at the Nursing Home and said her goodbyes.

# TENNYBOOTS!

Once she was home, after becoming acclimated to her room, she noticed that things weren't how she had left it. That entire first day home she raged. She stood in the doorway of her room and yelled at me first and when I left, Ashley. Frustrated with the way things were already going, I reminded Mama of our agreement that I would bring her home and attempt to care for her with support, but if I couldn't do it without harming myself, we would have to consider a permanent place in a nursing home. My reminding her of this angered her, and after I left, she called Russell and Edie asking if they knew a *hit* man who could knock me off because she was not going back to the nursing home. For the first two days at home, Mama wore us out.

She did not calm down for three days. My niece found her in a playful mood on the third day. Mama began to reveal what appeared to be her secrets. In all the stories she had told us, the memories she had shared, no one had ever heard what she seemed to be revealing. My nieces called me confused and not knowing what to believe about what Mama had revealed. I could not confirm nor deny the story she told, but I had an inkling that she might have confused some people and places and facts. Warming my way back into her good graces each day, on the seventh day she was home, I gently brought up the discussion.

"Hey Ma, I hear you're telling your secrets."

"What secrets?"

She had the silliest grin on her face, and was slouched in her big and comfortable, corduroy covered rocker. She was wearing her favorite red plaid pajamas, and she looked so young, coy even, and playful. I had asked Ashley to stay just out of the room where Mama could not see her, but within earshot, to confirm whatever she told me. With Ashley waiting in the wings to witness the revelation of secrets that had denied Mama entrance through the pearly gates, I pressed on.

"I hear you were telling Pinky your *secrets* the other day," I stretched out the word "secrets" as though we were girlfriends dishing dirt.

# TENNYBOOTS!

"Oh, I was just playing with her. I tell them lies all the time," she was still smiling and I swear she twirled her hair.

"Hmm. Something tells me that this one has some truth to it. You may have some facts confused, but a lot of the story seems true. I'm here to listen without judging if you are ready to tell it to me."

My voice was saccharine sweet, with a lot of *girlfriend* mixed in. I sat really close to her. If she thought I was judging her, I knew the game would be over.

Still looking coy and even amused as she began to speak, Mama took the lid off a decades old tale that had never made it into any of her stories. It was right there, easy on her lips all this time yet, she had never uttered a word of what she now revealed. She didn't stutter; she didn't fumble, she just spoke her truth. No denying it was the truth. Truth brings its own authority and broadcasts its own arrival. As soon as she unveiled it, I knew it to be true. I tried to read her face. Was she relieved? Did it even matter to her? Would she have taken it to her grave? Died with it? Mama's face gave up no clues. She turned her attention to the television, and I turned to my thoughts.

We never mentioned what she had revealed again. Ashley and I compared notes, and we had both heard the same thing. Mama had come back from the dead and did what she had to do. It was as simple as that, and we went on living our lives.

We went through four home attendants in ten days. And Mama was in and out of sorts the whole time. She and I had spent the Sunday before the seizures in the emergency room. Another UTI seemed the cause of her initial bad behavior. They couldn't get a line to inject the antibiotic intravenously so the doctors sent us home with a prescription antibiotic. The very next day on April Fool's Day, the seizures began.

Mama's stay at the hospital from April Fool's Day until the day she died was disorienting for her. Once again, a UTI had caused sepsis, which caused the seizures. Seven days in, they realized that the UTI was drug resistant and had to experiment with different medications. They also put Mama on a seizure medication. At 99, the MDA was all that Mama had; she didn't take any medications and had no prescriptions. A transfusion every six months, sometimes stretched out to a year, was all that kept her alive and well this last ten years. She awoke from the seizures and medicine cocktails with a very pronounced case of delirium. It was kind of cute at first; she thought she was in jail and was pleasant about it. I assumed that in a few days it would abate as the others had. But it did not. She became distrustful of the process and saying that they were trying to kill her; she had pleaded with us to get her out of there. She still knew who we were. For 16 weary days in her delirium, she devised sometimes silly ways to escape from the hospital. Two days before she died, it was a hat that would save her—she had sent me in search of a head covering for her white hair that would disguise her enough so that those who would see her dead would not recognize her. I had played along with her and brought napkins and placed on her head, but especially in her delirium she was no fool. She slapped the napkins from her head and yelled at me to go quickly and bring back a real turban or scarf for her head. Shooing my friend and me out of the room in search of a head covering with a sense of urgency, we obliged her.

Earlier in the hospital stay, I had sided with the medical staff and disguised her medicine in her food. When she found out she scolded me and would not even allow me to get near her for a few days. She stopped eating and even drinking for several days, so afraid that she was being killed. My friend had brokered a truce between Mama and me. She smiled at my friend when we came into her room that Saturday. She allowed her to feed her some yogurt and doughnuts. When I asked if she knew who I was, she smiled at me and said, of course I know who you are, Judy. I took the smile as a white flag that restored our being on good terms before her death. On the Friday before that I had sat with her, she berated me the entire time, telling me I could take my fat ass out of there, because she wanted nothing to do with me. She may have had a bout of delirium but my fat ass was still ripe for her attacks. Saturday she was pleasant shooing me out to find a hat, and on Sunday, there was nothing bitter between us. I had spent Sunday

# TENNYBOOTS!

night with her until she went to sleep. She told me to give her television to Ryder. Then she thought about it and said, "No, give it to both of them, Riley and Ryder." The talk of her end didn't spook me, I encouraged it, asking if she had anymore bequeaths. She said no, she was satisfied I knew what to do. So many times, before we had been here, this wasn't that different.

On Monday I had stayed away so as not to sign release papers to a nursing home. The doctor wanted to discharge her as medically there was nothing wrong with her. The nursing home she had just left had agreed to take her back until they found out she was non-compliant and combative. I asked the doctor to send her home instead, believing that if we got her home, we could get her back to normal. That request was emotional and reactive. To care for Mama in that state at home, even with help, would have been laborious. But I had asked my good friend if she could sit with Mama for six hours a day, she agreed. Mama did not want to return to a Nursing Home, and I really did not want to send her.

Cricket, Pinky, Ashley, Asia and the girls were the last ones to see her alive on Monday. They all reported that she was lethargic and quiet, a change from her being combative and restless. We attributed it to the drugs. She had not eaten the lunch that Cricket had brought her that day, nor the dinner that Ashley had cooked for her. Ryder had been unsuccessful in getting her to say much. Even so, when they left the hospital on Monday evening not one of them felt that it was the last time.

News of Mama's death traveled fast. Mama had left a great big empty space in many people's lives. Especially in her community. On the day of her death the young folks did an impromptu urban tribute, candles that spelled out M-A-M-A were lit in front of her bench. They poured bottles of Pepsi Cola in libation, an African tradition honoring the Ancestors that has devolved into a hood tribute as well. Seeing the candles spelling Mama and the large gathering crowd grieving Mama's death made it real for me, and for the first time that day, I cried. On the Saturday after Good Friday, we held a balloon release. Over 200 people came. We released 100 white balloons into the atmosphere to set Mama free.

# TENNYBOOTS!

    Her funeral was on a Wednesday morning. It had rained all of April, but on the day of the balloon release and the day of Mama's funeral the rain stopped and the sun sat high in the sky warming us with its rays. From ten in the morning until one o'clock in the afternoon Mama's home-going service was the place to be. The church held 400 people downstairs, and we took every seat. At least 100 people came through to pay their last respects but could not remain for the funeral. The common refrain heard since her death is the degree to which her community loved Mama. Everyone had a story of how Mama made them feel or what she had meant to them. When Mama died, the band stopped playing for the entire community.

****

# Epilogue

The Funeral had gone well. Enjoyable even—as much as a funeral can be enjoyable. Ashley had suggested that the family wear Mama's favorite color: royal blue and to dress up so we would look like people, a reference to Mama's requirement for any family member coming to visit her at church. We could not make her shame, so we had to look like people. Mama was laid out in her favorite royal blue suit too, with her 55-year-old Missionary Badge pinned over her heart. We had marched in to the song of Mama's youth: The Old Rugged Cross and enjoyed her favorite songs during the service. Speakers had spoken of Mama and nailed her personality and antics. After the Fifth Generation added Mama's name to the Roll of Ancestors, and once I was certain it was a funeral Mama could be proud of, for the first time in the week since her death, I allowed myself to stop conducting and take in the service.

The preacher was giving the eulogy for Mama with classic scripture that is the standard of proof for passage through the pearly white gates: 2 Timothy Chapter 4, Verse 7: She has fought a good fight, She has finished the course; She has kept the faith… when my thoughts trailed off.

"FINISH? At least Mama had finished. Her crown, according to Pastor Williams, was secured. For me, it was never even a certainty that I would make it out alive, let alone finish. At times, my death as the only sure way out was a pleasant preoccupation—and I was okay with that. Wasn't a dead martyr more authentic than a living one? The inscription etched on my afterlife in scarlet letters—Blessed Daughter Who Gave Her Life In Care of Her Aging Mother—would ensure my, my…what?"

# TENNYBOOTS!

Pastor Williams, in the tradition of long-winded Black Baptist preachers was revving up instead of winding down even though he had said he would say one more thing and sit down. Mama would say he was just getting loose. My niece, Pinky, sitting next to me, was on her feet now, her arms up in the air, shouting, "Hallelujah!"

Ticking off how Mama had accomplished this crown-reaping finish in the Biblical sense, the Pastor had backtracked to an earlier verse in 2 Timothy: "For I am already poured out like a drink offering," he had floated into the sanctuary where Wyatt Tee Walker had preached his fiery sermons.

"YES! SAY THAT! PREACH!" Now I was on my feet. He had my attention. Why! Why had I allowed myself to be poured out like a drink offering not only for the 134 straight days since Mama's hospitalization on December 3rd, but for the whole 10 years? The beginning had been easy enough. Clueless what my promise to take care of Mama in her old age entailed, I never allowed for the possibility that I would arrive here so abused and beat down. Oh, there was joy too and fun. But the abuse…

The pianist is playing softly in accompaniment with the sermon. The music is from one of Mama's favorite songs, "I Won't Complain." [1] I sing the lyrics to myself as the Preacher's eulogy drones on, But when I look around and I think things over all of my good days out-weigh my bad days, I won't complain.

Was Mama chiding me even in death? Touché old girl! That made me chuckle.

The Preacher was winding up his service with the illustration of Love. He cited a few chapters from the First Corinthian verse that is bandied about at every wedding: Love is patient, Love is Kind… Love keeps no record of wrongs…

But the love he speaks of is not the love the average person can attain. The theologian Bonhoeffer had cautioned folks that spiritual love was not easy. It was service and it was hard…

# TENNYBOOTS!

The eulogy was done. Her favorite Pastor had placed her in Heaven. My thoughts returned to the present as they opened the coffin for final viewing. The smile the mortician had chiseled onto her face made me believe her soul was pleased.

On Friday morning, two days after the funeral and too early for FedEx, someone laid on my doorbell with an impatient peal. Still asleep, I jumped out of bed to the intercom and asked, "Who is it?" "Special delivery," came the reply. Barefoot and navigating my long hallway without turning on lights, I reached the door and opened it just a crack, bed hair revealing my predicament. It had fallen below 40 degrees the night before and the old steam radiator near the door was hot and hissing. The letter carrier dropped a box into my open hands with no warning that the small size belied its great weight. I almost dropped it. He caught it at my knees and held it until I grabbed it more securely this time. I closed the door and turned on the foyer light to investigate the package. It was Mama. Her ashes had arrived in perfect Mama fashion, loud and bodacious and interrupting my sleep—I howled in laughter. Only Mama! I sat her on the fireplace mantle alongside the 60-year-old dentures in a green plastic holder that I could neither bear to look at, nor throw away. And there she sits. I am supposed to distribute her in nice blue vessels across the family, but something about disturbing Mama's ashes seems counter-intuitive.

The second half of April, and May and June passed without incident or anything memorable. I had great peace in that I had done my best and saw it through to the end. I soared. Things were the same, just without Mama, who had lived a long and full life. My predominant feeling was a sense of relief. Now was my time. And Mama had not stayed away. Birds came often and perched on the fire escape, outside my dining-room window, where she knew I would be—at the computer as she had accused me so many times when complaining about my coming late. Each time, the bird would squawk or chirp until it got my attention, and once I acknowledged Mama, the bird would stop and just hang out. I learned to stop on the street when I heard loud squawking and look for her in the birds. One would always persist until I spotted the loud one. The last bird that came was a Blue Jay, past its season, having decided

# TENNYBOOTS!

not to migrate south this year. It only tarried for a few minutes and then flew away.

But by July 3rd, I could not stop crying. The night before had been ordinary. But the next morning a profound sadness rolled out of bed with me and would not dissipate. If someone mentioned her, I cried. If they didn't mention her, I cried. The birds still came around, but I took neither comfort nor consolation from them as I had before. The sadness was weakening my will to exist outside of crying. My friend, Sheila, and I had aborted a road trip to the Southwest when Mama died. It was too hot to go south now, so I suggested we head north. I had to do something. We headed to a campground down on Cape Cod, and then to Acadia National Park in Maine. It rained the entire time in Maine and dense fog denied us the view from Cadillac Mountain. We returned to the Cape where the sun was shining. A loud squawking bird woke us up each morning. My friend, Mattie, was imploring me to look at a vintage Holiday Rambler travel trailer for sale to place on the campground. I had met her at the campground seven years ago when her husband, Mr. Bob, upon seeing me and my grandchildren tent camping remarked that we were the only ones who looked like him at the entire campground, so we'd better behave. Some years ago, I told her I wanted a camper, but with caring for Mama, it just never happened. Still sad, I was resisting even looking at it. But each morning the bird kept squawking and Mattie kept imploring me to at least look at the camper. On my last day, the couple who was selling it, Mike and Stacy, made an offer that I could not refuse. And Mama stopped squawking.

I spent five regenerative weeks on Cape Cod with my dear friends, Leslie and Deborah, each staying for a week or more. My daughter and the twins came at the end. For one full week, I slept. Mr. Bob and Mike took care of the trailer, as they had promised, and Mattie and Stacy took care of me. With each hour on the Cape, I shed not only the sadness, but the hard, the unpleasant and the bad of the past ten years. I cocooned myself in the good. The profound sadness that had rolled out of bed with me three months after Mama died was falling away. By the final week, leaving the Cape to return to my life was easy. The birds had continued to find me, but no longer squawking, she just hung around my healing.

# TENNYBOOTS!

\*\*\*\*

# Glossary

**Ass on her back**- idiomatic expression in the vernacular which means someone has an attitude, is ornery, or doesn't want to be bothered.

**Bosco**-brand name for a chocolate syrup used to make milk turn and taste chocolate

**Bringing Bones and Carrying Bones** – instigating confusion by telling each person by what the other had said in confidence

**Cadillacs**- Mama's first mispronunciation of cataracts which she continued to use

**Callahan**-a bayou in Opelousas Louisiana

**Cooter Brown**-a southern expression for a charismatic alcoholic

**Croppin**- sharecropping for short

**Cush**- a dish to eat made from cornbread and milk that originated in Senegambia as Kusha

**Dungarees**- denim pants now referred to as jeans

**Every Peas Pickin'**- southern expression for being involved in many things

**Gee nor haw**- as a mule goes, left or right

**Gully**- a water worn deep narrow gorge with steep sides

**Halves**-a contract to pay ½ of sharecropping profit to the owner of the plantation

**Hot**- something that was stolen from a retail establishment and being sold for less than retail price

**MOLST** -medical order for life sustaining treatment

**Mouth start to water**- salivation which typically precedes eating brought on by looking or smelling food

**No tea for the fever**-black idiom used by Langston Hughes which means a person who doesn't put up with nonsense

**Playing the dozens**-a competitive exercise of wits, which has the effect of numbing Black people to derogatory name calling

**Potwash**- a mispronunciation for patois-a dialect of the Creole people in Opelousas, LA

**Punchanella**- a children's game

**Press**- an armoire where clothing is kept

**Rican**-a branch from a Pecan tree, used for various purposes but especially for thrashing fruit and pecans out of trees to fall on the ground to be harvested

# TENNYBOOTS!

**Sad Sack**- an inept person, forlorn
**Safe**-a cupboard where food is kept
**Savoy Manor**-a ballroom hot-spot for music and public dancing in Harlem on Lenox Avenue, dubbed the "World's Finest Ballroom" that was in operation from 1926-1958 (Wikipedia)
**Short Rows**-farming expression for being almost done, as in farming the shortest rows in the field
**Stickin' Plaster-** expression meaning someone is very close to another person
**Tenny Boots** - black and white laced up boots worn by children and adults at the turn of the 20th century. 2)a name called Mama by children at a birthday party
**Thirds**-a contract to pay ⅓ of sharecropping profit to the owner of the plantation
**Turnrow**-a strip of usually uncropped land at the side or end of a field upon which a plow may be turned. (Merriam-Webster dictionary)
**Waked**- to have a body lie in repose in a funeral home, or in a house
**Wooden nickels**-slang for not to be fooled. Wooden nickels have no monetary value.

# Who's Who In the Family

*(First Names Only)*
Eddie Edwards (Rest In Peace)- January 12, 1924- December 19, 1999
Matriarch: Florence Edwards (Rest in Peace)-October 23, 1919- April 16, 2019
5 living generations until Mama's death
Mama has three daughters: Edie, Gay and Judy
Edie has three children: Robin, Kitt and Nakia
Robin has three children: Bruce, Alexis and April
Bruce has one daughter: Kennedy
Alexis has one daughter: Me Kenzie
Kitt has one daughter: Lyndsey
Nakia has one daughter: Destiny
Gay(Rest In Peace) February 27, 1951- November 27, 1996
Gay has three children: Shonda (Pinky) Russell, Nikki
Shonda Gay has three children: Ashley who lived with Mama, Asia, Robert Devante "Vanni"
Ashley has two girls, who lived with Mama: Ryder, Riley
Asia has a dog, Harley
Russell has one child: Tyquasia
Tyquasia has three children: D.J., Kaylee, Amir
Nikki has eight children: Raven, Sara, Erin, Damani, Quadir, Rayelle, Sydney, Rodney
Raven has one daughter: Payton, who Mama calls Paylee
Sara was raised by Mama and has one son: Hunter
Judy has one daughter: Kristen(Cricket)
Cricket has twins: Chloe and Elijah

**Maternal Ancestors**:
Florence Edwards
Mother: Malinda King: Allen 1896-1966
Maternal Grandfather: Boneparte "Bonny" King 1859-1945
Maternal Great Grandmother: Melinda Mouton King 1834
Maternal Great Grandfather: Robert King 1820-1860 (S.C.?)
Maternal 2nd Great Grandfather: Robert or W King
Maternal Grandmother: Mary Jane Woods 1861-1906

# TENNYBOOTS!

Maternal Great Grandmother: Cecilia Woods Hill 1840
Maternal Great Grand Father: Unknown
Maternal 2nd Great Grandmother: Jane Anne Stilley
Maternal 2nd Great Grandfather:Phillip Woods

Father: George Wilson 1893-1918(19)
Paternal Grandmother: Fanny Wilson 1863
Paternal Grandfather: Ben Wilson 1837
Paternal Great Grand Mother: Fannie Wilson 1812
Paternal Second Great Grand Mother: Dolly Robinson 1789-1870

****

## About the Author

**Judy Edwards** born in Harlem, too late for the Harlem Renaissance, much to her dismay. A born and bred Harlemite, she embodies its soul. Daughter, biological mother of an only child but mother to many, and grandmother is how she defines herself. Trained as a social justice lawyer, at the CUNY School of Law, Judy was born an advocate to the underdog. In writing this memoir, and memorializing her decade of care giving her fiercely independent mother, she endeavors to give voice to the aging and the caregiver who often silently endures the burden.

# TENNYBOOTS!

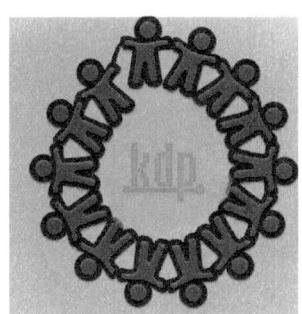

www.ingramcontent.com/pod-product-compliance
Lightning Source LLC
Chambersburg PA
CBHW020353170426
43200CB00005B/150